Popular Complete Smart Series

Complete
MathSmart

Grade
12

 Proud Sponsor of Math Team Canada 2019

Credits

Artwork (Front Cover "3D White Sphere" Senoldo/123RF.com)

Copyright © 2017 Popular Book Company (Canada) Limited

MathSmart is a registered trademark of Popular Book Company (Canada) Limited, used under licence.

All rights reserved. No part of this publication may be reproduced, stored in a retrieval system, or transmitted in any form or by any means, electronic, mechanical, photocopying, recording or otherwise, without the prior written permission of the Publisher, Popular Book Company (Canada) Limited.

Printed in China

ISBN: 978-1-77149-223-2

ISBN: 978-1-77149-223-2

Overview

Complete MathSmart is our all-time bestselling series. *Complete MathSmart* Grade 12 is designed to strengthen students' math foundation, allow them to demonstrate their understanding by applying their knowledge and skills to solve real-world problems, and provide them with an opportunity to evaluate their own learning progress.

This workbook covers the three courses of the Mathematics curriculum:
- Advanced Functions
- Calculus and Vectors
- Mathematics of Data Management

The concepts introduced in each course are included in this workbook in the testing practice format. Each practice test starts with a list of test areas which highlights the topics covered in the test. Each test begins with basic multiple-choice questions followed by questions that increase in the level of difficulty, which is similar to the test format that students encounter in schools. All the questions are classified into four categories of knowledge and skills in mathematics as the achievement chart set in the curriculum. The four categories can help students make judgements about their own work.

The four categories are:
- Knowledge and Understanding
- Application
- Communication
- Thinking

Cumulative tests are provided at the end of each section for students to recapitulate the fundamental concepts and skills they have learned. They are ideal as testing practice to prepare students for the Math examination in school.

At the end of this workbook is an answer key that provides thorough solutions with the crucial steps clearly presented to help students develop an understanding of the correct strategies to arrive at the solutions. It also provides an opportunity for students to identify their strengths and weaknesses in making connections of their knowledge and the correct approaches in solving math problems. In addition, a handy reference containing definitions and formulas is included to provide quick and easy access for students whenever needed.

Complete MathSmart will undoubtedly reinforce students' math skills and strengthen their conceptual foundation that is a prerequisite for exploring mathematics further in their education.

 Contents

ISBN: 978-1-77149-223-2

Mathematics of Data Management

ISBN: 978-1-77149-223-2

Complete MathSmart 12
Advanced Functions

ISBN: 978-1-77149-223-2

Polynomial Functions

TEST AREAS

- understanding the characteristics of polynomial functions
- identifying even and odd functions
- determining the equation of a polynomial function
- understanding the transformations of functions

Knowledge and Understanding

Circle the correct answers.

① Which is an odd function?

A. $y = 2x^3 - 3x + 2$

B. $y = 3x^2 + 2x + 1$

C. $y = -3x^5 - x$

D. none of the above

② Which is an even function?

A. $y = x^2(x^3 + 3x)$

B. $y = -x(x^3 + x^5)$

C. $y = x^2(x^2 + 3x)$

D. $y = x^2 - 5x + 1$

③ The end behaviours of the graph of $f(x) = (x - 1)(x - 3)^2$ can be described as:

A. As $x \to \infty$, $y \to \infty$ and as $x \to -\infty$, $y \to -\infty$.

B. As $x \to \infty$, $y \to \infty$ and as $x \to -\infty$, $y \to \infty$.

C. As $x \to \infty$, $y \to 0$ and as $x \to -\infty$, $y \to -\infty$.

D. As $x \to \infty$, $y \to 0$ and as $x \to -\infty$, $y \to 0$.

④ The end behaviours of the graph of $f(x) = -x(x + 2)^3$ can be described as:

A. As $x \to \infty$, $y \to \infty$ and as $x \to -\infty$, $y \to -\infty$.

B. As $x \to \infty$, $y \to -\infty$ and as $x \to -\infty$, $y \to -\infty$.

C. As $x \to \infty$, $y \to 0$ and as $x \to -\infty$, $y \to -\infty$.

D. As $x \to \infty$, $y \to \infty$ and as $x \to -\infty$, $y \to 0$.

⑤ Which shows the graph of $y = x^4$?

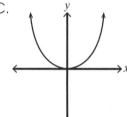

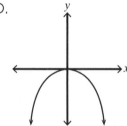

⑥ Which function has roots at -2, 2, and 3, and a y-intercept of -6?

A. $f(x) = \frac{1}{2}(x + 2)(x + 3)(x - 2)$

B. $f(x) = \frac{1}{3}(x - 2)^2(x + 2)(x - 3)$

C. $f(x) = \frac{1}{4}(x + 2)^2(x - 2)(x - 3)$

D. $f(x) = \frac{1}{6}(x - 3)^2(x^2 - 4)$

⑦ A fourth degree polynomial cannot have

A. two real roots.

B. four real roots.

C. five real roots.

D. no real roots.

⑧ Write the answers using set notation and interval notation.

a.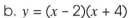

_____ _____

b. $y = (x - 2)(x + 4)$ **Domain:**

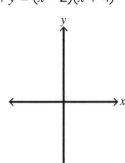

_____

_____

Range:

_____

_____

c. 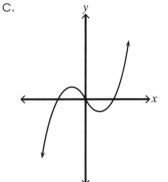 **Domain:**

_____

_____

Range:

_____

_____

⑨ Find the coordinates of the y-intercept of each function.

a. $y = (x + 2)^2(x - 3)(x + 1)$ _____

b. $y = 4(x + 3)^2(x - 4)$ _____

c. $y = -2x^3 + 3x^2 - x + 5$ _____

d. $y = -2(x + 1)(x - 3)(x + 2)(x - 5)(x - 1)$ _____

⑩ Use finite differences to determine the type of polynomial function each set of data represents.

a.

x	y
-2	5
-1	0
0	-3
1	-4
2	-3

_____

b.

x	y
2	6
3	0
4	0
5	12
6	42

_____

⑪ Find the roots and the multiplicity of each root for each function.

a. $y = x^2(x + 3)(x - 1)^2$

c. $y = (x^2 - x - 12)(x - 2)^5$

_____

b. $y = (x - 1)(x + 2)^3(x + 3)^2$

⑫ Determine the factored form of the function in the graph.

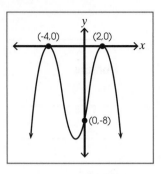

⑬ Determine the standard form of each function.

a. $y = (x + 2)^2(x - 3)$

b. $y = 1 - \dfrac{1}{2}(x + 3)^2(2 + x)$

⑭ State the degree of each function and describe the end behaviours of its graph.

	Degree	End Behaviours	
		$a > 0$	$a < 0$
$y = ax^2 + bx + c$			
$y = ax^3 + bx^2 + cx + d$			
$y = ax^4 + bx^3 + cx^2 + dx + e$			
$y = ax^5 + bx^4 + cx^3 + dx^2 + ex + f$			

⑮ Sketch each polynomial function.

Ⓐ $y = (x + 2)^2(x - 2)^3$

Ⓑ $y = -(x + 2)(x - 1)^3$

Ⓒ $y = x^4 + 16x^3 + 96x^2 + 256x + 256$

Ⓓ $y = -x^5 - 4x^4 - 4x^3$

Ⓐ

Ⓑ

Ⓒ

Ⓓ

ISBN: 978-1-77149-223-2

Complete the table of the transformations for $y = x^3$.

	A	B	C
Transformed Form	$y = 4(x - 1)^3 - 32$	$y = -(x + 2)^3 + 8$	
Standard Form			$y = 8x^3 - 27$
Factored Form			
x-intercept(s)			
y-intercept			

⑰ Write the general equation for the family of functions with roots at the given points, all with a multiplicity of 1.

a.

roots
-5, -2, 2, and 5

_____

b.

roots
-3, -2, 0, 1, and 4

_____

⑱ Determine the equation of the polynomial function with a double root of 3, a root of 1, and the y-intercept at 9. Then sketch it.

⑲ Sketch the graph of the function below. Label the roots and the y-intercept on the graph.

$$y = -x(x - 2)^2(x + 3)$$

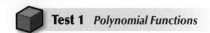

Application

⑳ Ezra's Eatery has a profit function $P(x) = -2x^2 + 7x - 3$, where x is the number of burgers sold in hundreds and $P(x)$ is the profit in thousands of dollars. Sketch a graph of the profit function and determine the number of burgers Ezra should sell to maximize the profit.

㉑ The course of Noah's cruise ship can be mapped by the function $d(x) = 2x^3 - 22x^2 + 78x - 90$, where x is the distance travelled in 100 km east and $d(x)$ is the distance travelled in 100 km north. Sketch a graph of the journey. How far east will the ship have travelled if the ship travelled 1800 km north?

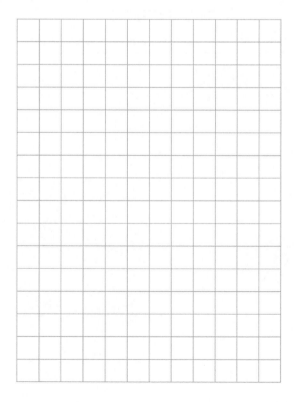

Communication

㉒ Describe the transformations applied to $y = x^3$ to get $y = -\frac{1}{3}(2x + 10)^3 + 4$.

㉓ What is the minimum number of real roots a quintic function can have? What is the maximum? Explain.

㉔ Write the definition of an even function and that of an odd function. Give an example of an odd function, an even function, and a function that is neither.

㉕ Explain why $f(x) = x^4 + 2x^2 + 1$ cannot be factored using the factor theorem.

Thinking

㉖ Determine the equation of the function with each set of points.

a.

x	y
0	3
1	6
2	13
3	24
4	39
5	58

b.

x	y
0	1
1	4
2	1
3	-20
4	-71
5	-164

㉗ Sketch the graph of the function $f(x) = (4 - x)(1 - x)^3(x + 2)^2$. Then write the information of the function.

degree: _____

y-intercept: _____

leading coefficient: _____

end behaviours: _____

_____

roots (multiplicities): _____

_____

㉘ Give two examples of equations that satisfy the following conditions.

a. • degree 3
• a double root at 2
• a root at 7

_____

_____

b. • degree 4
• as $x \to -\infty$, $y \to -\infty$
• double roots at -7 and 7

_____

_____

c. • a double root at 2
• a double root at -5
• end behaviours: as $x \to \infty$, $y \to -\infty$ and as $x \to -\infty$, $y \to \infty$

_____

_____

d. • degree 3
• leading coefficient of -2
• a double root at 0

_____

_____

㉙ Complete the tables of the original function and the corresponding points of the transformed function. Sketch both functions in the graph. Determine the point of intersection.

Original function:

$$y = x^3$$

x	y
-3	
-2	
-1	
0	
1	
2	
3	

Transformed function:

$$y = \frac{1}{2}(\frac{1}{2}(x+2))^3 + 4$$

x	y
-8	-9.5

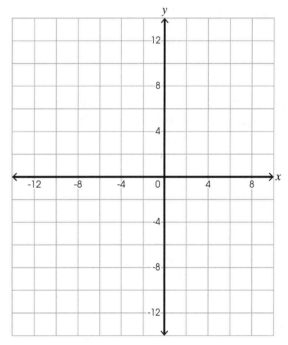

_____

Test 2 Polynomial Equations and Inequalities

TEST AREAS

- factoring polynomials using synthetic division and polynomial division
- applying the remainder theorem and the factor theorem
- solving polynomial equations and inequalities
- graphing polynomial equations and inequalities

Knowledge and Understanding

Circle the correct answers.

① What values of x will the function $y = (x + 2)(x - 3)(x + 4)$ be positive?

A. $x < -4, -2 < x < 3$

B. $x < -3, 4 < x < 2$

C. $-4 < x < -2, x > 3$

D. $-3 < x < 2, x > 4$

② What values of x will the function $y = -x(x - 2)^2(x + 3)$ be positive?

A. $x < -3$

B. $0 < x < 2$

C. $-3 < x < 0$

D. $x > 2$

③ Which of the following polynomials are factors of $x^3 + 5x^2 - x - 5$?

A. $x - 1$

B. $x + 1$

C. $x + 5$

D. all of the above

④ What is the remainder if $x - 3$ is divided into $x^3 + 2x^2 - 3x - 5$?

A. -5   B. 31

C. 19   D. -31

⑤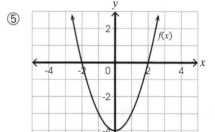

According to the graph, for what values of x will $f(x) > 0$?

A. $x > -2, x > 2$

B. $x < -2, x > 2$

C. $-2 < x < 2$

D. $x > 0$

⑥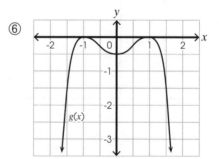

Given the graph of $g(x)$, when is the function negative?

A. $x < -1, x > 1$

B. $x \in \mathbb{R}$

C. $-1 < x < 1$

D. $x < -1, -1 < x < 1, x > 1$

ISBN: 978-1-77149-223-2

Write the multiplication statements.

    a. $(2x^3 - 15x^2 - 12x + 12) \div (x - 3)$ b. $\dfrac{3x^3 + x^2 - 4x - 6}{x + 2}$

⑧ Solve each polynomial using the method specified.

a. by factoring	b. by synthetic division	c. by polynomial division
$4x^3 - 20x^2 + 25x = 0$	$x^3 + 2x^2 - 5x - 6 = 0$	$x^3 - 5x^2 - 2x + 24 = 0$

⑨ Solve $2x^3 - 7x^2 - 17x + 10 > 0$ graphically.

⑩ Solve $t^3 - 8t^2 - 5t + 84 < 0$ using a factor table.

⑪ Find the equation $P(x)$ of a function that satisfies the given conditions.

- $(x + 2)$ and $(x + 1)$ are factors
- has a degree of 3
- $P(\frac{1}{2}) = 0$ and $P(1) = 12$

⑫ Determine the value of m if $x = 1$ is a root of the equations given.

a. $mx^4 + (2m + 1)x^3 + (3 + m) = 0$

b. $3mx^3 - (4 - m)x - 2m = 0$

Application

⑬ A cargo has a width of $(2x - 7)$, a length of $(2x + 3)$, and a height of $(x - 2)$. If the volume of the cargo is 117 m³, what are the dimensions?

⑭ Edward is making a cardboard box by cutting square corners of a 32 cm by 28 cm sheet. If the box needs a volume of 1920 cm³, what are the possible dimensions of the box?

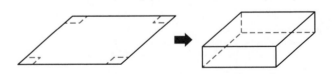

     ISBN: 978-1-77149-223-2

⑮ A new cage is built at a petting farm. The volume of the cage, in m³, can be modelled by the function $V(x) = 2x^3 + 7x^2 + 2x - 3$. What are the dimensions of the cage in terms of x? What are the dimensions when $x = 2$?

⑯ Leo kicks a ball into the air. The height of the ball in metres with respect to time t in seconds can be modelled by the function $H(t) = -25t^3 + 25t^2 + t$. When will its height be greater than 1 m from the ground?

⑰ Avery and Christine are selling boxes of cookies to raise money for the protection of animal welfare. They estimate that at a price of x dollars per box, the weekly cost $C(x)$ and the revenue $R(x)$, in hundreds of dollars, can be modelled by:

$$C(x) = 28 - 2x \qquad R(x) = 9x - x^2$$

At what price per box can they sell the cookies in order to make a profit?

⑱ Katie is flying a remote-controlled helicopter. If the height h in metres above the ground at the end of t minutes is given by $h(t) = 112t - 16t^2$, find the interval of time for which the helicopter is 160 m above the ground or higher.

⑲ Adrian drove a truck to deliver a couch from a warehouse to a customer. The distance from the warehouse in kilometres at time t in hours can be modelled by $d(t) = -2t^3 + 15t^2 - 4t$. When was he over 21 km from the warehouse?

⑳ A ball rolled off a shelf. The height of the ball in decimetres and the distance it travelled across the floor in metres can be modelled by the function $H(d) = -d^4 + 8d^3 - 16d^2 + 16$ before a cat popped it. How far is the ball away from the shelf when it is greater than 7 dm above the ground?

ISBN: 978-1-77149-223-2

Communication

㉑ Explain the steps you would take to solve the inequality $f(x) > 0$, where $f(x) = 2x^3 - x^2 - 13x - 6$. You do not need to solve the inequality.

㉒ When solving for $P(x) \geq 0$, it was found that $P(x)$ has 4 zeroes at a, b, c, and d. How many intervals do you need to test to solve the inequality using a factor table, and what are the intervals in terms of a, b, c, and d?

㉓ Given that $f(x) = x^3 - 2x^2$, $g(x) = 3x + 2$, and $h(x) = x^3 - 2x^2 - 3x - 2$, explain why solving for $f(x) > g(x)$ is the same as solving for $h(x) > 0$.

㉔ Would you use polynomial division or synthetic division to find $(x^3 - 64) \div (x^2 + 8x + 16)$? Explain.

Thinking

㉕ Write the multiplication statement.

$$\frac{12x^2 + 4x^3 + 3 + 3x}{2x + 1 + x^2}$$

㉖ Find the values of a and b if $ax^4 + 3x^3 - bx^2 + 2$ has a remainder of 4 when divided by $(x - 1)$ and a remainder of 56 when divided by $(x + 3)$.

㉗ Solve $4x^4 - x^2 + 6 \le 12x^3 - 3x + 6$ using a factor table.

㉘ Solve $3x^4 + 2x^2 + 4x > x^4 - x^3 + 15x^2 - 2x$ graphically.

㉙ Solve $\dfrac{x^3 + 6x^2 + 9x + 20}{x^3 - 25x} < 0$ using a factor table.

㉚ Create two possible cubic inequalities that correspond to the following solutions: $x < -4$ and $3 < x < 5$. Sketch the graphs.

㉛ Solve $-3x^3 + 5x^2 + x + 8 < 3x^3 - 2x + 10 < -2x^3 + 6x^2 + 97x - 10$. Use a number line to show the final answer.

Rational Functions

TEST AREAS

- understanding reciprocal functions
- graphing rational functions
- solving rational equations and inequalities
- determining the asymptotes, end behaviours, and discontinuities of rational functions

---

Knowledge and Understanding

Circle the correct answers.

① What is the horizontal asymptote of $f(x) = \dfrac{x - 2}{4x - 1}$?

    A. $y = 2$ B. $y = \dfrac{1}{4}$

    C. $y = \dfrac{3}{2}$ D. no horizontal asymptotes

② What is the vertical asymptote of $f(x) = \dfrac{x - 1}{4x - 6}$?

    A. $x = 1$ B. $x = 3$

    C. $x = \dfrac{3}{2}$ D. $x = \dfrac{1}{4}$

③ Which is a reciprocal function?

    A. $f(x) = \dfrac{(x - 1)}{(x + 2)(x - 3)}$ B. $f(x) = \dfrac{1}{(x + 3)(x - 2)}$

    C. $f(x) = \dfrac{x^2 + 3x - 10}{x^2 - x - 6}$ D. all of the above

④ What is/are the x-intercept(s) of $f(x) = \dfrac{(x - 2)^2}{x + 3}$?

    A. (-3,0)   B. (2,0)   C. (2,0) and (-3,0)   D. no x-intercepts

⑤ What is the y-intercept of $f(x) = \dfrac{x + 4}{x^2 - 3x}$?

    A. (0,-4)   B. $(0,-\dfrac{4}{3})$ C. (0,0)   D. no y-intercepts

⑥ What is the point discontinuity of $f(x) = \dfrac{4(x + 2)}{(x + 5)(x + 2)}$?

    A. (-2,-2)   B. $(-2,\dfrac{4}{3})$ C. $(2,\dfrac{1}{2})$ D. $(2,\dfrac{4}{3})$

⑦ Consider the rational functions in the table below.

a. Check the types of discontinuities each function has.

	$f(x) = \dfrac{x(x-1)(x+3)}{x^2-4}$	$f(x) = \dfrac{2x^2+5x+2}{x+2}$	$f(x) = \dfrac{3x^2-2x+5}{(x+1)(x-7)}$
point discontinuity			
vertical asymptote			
horizontal asymptote			
oblique asymptote			

b. Describe how you determine whether each type of discontinuity exists.

_____

⑧ Match each function with its graph.

Ⓐ $f(x) = \dfrac{2x-1}{x+2}$

Ⓑ $f(x) = \dfrac{x^2-1}{x-1}$

Ⓒ $f(x) = \dfrac{1}{x^2+2x-3}$

Ⓓ $f(x) = \dfrac{3x^2+x-2}{3x-2}$

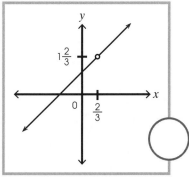

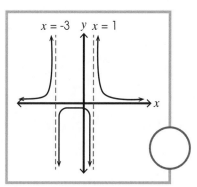

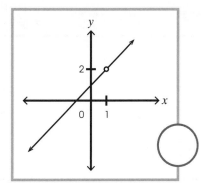

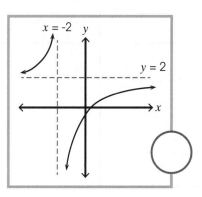

⑨ Determine the equations of all the asymptotes and point discontinuities if there are any.

a. $f(x) = \dfrac{3x^2 + 2x - 5}{x(x - 1)}$

b. $f(x) = \dfrac{2x^2 + 1}{x^2 + x - 20}$

⑩ Sketch the rational functions. Label the key points and asymptotes. Complete the table.

a. $f(x) = \dfrac{3x - x^2}{2x - 6}$

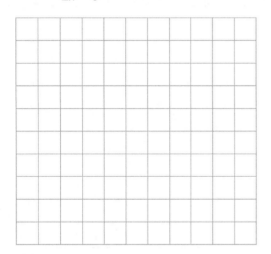

b. $f(x) = \dfrac{4x^2 - 25}{2x^2 - x - 15}$

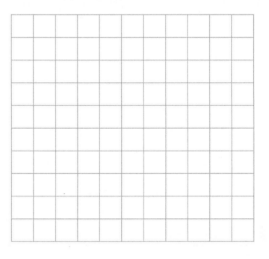

	domain	range	asymptotes	positive and negative intervals	intervals of increase or decrease
$f(x) = \dfrac{3x - x^2}{2x - 6}$					
$f(x) = \dfrac{4x^2 - 25}{2x^2 - x - 15}$					

ISBN: 978-1-77149-223-2

⑪ Solve the equations.

a. $\dfrac{x+5}{x-3} = \dfrac{2}{3}$

b. $\dfrac{3x+2}{4x-1} = \dfrac{7}{1-4x}$

⑫ Solve each inequality. Graph the solutions on a number line.

a. $\dfrac{x^2+4x+3}{x^2+4x+4} > 0$

b. $\dfrac{x^2+2x-3}{x^2+3x-4} < 0$

Application

⑬ A reusable heating pack can generate heat for $H(x) = \dfrac{20}{x+5}$ in hours, where x is the number of times the heating pack has been used.

a. For how many hours can the heating pack generate heat when it is brand new?

b. After how many uses will the heating pack generate heat for only 30 minutes?

ISBN: 978-1-77149-223-2

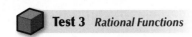

⑭ The number of weeds in a garden after x weeks is given by $w(x) = \dfrac{56(1 + 0.5x)}{8 + 0.04x}$.

a. How many weeds were there when $x = 0$?

b. How many weeds will there be after 10 weeks?

c. When will there be 100 weeds?

⑮ The sales price of a book can be modelled based on the cost of printing, x, in dollars. A textbook is sold for $\dfrac{40x + 10}{x + 2}$. What is the price range of the textbook?

⑯ The remaining battery charge, in 10 000 mAh, in cellphones is dependent on the usage time represented by x in hours. The remaining battery charge in Hailey's phone is modelled by $H(x) = \dfrac{x^2 - 9}{-4x - 3}$ and that in Cory's phone is modelled by $C(x) = \dfrac{-x + 7}{5x + 1}$. When will Hailey's phone have more remaining battery charge than Cory's phone?

Communication

⑰ Lisa's solution to a rational inequality is shown. Is she correct? If not, what error did she make? Explain.

$$\frac{3x+2}{x+1} > 2$$
$$3x + 2 > 2(x + 1)$$
$$3x + 2 > 2x + 2$$
$$3x + 2 - 2x - 2 > 0$$
$$x > 0$$

⑱ Describe the differences between a point discontinuity and an asymptote graphically.

⑲ List the cases of asymptotes with respect to the degrees of the numerator and denominator in a rational function for $f(x) = \dfrac{p(x)}{q(x)}$.

⑳ Compare the functions $f(x) = \dfrac{x^2 + 5x + 6}{x^2 + 7x + 12}$ and $g(x) = \dfrac{x + 2}{x + 4}$. List all the similarities and differences.

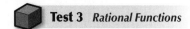

Thinking

㉑ Determine the equations of the rational functions.

a.

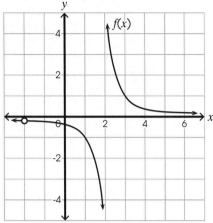

b.

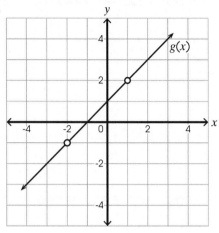

㉒ Find an equation to each rational function with the given properties.

a. • vertical asymptotes at $x = 1$ and $x = 2$

  • horizontal asymptote at $y = 0$

b. • horizontal asymptote at $y = \frac{1}{3}$

  • x-intercept at $(2,0)$

c. • point discontinuity at $x = \frac{1}{2}$

  • horizontal asymptote at $y = 3$

d. • y-intercept at $(0,\frac{1}{8})$

  • vertical asymptote at $x = -2$

ISBN: 978-1-77149-223-2

㉓ Create a rational function that has no point discontinuities or vertical asymptotes, but has a horizontal asymptote at $y = 0$ and y-intercept at $(0,2)$.

㉔ Consider $f(x) = \dfrac{x+2}{x^2}$.

a. Find the point(s) of intersection of $f(x)$ and its reciprocal, $g(x)$, algebraically.

b. Find the intervals when $f(x) > g(x)$.

㉕ Find the reciprocal of the function in the graph. Draw the reciprocal function and then find the point(s) of intersection.

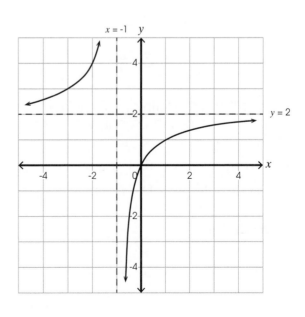

Trigonometric Functions

TEST AREAS

- converting angles between radians and degrees
- understanding trigonometric functions and their reciprocals
- graphing transformations of trigonometric functions
- modelling real-life problems using trigonometric functions

Knowledge and Understanding

Circle the correct answers.

① Convert 240° to radians.

A. $\frac{2\pi}{3}$ B. $\frac{4\pi}{3}$

C. $\frac{3\pi}{4}$ D. $\frac{5\pi}{4}$

② Convert $\frac{5\pi}{30}$ to degrees.

A. 45°   B. 150°

C. 30°   D. 60°

③ What is the measure of the angle in radians if the arc length is 60 cm and the radius is 18 cm?

A. $\frac{3}{10}$ B. $\frac{10}{3}$

C. $\frac{3\pi}{10}$ D. $\frac{10\pi}{3}$

④ What is the arc length of a circle with a radius of 12 cm and a central angle of 255°?

A. 8.5 cm   B. 12π cm

C. 24π cm   D. 17π cm

⑤ Evaluate $\tan \frac{7\pi}{6}$.

A. $\sqrt{3}$ B. $-\frac{\sqrt{3}}{2}$

C. $\frac{\sqrt{3}}{2}$ D. $\frac{1}{\sqrt{3}}$

⑥ Evaluate $\sec \frac{5\pi}{3}$.

A. $\frac{\sqrt{3}}{2}$ B. $-\frac{2}{\sqrt{3}}$

C. 2   D. -2

⑦ What is the range of $y = \sin x$?

A. $\{y \in \mathbb{R}\}$

B. $\{y \in \mathbb{R} \mid y > 0\}$

C. $\{y \in \mathbb{R} \mid -1 \leq y \leq 1\}$

D. $\{y \in \mathbb{R} \mid y \neq 0\}$

⑧ What is the domain of $y = \tan x$?

A. $\{x \in \mathbb{R}\}$

B. $\{x \in \mathbb{R} \mid x \neq 2\pi\}$

C. $\{x \in \mathbb{R} \mid -\pi \leq x \leq \pi\}$

D. $\{x \in \mathbb{R} \mid x \neq \frac{(2n + 1)\pi}{2}, n \in \mathbb{I}\}$

⑨ What is the period for the function $y = \tan 2x$?

A. $\frac{\pi}{4}$ B. $\frac{\pi}{2}$

C. π D. 2π

⑩ Convert the angles between degrees and radians. Then evaluate the exact values of the trigonometric ratios of θ.

a.

$\theta = 60°$

↓

$\theta = $ _____

• $\tan \theta$

• $\csc \theta$

b.

$\theta = \dfrac{3\pi}{4}$

↓

$\theta = $ _____

• $\sin \theta$

• $\cot \theta$

c.

$\theta = 1020°$

↓

$\theta = $ _____

• $\sec \theta$

• $\cos \theta$

⑪ Solve for θ in radians if $0 \le \theta \le 2\pi$.

a. $\tan \theta = -1$

b. $\sin \theta = -\dfrac{\sqrt{3}}{2}$

c. $\sec \theta = -\sqrt{2}$

⑫ Find the angles in radians if the terminal arms pass through the given points. Round your answers to 2 decimal places.

a. (-2,3)

b. (7,-6)

c. (-4,-8)

⑬ What are the maximum value and the minimum value of the function $y = 3\cos(2x) - 1$?

⑭ Find the period of each function.

a. $y = -\sin\left(\frac{\pi}{2}(x + 1)\right)$

b. $y = 2\tan\left(\frac{\pi}{6}x - 2\pi\right) + 1$

⑮ If the minimum value of a sine function is -2 and the maximum value is 10,

a. what is the amplitude?

b. what is the vertical translation?

⑯ Consider the function $y = -2\sin\left(x + \frac{\pi}{3}\right) - 1$. State the following.

a. amplitude _____

b. horizontal translation _____

c. period _____

d. vertical translation _____

⑰ Write an equation that matches each description. Then graph it for $-2\pi \le x \le 2\pi$.

a. **sine function**

- amplitude of 2

- period of π

- horizontal translation of $\frac{\pi}{2}$ to the right

- vertical translation of 3 units up

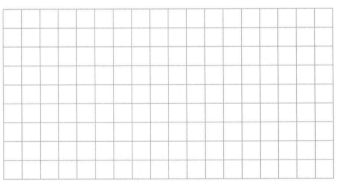

b. **cosine function**

- reflection in the x-axis

- amplitude of $\frac{1}{2}$

- period of 4π

- horizontal translation of π to the left

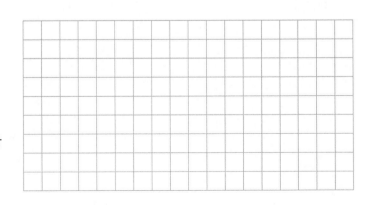

ISBN: 978-1-77149-223-2

Application

⑱ The hypotenuse of an isosceles right triangle is the chord of a circle. The legs of the triangle are the radii of the circle. The length of the chord is 18 cm. Determine the length of the arc subtended by the chord.

⑲ A racing bicycle is travelling on a curve along a track. The curve can be represented as an arc of a circle with a radius of 0.5 km. If the bicycle's speed is 28 km/h, what is the angle of the curve in radians through which the bicycle will cover in 45 seconds?

⑳ The tides of an island vary between a minimum of 0.85 m and a maximum of 2.25 m over 6.2 hours. The depth of the tides, in metres, as a function of time, in hours, can be described by a sine function. Find a function where $t = 0$ corresponds to the time when the tide is at its lowest.

㉑ The population, P, of a ski-resort town, as a function of the number of months, n, into the year can be described by a cosine function. The maximum population is about 15 000 people at the beginning of the year and the minimum population is about 500 people in June.

a. What is the population at the end of July, rounded to the nearest whole person?

b. At the end of which month(s) will the population be around 11 375?

Communication

㉒ Describe the similarities and differences between $y = \sin x$ and $y = \cos x$.

㉓ Consider the reciprocal trigonometric functions.

a. Describe their relationships with the corresponding primary trigonometric functions on vertical asymptotes, periods, domains, and ranges.

b. State the vertical asymptotes, period, domain, and range of each reciprocal function.
- $y = \csc \theta$
- $y = \sec \theta$
- $y = \cot \theta$

㉔ Explain the advantages of expressing angles in radians over degrees. Give an example.

ISBN: 978-1-77149-223-2

Thinking

㉕ Model the graph below with a sine function and a cosine function.

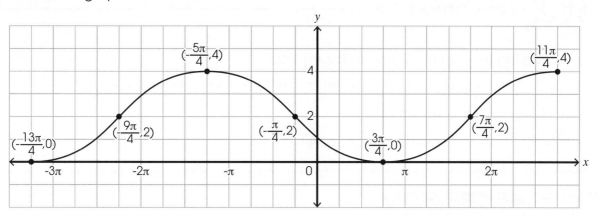

a. sine function   b. cosine function

㉖ A sine function has an amplitude of 3, a period of π, and a vertical translation of 1 unit up. If it passes through the point $(\frac{\pi}{3},1)$, what is the horizontal translation?

㉗ Determine the values of a and c for the function $y = a \cos (x + \frac{\pi}{6}) + c$ if this function has $\frac{\pi}{6}$ as one of its x-intercepts and it passes through $(\frac{5\pi}{6},-3)$.

Trigonometric Equations

- identifying equivalent trigonometric equations
- applying the compound angle formulas and the double angle formulas
- proving trigonometric identities
- solving linear and quadratic trigonometric equations

Knowledge and Understanding

Circle the correct answers.

① Which of the following is equal to $\sin \theta$?

A. $\cos \theta$

B. $\cos (\theta - \frac{\pi}{2})$

C. $\cos (\theta + \frac{\pi}{2})$

D. $-\cos \theta$

② Which of the following is equal to $\cos \theta$?

A. $-\cos \theta$

B. $\cos (-\theta)$

C. $\sin (\theta - \frac{\pi}{2})$

D. $\sin (-\theta)$

③ Which one is an even function?

A. $f(\theta) = \sin \theta$

B. $f(\theta) = \cos \theta$

C. $f(\theta) = \cot \theta$

D. none of the above

④ Which one is an odd function?

A. $f(\theta) = \sin \theta$

B. $f(\theta) = \tan \theta$

C. $f(\theta) = \csc \theta$

D. all of the above

⑤ Which one is equal to $\sin (a + b)$?

A. $\sin a \cos b - \cos a \sin b$

B. $\cos a \cos b - \sin a \sin b$

C. $\sin a \cos b + \cos a \sin b$

D. $\cos a \cos b + \sin a \sin b$

⑥ Which one is equal to $\cos 2\theta$?

A. $\cos^2 \theta - \sin^2 \theta$

B. $2 \cos^2 \theta - 1$

C. $1 - 2 \sin^2 \theta$

D. all of the above

⑦ Which one is equal to $\tan (x - y)$?

A. $\dfrac{\tan x - \tan y}{1 + \tan x \tan y}$

B. $\dfrac{2 \tan x}{1 - \tan^2 x}$

C. $\dfrac{\tan x + \tan y}{1 - \tan x \tan y}$

D. $\dfrac{1 - \tan^2 x}{2 \tan x}$

⑧ Which of the following is a Pythagorean identity?

A. $\sin^2 x + \cos^2 x = 1$

B. $1 + \tan^2 x = \sec^2 x$

C. $1 + \cot^2 x = \csc^2 x$

D. all of the above

⑨ Express each as a single trigonometric function.

For the trigonometric identities, go to page 192.

a. $\sin\left(\frac{\pi}{2} - \theta\right)$

b. $\cos(5\theta)\cos(4\theta) - \sin(5\theta)\sin(4\theta)$

c. $2\sin\left(\frac{\pi}{6}\right)\cos\left(\frac{\pi}{6}\right)$

d. $1 - 2\sin^2(2\theta)$

⑩ Evaluate and determine the exact values.

a. $\dfrac{\sin\frac{\pi}{3}\tan\frac{\pi}{6}}{\csc\frac{\pi}{4}}$

b. $\sec\frac{5\pi}{3}\cot\frac{\pi}{6} - \tan\frac{3\pi}{4}$

c. $\sin\left(\frac{5\pi}{4} - \frac{2\pi}{3}\right)$

d. $\dfrac{\tan\frac{7\pi}{8} - \tan\frac{5\pi}{8}}{1 + \tan\frac{7\pi}{8}\tan\frac{5\pi}{8}}$

e. $\sec^2\left(\frac{11\pi}{6}\right) - \csc^2\left(\frac{7\pi}{4}\right)$

f. $\cos\frac{5\pi}{12} + \cos\frac{\pi}{12}$

⑪ Match the equivalent expressions. Then prove algebraically that they are equal.

A csc x •

B sin $2x$ •

C sec^2 x + 2 tan x •

D cos^2 x − sin^2 x •

• cos $3x$ cos x + sin $3x$ sin x

• $(1 + \tan x)^2$

• sec x cot x

• $\dfrac{2 \cot x}{\csc^2 x}$

A

B

C

D

⑫ Solve each equation in the given range.

a. cos $\theta = \dfrac{1}{2}$ when $0 \le x \le \pi$

b. sin^2 $\theta = \dfrac{1}{4}$ when $\pi \le x \le 2\pi$

c. $\sqrt{3}$ sec $\theta + 2 = 0$ when $\pi \le x \le 2\pi$

d. csc^2 $\theta - 2 = 0$ when $0 \le x \le \pi$

ISBN: 978-1-77149-223-2

Application

⑬ A 1-m tall painting is hung 0.8 m down from the ceiling. A spotlight is mounted on the ceiling so that the angles of depression are equal as shown. Determine the distance of the spotlight from the wall, L.

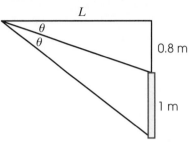

⑭ The average weekly temperature of Toronto can be modelled by $T(w) = -24 \cos \left(\frac{2\pi}{52} w\right) + 8$ in degree Celsius, where w is the number of weeks into a year. At which weeks in the year is the average temperature 20°C?

⑮ The distance in kilometres of a streetcar away from the station is modelled by $d(t) = -6 \sin \left(\frac{\pi}{10}(t + 5)\right) + 6$, where t is the time in minutes. Each round trip takes 20 minutes. When will the streetcar be 8 km away from the station in the next 30 minutes?

⑯ The water level in metres at a pier can be modelled by $w(t) = 4 \cos^2 \left(\frac{\pi}{12} t\right)$, where t is the time of day in 24 hours. What time of day will the water level be 1 m?

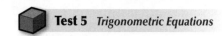

Communication

⑰ Describe how the compound angle formulas and double angle formulas are related when the compound angles are the same.

⑱ Describe how the Pythagorean identity $\sin^2 \theta + \cos^2 \theta = 1$ holds true using the unit circle.

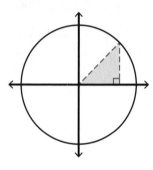

⑲ Explain why $(\sin \theta - 2)(\cos \theta + 2) = 0$ has no solutions.

⑳ To solve for $\tan x = -1$, Jason used a calculator and found that $\tan^{-1} (-1) = -45$. He says, "Since $\tan x$ is negative, it must be in quadrants 2 or 4. So x is $\pi - 45$ or $2\pi - 45$." Point out the mistake Jason made in his statement.

Thinking

㉑ Prove the following identities.

a. $\sin^4 x - \cos^4 x = 2\sin^2 x - 1$

b. $\cos\left(\frac{3\pi}{4} - x\right) - \sin\left(\frac{3\pi}{4} + x\right) = -\sqrt{2}\,(\cos x - \sin x)$

c. $\dfrac{\sin 2x}{1 - \cos 2x} = \cot x$

d. $\dfrac{1}{\sin A\,(\tan A + \cot A)} = \cos A$

㉒ Solve where $0 \le x \le 2\pi$.

a. $\sin 2x = \cos x$

b. $(2\cos x - \sqrt{3})\cot x = 0$

c. $\tan^2 x = 3 - 2\tan x$

d. $4\sin^2 x = 6 + 5\sin x$

Test 6

Exponential and Logarithmic Functions

TEST AREAS

- understanding exponential and logarithmic functions
- identifying transformations of logarithmic functions
- applying laws of logarithm
- solving problems with exponential and logarithmic functions

---

Knowledge and Understanding

Circle the correct answers.

① Evaluate $\log_9 1$.

    A. 1   B. 9

    C. 0   D. -1

② Evaluate $3^{\log_3 2}$.

    A. 2   B. 3

    C. 9   D. 27

③ State the inverse of $y = a^x$.

    A. $-x = a^y$ B. $\log_a y = x$

    C. $y = a^{-x}$ D. $\log_a x = y$

④ State the inverse of $y = \log_3 x$.

    A. $\log_y 3 = x$ B. $3^y = x$

    C. $3^x = y$ D. $1 = x^{\log_3 y}$

⑤ If $\log_{10} 5 = m$ and $\log_{10} 3 = n$, what is the value of $\log_{10}(\frac{50}{3})$?

    A. $m + n$ B. $m - n$

    C. $m + n - 1$ D. $m - n + 1$

⑥ Which function corresponds to the graph?

    A. $y = 2^x$

    B. $y = (\frac{1}{2})^x$

    C. $y = \log_2 x$

    D. $y = \log_{\frac{1}{2}} x$

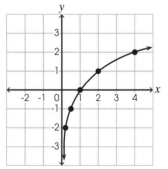

⑦ What is the vertical asymptote of $y = -3 \log_{10}(x - 1) + 2$?

    A. $x = -3$ B. $x = 1$

    C. $x = 2$ D. $x = 0$

⑧ What is the domain of $y = 2 \log_3(x - 2) + 1$?

    A. $\{x \in \mathbb{R}\}$ B. $\{x \in \mathbb{R} \mid x > 0\}$

    C. $\{x \in \mathbb{R} \mid x > 1\}$ D. $\{x \in \mathbb{R} \mid x > 2\}$

⑨ What is the range of $y = 4(2^x) - 5$?

    A. $\{y \in \mathbb{R}\}$ B. $\{y \in \mathbb{R} \mid y > -5\}$

    C. $\{y \in \mathbb{R} \mid y > 0\}$ D. $\{y \in \mathbb{R} \mid y > 4\}$

⑩ Solve the equations.

a. $\log_2 64 = x$

b. $\log_{25} x = 0.5$

c. $\log_x 9 = \frac{2}{3}$

d. $5^{x+8} = \frac{1}{25}$

e. $8^{2x-1} = 16^{x-1}$

f. $x = \log_2(\frac{1}{\sqrt{8}})$

g. $36(3^{3x+1}) = 4$

h. $\log_3(5x - 1) = 2$

i. $\log_x 5 - \log_x 2 = 1$

⑪ Complete the table. Then solve for x.

	Exponential Form	Logarithmic Form
A	$x = 5^3$	
B	$3x = \sqrt{6}$	
C		$\log_x(\frac{1}{9}) = -2$
D		$\log_2(\frac{2}{x}) = \frac{3}{2}$
E	$2x^{-3} = \frac{27}{4}$	
F		$\frac{1}{2}\log_2 8 = \frac{x}{4}$

A

B

C

D

E

F

ISBN: 978-1-77149-223-2

⑫ Express as a single logarithm.

a. $2 \log 2 + \log 25$

b. $\frac{1}{2} \log_2 5 - \log_2 10$

c. $\log_3 7 - \log_3 9 + \log_3 20$

d. $1 - (\log_5 10 + 2 \log_5 3)$

⑬ Make a sketch of each graph. Then find the properties of the function.

a. $f(x) = \log (x + 2) - 1$

Domain:

_____

Range:

_____

Asymptote(s):

_____

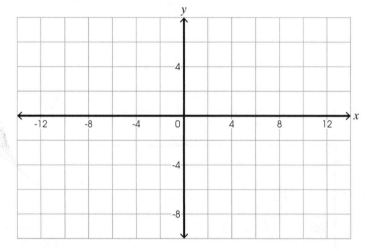

b. $f(x) = -\log (2(x - 1)) + 3$

Domain:

_____

Range:

_____

Asymptote(s):

_____

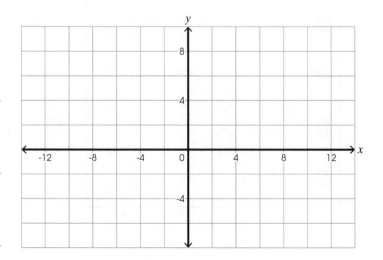

ISBN: 978-1-77149-223-2

Application

⑭ A difference of 1 magnitude on the Richter magnitude scale corresponds to a 10-time change of an earthquake's intensity. An earthquake registered a magnitude of 8.2. It was followed by an aftershock with a magnitude of 7.1. How many times more intense was the initial earthquake than the aftershock?

⑮ An increase of 1 pH unit represents a 10-time reduction in the concentration of hydrogen ions (H^+) in a solution. A glass of water was measured to have an H^+ concentration of 0.000 023 mol/L. What is the pH of the water? Round your answer to 2 decimal places.

⑯ A strain of bacteria doubles every 30 minutes. How many hours will it take for the strain to grow from 400 to 51 200 bacteria?

⑰ At what annual interest rate will $500 grow to $2000 in 18 years compounded annually?

⑱ A car is currently worth $11 579. The car was worth $21 000 when it was first purchased 3 years ago. What is the annual depreciation rate of the car? Round your answer to the nearest whole percent.

⑲ The half-life of carbon-14 is 5730 years.

a. How long does it take for 3000 mg of carbon-14 to decay to 375 mg?

b. A fossil was formed 8680 years ago. If the fossil contains 280 mg of carbon-14 now, how much carbon-14 was there initially?

⑳ An unknown isotope decayed from 2100 mg to 1750 mg after 1 day. What is the half-life of the isotope?

㉑ A clock tower's sound level is modelled by $C(d) = 90(10^{-0.4d})$ in dB, where d is the distance in kilometres from the tower. How far away from the clock tower will the sound level be 20% of the original 90 dB sound?

㉒ Kyle kept track of his savings in a compounded interest account. Write an equation that models his savings over time. How long will it take for the initial investment to double?

Kyle's Savings

Year	Amount ($)
0	5000
1	5200
2	5408
3	5624.32
4	5849.29
5	6083.26

ISBN: 978-1-77149-223-2

Communication

㉓ Describe the transformations applied to the base function $f(x) = \log x$ in order to obtain the function $g(x) = -2 \log (3(x - 2)) - 5$.

㉔ Explain why in logarithmic expressions $\log_a b$ where $a > 0$, b must be a positive number.

㉕ Describe the difference between $\log x^2$ and $(\log x)^2$. Provide an example.

㉖ List the steps to finding the inverse of a logarithmic function algebraically and graphically.

Thinking

㉗ Evaluate the following without using a calculator. Show your work. Use fractions when appropriate.

a. $\log_{\frac{1}{3}}\sqrt{27}$

b. $\log_2\sqrt{96} - \log_2\sqrt{3}$

㉘ Factor as needed. Then solve for x. Round your anwers to 2 decimal places when necessary.

a. $5^{x+2} + 5^x = 650$

b. $6(2^x) = 5(3^x)$

c. $3^{x^2} = \dfrac{27}{9^x}$

d. $4^{2x} = 3^{x-1}$

e. $(2^x - 1)^2 = 16$

f. $2^{2x} + 2^{x+2} - 2^5 = 0$

ISBN: 978-1-77149-223-2

㉙ Consider the logarithmic equation $y = \dfrac{1}{2} \log(3(x-1)) + 2$.

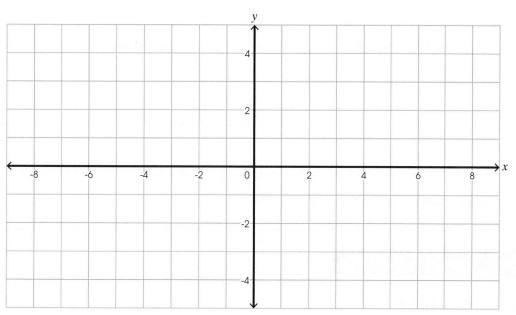

a. Sketch the graph of the function. Find its properties.

Domain: _____

Range: _____

Asymptote(s): _____

b. Sketch the inverse of the function without the use of algebra. Find its properties.

Domain: _____

Range: _____

Asymptote(s): _____

㉚ Show that $\log_a x = \dfrac{\log x}{\log a}$.

㉛ Show that $\log_4 a = \log_2 \sqrt{a}$.

ISBN: 978-1-77149-223-2

Rates of Change

TEST AREAS

- understanding average and instantaneous rates of change
- finding rates of change in polynomial, rational, trigonometric, exponential, and logarithmic functions
- identifying greatest and least rates of change algebraically and graphically
- solving problems using rates of change

Knowledge and Understanding

Circle the correct answers.

① Which formula determines the average rate of change?

A. $\dfrac{f(x_1) + f(x_2)}{x_1 + x_2}$ B. $\dfrac{f(x + h) - f(x)}{h}$ C. $\dfrac{f(x_2) - f(x_1)}{x_2 - x_1}$ D. $\dfrac{f(x + h) + f(x - h)}{2h}$

② Which of the following is the difference quotient?

A. $\dfrac{f(a_1) + f(a_2)}{a_1 + a_2}$ B. $\dfrac{f(a + h) - f(a)}{h}$ C. $\dfrac{f(a_2) - f(a_1)}{a_2 - a_1}$ D. $\dfrac{f(a + h) + f(a - h)}{2h}$

③ What is the instantaneous rate of change of a polynomial function at its turning point?

A. 1 B. undefined C. ∞ D. 0

④ In a logarithmic function, what is the instantaneous rate of change for small values of x?

A. close to 0 B. very large C. very small D. none of the above

⑤ Consider the given graph.

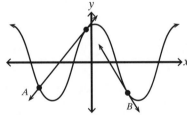

a. What is Line A?

A. secant line B. sine function
C. tangent line D. cosine function

b. What is Line B?

A. secant line B. sine function
C. tangent line D. cosine function

⑥ Where on a rational function does its instantaneous rate of change approach 0?

A. at its vertical asymptote

B. at its horizontal asymptote

C. near its vertical asymptote

D. near its horizontal asymptote

⑦ Which of the following has an instantaneous rate of change of 0?

A. a sine function at its maximum

B. a cosine function at its minimum

C. a quadratic function at its vertex

D. all of the above

  ISBN: 978-1-77149-223-2

⑧ Find the average rate of change of each function $f(x)$ over the given interval.

a. $f(x) = 3x^2$, for $-1 \leq x \leq 2$

b. $f(x) = x^3 - 2x + 1$, for $-2 \leq x \leq 3$

c. $f(x) = \dfrac{1}{x} + 4$, for $x \in [4,8]$

d. $f(x) = 2\sin x - 1$, for $x \in [-1,1]$

e. $f(x) = 2^x - 3$, for $2 \leq x \leq 4$

f. $f(x) = -\log 2x$, for $0.5 \leq x \leq 5$

⑨ Consider the function $f(x) = \sin(x + 2\pi) - \dfrac{1}{2}$ for $0 \leq x \leq 2\pi$.

a. Find an interval in which the function $f(x)$ has an average rate of change that is 0.

b. Find an interval in which the average rate of change is negative.

⑩ Consider the function $f(x) = x^4 + 2x^3 - 3x^2 - 4x$. Determine whether $(-2,-4)$ is a local maximum, a local minimum, or neither.

ISBN: 978-1-77149-223-2

⑪ Estimate the instantaneous rate of change for each function at the given value of x.

a. $f(x) = -3x^2 + 5x$ at $x = 2$

b. $f(x) = 2x^3 - 3x^2 - 3x + 2$ at $x = -2$

c. $f(x) = \dfrac{2x}{x - 1}$ at $x = -1$

d. $f(x) = \dfrac{1}{2}\cos 2x$ at $x = \dfrac{3\pi}{4}$

e. $f(x) = 25(1.8)^{-x}$ at $x = 6$

f. $f(x) = 49 \log x - 14$ at $x = 16$

Application

⑫ A bathtub is being drained. The volume, $V(t)$, in litres, of the water remaining in the bathtub after t minutes can be modelled by the function $V(t) = 1.4(5 - t)^3$.

a. What is the average rate of change of volume during the first 2 minutes?

b. Estimate the instantaneous rate of change of volume at 4 minutes. Is the function increasing or decreasing?

     ISBN: 978-1-77149-223-2

⑬ The demand function for doughnuts is given by $p(x) = \dfrac{3}{x^2 + x + 2}$. The x is the number of doughnuts sold in thousands, and the price per doughnut, $p(x)$, is in dollars.

a. What is the revenue function, $R(x)$, of the doughnuts?

b. Estimate the marginal revenue for $x = 0.7$.

⑭ The horizontal distance, in centimetres, of a pendulum from one side to the other is given by $d(t) = 5 \cos(\pi t) + 5$, where t is the time in seconds. Estimate the instantaneous speed of the pendulum at 3.5 s.

⑮ Michael invests $1400 with an interest rate of 12%, compounded twice annually. Estimate the instantaneous rate of change when Michael doubles his initial investment.

⑯ The memory retention of a person, as a percent over time in t minutes, is given by $m(t) = -15 \log(t + 0.0216) + 75$. What are the average rates of change after 20 minutes and after 8 hours?

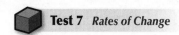

Communication

⑰ How does a secant line passing through the point (x_1, y_1) relate to the instantaneous rate of change at (x_1, y_1)?

⑱ What is the difference between finding the average rate of change and the instantaneous rate of change?

⑲ When will the least and greatest instantaneous rates of change occur in a sinusoidal function?

⑳ What will the instantaneous rate of change be as x approaches a horizontal asymptote and a vertical asymptote?

Thinking

㉑ Find the equation of the tangent for each function at the given value of x.

 a. $f(x) = 3x^2 + 7x - 2$ at $x = 2$

 b. $f(x) = \dfrac{2}{x + 6}$ at $x = -3$

㉒ Find the instantaneous rate of change for each function algebraically.

 a. $f(x) = x^3$

 b. $g(x) = -\dfrac{3}{x}$

㉓ Refer to the functions in Question 22. Find the values of x which have the instantaneous rate of change of 27.

 a. $f(x)$

 b. $g(x)$

Test 8 Combining Functions

TEST AREAS

- understanding combinations of functions through addition, subtraction, multiplication, division, and composition
- exploring combinations of functions graphically, numerically, and algebraically
- identifying characteristics of combinations of functions
- modelling and solving real-life problems using combinations of functions

Knowledge and Understanding

Circle the correct answers.

① The ordered pairs of $f(x)$ and $g(x)$ are given.

> $f = \{(2,1), (3,2), (4,5), (6,7)\}$
> $g = \{(1,2), (2,6), (4,4), (7,4)\}$

a. What is $f + g$?

A. $\{(3,3), (5,8), (10,9), (13,11)\}$

B. $\{(1,2), (2,7), (3,2), (4,9), (6,7), (7,4)\}$

C. $\{(2,7), (4,9)\}$

D. $\{(2,2), (3,6), (4,5), (6,4)\}$

b. What is $f \times g$?

A. $\{(2,2), (6,12), (16,20), (42,28)\}$

B. $\{(2,6), (4,20)\}$

C. $\{(4,6), (16,20)\}$

D. $\{(1,2), (3,2), (6,7), (7,4)\}$

② When $h(x) = x^2 + 3$ and $k(x) = -2x$, what is $(h - k)(3)$?

A. 6   B. 18

C. 39   D. 50

③ When $m(x) = 2x + 1$ and $n(x) = \sqrt{x - 1}$, what is $(m \div n)(10)$?

A. 6   B. 7

C. 15   D. 21

④ Consider the graphs of $f(x)$ and $g(x)$.

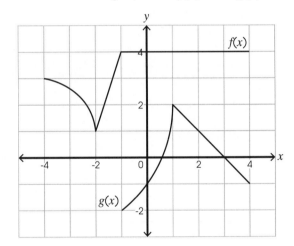

a. What is $(f \circ g)(2)$?

A. 0   B. 4

C. 2   D. -1

b. What is $(g \circ f)(-1)$?

A. 1   B. -2

C. -1   D. 2

c. What is $(f \circ f)(0)$?

A. 1   B. 4

C. -3   D. -2

d. What is $(g \circ g)(1)$?

A. 4   B. -2

C. 1   D. 0

ISBN: 978-1-77149-223-2

⑤ Use the given functions to create the combined functions. Then match each combined function with its graph.

$$f(x) = -2x^2 + 1 \qquad g(x) = 1.2^x \qquad h(x) = 2\sin x$$

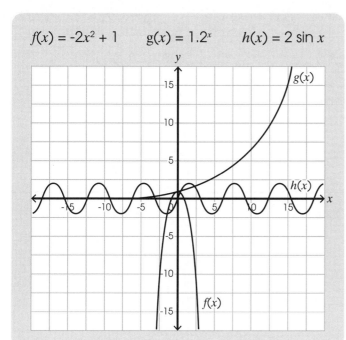

A $(g + h)(x)$

B $(f \times g)(x)$

C $(h - g)(x)$

D $(f \div g)(x)$

Note: The graphs of the combined functions below are in bold.

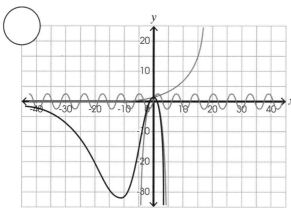

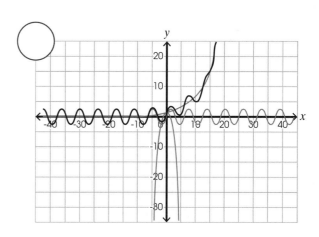

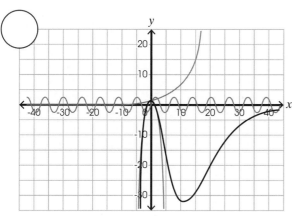

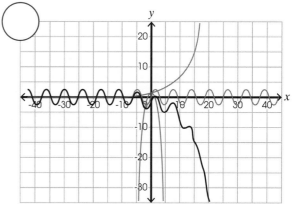

ISBN: 978-1-77149-223-2

⑥ Find the combined functions. State the domain of each.

| $f(x) = \dfrac{1}{x^2}$ $\quad g(x) = 2^x$ | $f(x) = \sin x \quad g(x) = \log x$ | $f(x) = \sqrt{2x + 3} \quad g(x) = x - 1$ |

a. $(f + g)(x)$

c. $(f \div g)(x)$

e. $(g \times f)(x)$

_____

_____

_____

b. $(f \circ g)(x)$

d. $(g \circ f)(x)$

f. $(f \circ g)(x)$

_____

_____

_____

⑦ Solve for x in the given interval using a guess and improvement strategy.

a. $3^x - 4 = -x^3$, $-2 \le x \le 2$

b. $\log x = \cos x$, $\pi \le x \le 2\pi$

c. $\sqrt{x + 6} - 1 = \dfrac{4}{x^2}$, $-6 \le x \le 2$

d. $|x| - 2 = x^4 - 10x^2 + 9$, $-4 \le x \le 4$

Application

⑧ The revenue and operating cost of a car wash facility are given by $R(x) = 12x - 0.5x^2$ and $C(x) = 2x + 4$, where x represents the number of cars washed.

a. What is the profit function, $P(x)$?

b. What is the profit when 15 cars are washed?

c. Will washing 10 cars make the maximum profit?

⑨ Mr. Travis tracks his students' test scores and the number of hours they studied. He found that his students score an average of 27 marks when they do not study and an average of 65 marks when they study for 3 hours. The test is out of 100 marks.

a. Use a logistic model to write a function of average test scores on the number of hours studied.

b. Use the model to estimate how long the students need to study to get an average of 80 marks.

c. Use the model to estimate the average rate of change of test marks over the first 5 hours of studying.

⑩ The radius in centimetres of a growing orange can be modelled by $r(t) = 4 - 4(0.65^t)$, where t is the time grown in months.

   a. What is the maximum radius of an orange?

   b. Assuming the orange is a perfect sphere, write the function $V(t)$ where the volume is given in cm^3.

   c. What is the volume of the orange if it is picked at 10 months?

⑪ To restore a forest's ecosystem, ecologists reintroduced a plant species and the recent growth of this species is recorded in the table. The maximum number of plants is 940.

Year	2005	2006	2007	2008	2009	2010	2011	2012	2013	2014
No. of Plants	85	134	204	297	409	529	641	734	805	854

   a. Make a graph for the set of data and write the function $n(t)$, where n is the number of plants and t is the year.

   b. Use the function to extrapolate the number of plants in the year 2020.

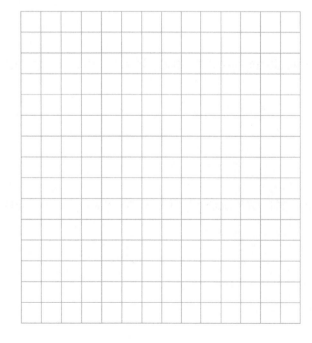

   c. 10 plants were initially introduced to the forest. In which year were they introduced?

Communication

⑫ What is known about the functions $f(x)$ and $g(x)$ if $(f + g)(x) = 0$? Describe their graphs.

⑬ Describe how the domain of a combined function is determined.

⑭ If $f(x) \neq g(x)$, is it always true that $(f \circ g)(x) \neq (g \circ f)(x)$? Give an example to support your reasoning.

⑮ Explain why $(f \circ f^{-1})(x) = x$. Give an example.

⑯ Write the functions of the exponential model and the logistic model. Compare their limits.

ISBN: 978-1-77149-223-2

Thinking

⑰ Create a linear function $f(x)$ and a quadratic function $g(x)$ such that they satisfy the two conditions stated below.

$$(f + g)(x) = -2x^2 - 2x + 5$$
$$(f - g)(x) = 2x^2 - 8x + 1$$

⑱ A quadratic function of the form $f(x) = x^2 + n$ and a linear function of the form $g(x) = px + q$ have the following properties:

$(f + g)(0) = -6$ $(f \times g)(-2) = 4$

$(f - g)(0) = 2$ $(\frac{f}{g})(-1) = 1$

a. Solve for n and p to find the functions $f(x)$ and $g(x)$ that satisfy all the properties above.

b. Solve for x if $(f \circ g)(x) = (g \circ f)(x)$.

⑲ a. Given $f(x) = \sqrt{x^3 + 2}$, determine $p(x)$, $q(x)$, and $r(x)$ such that $f(x) = p(q(r(x)))$. State the domain of each function.

b. Determine $r(q(p(x)))$ and its domain.

c. Determine $p(q(r^{-1}(r(x))))$ and its domain.

⑳ Use the graphs of $f(x)$ and $g(x)$ to draw the combined functions.

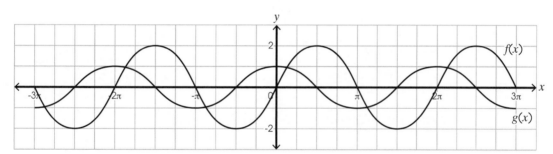

a. $(f - g)(x)$

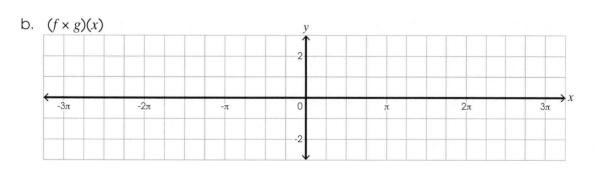

b. $(f \times g)(x)$

ISBN: 978-1-77149-223-2

Knowledge and Understanding

Circle the correct answers.

① What are the end behaviours of the function $f(x) = (x - 2)^2(x - 1)$?

A. As $x \to \infty$, $y \to \infty$ and as $x \to -\infty$, $y \to -\infty$.   B. As $x \to \infty$, $y \to \infty$ and as $x \to -\infty$, $y \to \infty$.

C. As $x \to \infty$, $y \to -\infty$ and as $x \to -\infty$, $y \to -\infty$.   D. As $x \to \infty$, $y \to -\infty$ and as $x \to -\infty$, $y \to \infty$.

② If $f(x) = x^3 + 2x^2 - 20$ is divided by $(x - 1)$, what will the remainder be?

A. -23   B. -20   C. -17   D. 0

③ How many x-intercepts does the function $f(x) = \frac{1}{2}(x - 1)(x + 3)(x - 2)$ have?

A. 1   B. 2   C. 3   D. 4

④ What is the exact value of $\cos\left(\frac{\pi}{8}\right) \cos\left(\frac{3\pi}{8}\right) - \sin\left(\frac{\pi}{8}\right) \sin\left(\frac{3\pi}{8}\right)$?

A. $\frac{\pi}{2}$ B. 0   C. $-\frac{\pi}{2}$ D. $\frac{1}{\sqrt{2}}$

⑤ Consider the function $y = 2\cos\left(\frac{\pi}{6}x - \pi\right) + 1$. Which value is the horizontal translation of the function?

A. $\frac{\pi}{6}$ B. π C. 1   D. 6

⑥ Where will a hole appear in $y = \frac{x - 2}{x^2 - x - 2}$?

A. $x = -2$ B. $x = -1$ C. $x = 1$ D. $x = 2$

⑦ Consider $f(x) = 2^x$. Which of the following is equivalent to $2f(x)$?

A. $y = f(2x)$ B. $y = f(x + 1)$ C. $y = f(x) + 2$ D. $y = f(x) + 1$

⑧ What is the asymptote of $f(x) = \frac{2x + 3}{x - 4}$?

A. $x = 4$ B. $y = 4$ C. $x = -\frac{3}{2}$ D. $y = \frac{2}{3}$

⑨ If $f(x) = x^2 + 1$ and $g(x) = \frac{1}{x}$, what will the value of $(f \circ g)(2)$ be?

A. $\frac{1}{5}$ B. 5   C. $\frac{5}{4}$ D. $\frac{9}{4}$

⑩ What is the average rate of change for $f(x) = 2^x + x^2$ on the interval $x \in [0, 3]$?

A. $\frac{16}{3}$ B. $\frac{17}{3}$ C. 6   D. $\frac{19}{3}$

⑪ Which of the following is equivalent to the instantaneous rate of change?

A. the curve of best fit   B. the slope of the line of best fit

C. the slope of the tangent line   D. the slope of the secant line

ISBN: 978-1-77149-223-2

⑫ Solve for x.

    a. $3x^4 - 7x^3 - 13x^2 + 23x - 6 = 0$ b. $\log_7(x + 4) + \log_7(x - 2) = 1$

    c. $\tan x = \dfrac{1}{\sin 2x}, \; 0 \le x \le \pi$ d. $4^{2x} = 8^{x - 1}$

    e. $2 \log_x 16 = \log_x 4 + 2$ f. $4 \sin x \cos x - 1 = 0, \; 0 \le x \le \dfrac{\pi}{2}$

⑬ For each graph, determine the minimum degree of its function and whether its leading coefficient is positive or negative.

a.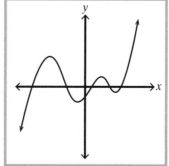

b.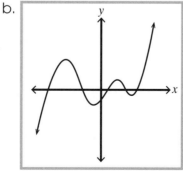

c.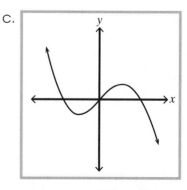

| degree | leading coefficient | | degree | leading coefficient | | degree | leading coefficient |

ISBN: 978-1-77149-223-2

⑭ Make a sketch of the rational functions. Label the key points and asymptotes. Then list their characteristics.

a. $f(x) = \dfrac{2x^2 - 3x - 2}{2x - 4}$

b. $f(x) = \dfrac{2x^2 - 7x - 4}{2x^2 + 7x + 3}$

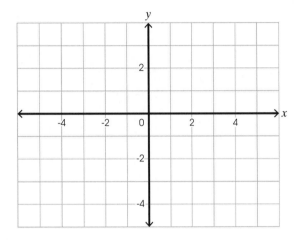

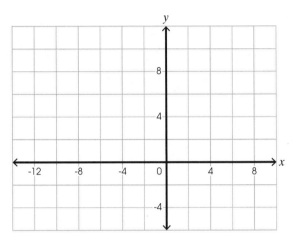

_____   _____
  domain   range

_____   _____
  domain   range

_____
  positive and negative intervals

_____
  positive and negative intervals

⑮ Find the average rates of change of the functions and the instantaneous rates of change of the combined functions.

a. Find the average rates of change.

$f(x) = x^3 - 64,\ x \in [0, 4]$

$g(x) = \dfrac{1}{x - 4},\ x \in [-2, 0]$

$m(x) = \log_8(2x^2),\ x \in [1, 8]$

$n(x) = 0.6(8^x),\ x \in [-1, 1]$

b. Find the instantaneous rates of change.

$(f \times g)(x)$ at $x = 3$

$(n \circ m)(x)$ at $x = -3$

ISBN: 978-1-77149-223-2

⑯　Consider the given graph. Answer the questions.

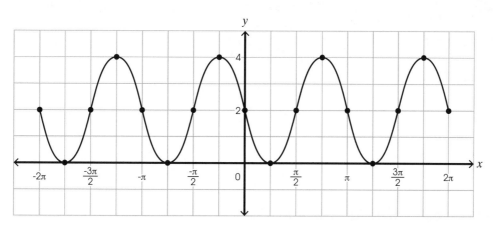

a. State the characteristics.

period: _____

amplitude: _____

maximum value: _____

minimum value: _____

domain: _____

range: _____

b. Model the graph using a sine function and a cosine function.

c. What are the greatest and the least instantaneous rates of change?

⑰　Solve the inequalities.

a. $x^3 + 6 \geq x(2x + 5)$

b. $\dfrac{x}{x + 6} < \dfrac{1}{x + 2}$

ISBN: 978-1-77149-223-2

Application

⑱ The population of a small town is modelled by the function $P(t) = -2t^3 + 54t^2 - 40t + 21\,000$, where t represents the number of years since 2015.

a. What will the population be in the year 2020?

b. When will the population fall below 14 400?

c. Determine the average rate of change of the population from 2018 to 2028.

d. Approximate the instantaneous rate of change in the year 2037.

⑲ Gunter borrows $1500 at an annual interest rate of 12% and invests all of it at 1% monthly interest rate.

a. How much will Gunter gain in total after 5 years?

b. Approximate the instantaneous rate of change for Gunter's net gain in 10 years.

⑳ The value of a machinery in thousands of dollars as a function of the time t in months can be modelled by $V(t) = \dfrac{4t + 750}{t + 30}$. It was paid monthly and the total payment in thousands of dollars can be modelled by $P(t) = 0.25t + 3$.

a. After how many months will the value of the machinery decrease by 39%?

b. What is the minimum value of the machinery?

c. After how many months will the total payment exceed the value of the machinery?

㉑ Camilla is running on a treadmill. The speed in m/s over time can be modelled by the function $V(t) = \sin\left(\dfrac{\pi}{10}t\right) + 0.6t - 0.01t^2$, where t is the time in minutes.

a. What is her speed at 30 minutes?

b. Is Camilla running at the maximum speed at 50 minutes?

c. What is the average rate of change for speed from 20 min to 25 min?

ISBN: 978-1-77149-223-2

㉒ The height of a hill relative to its width x in metres can be modelled by the function
$h(x) = -100 \log ((x - 90)^2 + 1900) + 400$.

a. What is the total width of the hill?

b. What is the instantaneous rate of change at a width of 130 m?

c. Is the maximum height of the hill at $x = 90$?

㉓ Dr. Kim uses a model to predict the number of students infected with a virus at a school over the school year. The model is $S(x) = (f \circ g \circ h)(x)$, where $f(x) = x^{-1}$, $g(x) = x + 0.005$, $h(x) = 0.95^x$, and x is the number of school days.

a. Write the model as a logistic function.

b. What is the predicted maximum number of students infected?

c. How many days will it take for 80% of the students to be infected?

ISBN: 978-1-77149-223-2

Communication

㉔ Describe the end behaviours of a polynomial function of 5th degree with a positive leading coefficient. What are all the possible numbers of x-intercepts? Give examples.

㉕ Determine the asymptotes of the function $f(x) = \dfrac{(x + 3)(x - 2)}{(x + 1)}$ and its reciprocal.

㉖ Describe the transformations needed to change $f(x) = -2\cos(3x) - 4$ to $g(x) = \dfrac{1}{2}\cos(\dfrac{\pi}{4}x) + 3$.

㉗ Consider the functions $f(x) = \log x$ and $g(x) = 10^x$. Are $(f \circ g)(x)$ and $(g \circ f)(x)$ equal? Explain.

Cumulative Test

Thinking

㉘ Determine the exact values of x.

a. $\log_4(x - 2) = \log_2(2x - 5)$

b. $\sin 2x - 2 = 2(\sin x - \cos x)$, $0 \le x \le 2\pi$

c. $2^{2x} + 2^{x+2} - 2^5 = 0$

d. $\cos^3 x + \sin^3 x = 0$, $-\dfrac{\pi}{2} \le x \le \dfrac{\pi}{2}$

㉙ Solve the inequalities.

a. $\dfrac{\tan x}{\log x} < 0$, $0 \le x \le \pi$

b. $\dfrac{\sqrt{x + 2}}{2^x - 1} < 0$, $-4 \le x \le 4$

c. $10^{\sin x} - 1 \ge 0$, $0 \le x \le 2\pi$

d. $2\cos^2 x \ge -\cos x + 1$, $-\pi \le 0 \le \pi$

㉚ Consider the given functions and answer the questions.

$$f(x) = 2x^2 + x - 3 \qquad g(x) = x^3 - 1$$

a. Sketch $h(x)$ for $h(x) = g(x) - f(x)$.

b. Find the instantaneous rate of change of $h(x)$ at $x = -1$.

c. Find an interval of x for which the average rate of change is 0.

㉛ Prove the identities.

a. $\dfrac{\cos \theta - \sin 2\theta}{\cos 2\theta + \sin \theta - 1} = \cot \theta$

b. $\sin 2x \tan^2 x = \dfrac{2 - 2 \cos^2 x}{\cot x}$

ISBN: 978-1-77149-223-2

ISBN: 978-1-77149-223-2

Complete MathSmart 12
Calculus and Vectors

ISBN: 978-1-77149-223-2

Test 1 Limits

 TEST AREAS

- simplifying and rationalizing radical expressions
- determining the slope of a tangent and rates of change
- exploring the limits of a function and its properties
- understanding discontinuities

Knowledge and Understanding

Circle the correct answers.

① Which of the following is equal to $\dfrac{3}{\sqrt{2}}$?

A. $\dfrac{\sqrt{2}}{3}$ B. $\dfrac{3\sqrt{2}}{2}$

C. $\dfrac{2}{\sqrt{3}}$ D. $\dfrac{2\sqrt{2}}{3}$

② Which of the following is equal to $\dfrac{\sqrt{5} - \sqrt{3}}{2}$?

A. $\dfrac{\sqrt{5} + \sqrt{3}}{2}$ B. $\dfrac{1}{\sqrt{5} - \sqrt{3}}$

C. $\dfrac{1}{2(\sqrt{5} - \sqrt{2})}$ D. $\dfrac{1}{\sqrt{5} + \sqrt{3}}$

③ What is the slope of the tangent of $y = x^2 - 2x$ at $x = 2$?

A. 0 B. 1
C. 2 D. 4

④ What is the slope of the tangent of $f(x) = \sqrt{x - 5}$ at $x = 9$?

A. $\dfrac{1}{2}$ B. $\dfrac{1}{4}$

C. $\dfrac{1}{5}$ D. $\dfrac{1}{9}$

⑤ What is the average rate of change of $f(x) = 4x(x - 3)$ for $2 \le x \le 5$?

A. -8
B. 3
C. 16
D. 40

⑥ Which is the value of $\lim\limits_{x \to 0} x + 3$?

A. -3
B. 0
C. 3
D. 6

⑦ Which of the following functions is continuous at $x = -3$?

A. $f(x) = 2x^2$ B. $f(x) = \sqrt{x + 3}$

C. $f(x) = \dfrac{1}{x + 3}$ D. $f(x) = \begin{cases} x, & \text{if } x > -3 \\ -x, & \text{if } x \le -3 \end{cases}$

⑧ What is the discontinuity shown in the graph?

A. point discontinuity
B. jump discontinuity
C. infinite discontinuity
D. none of the above

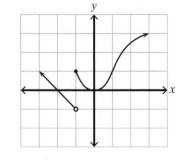

ISBN: 978-1-77149-223-2

⑨ Rationalize the denominator or numerator as specified for each expression. Write your answer in simplest form.

denominator	numerator

a. $\dfrac{\sqrt{7} + \sqrt{2}}{\sqrt{3}}$

c. $\dfrac{\sqrt{7} + \sqrt{2}}{\sqrt{3}}$

b. $\dfrac{4\sqrt{5} - 2\sqrt{3}}{3\sqrt{2}}$

d. $\dfrac{4\sqrt{5} - 2\sqrt{3}}{3\sqrt{2}}$

⑩ Evaluate the limits algebraically.

a. $\lim\limits_{x \to 3} x$

b. $\lim\limits_{x \to \text{-}2} (x - 2)$

c. $\lim\limits_{x \to 2} 3x$

d. $\lim\limits_{x \to \text{-}1} x^2$

e. $\lim\limits_{x \to 1} ((x - 1)(x + 2))$

f. $\lim\limits_{x \to 4} \dfrac{(x + 3)}{(x - 2)}$

ISBN: 978-1-77149-223-2

⑪ Sketch a graph of each function. Then answer the questions.

a. $f(x) = -\frac{1}{2}x^2$

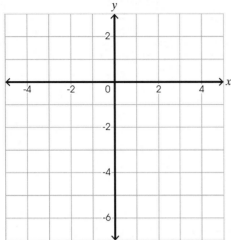

b. $f(x) = \sqrt{x - 1}$

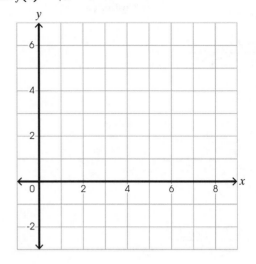

• What is $\lim\limits_{x \to -1} f(x)$?

• What is $\lim\limits_{x \to 5} f(x)$?

• Determine the equation of the tangent at $x = -1$.

• Determine the equation of the tangent at $x = 5$.

⑫ Consider the given function. Answer the questions.

a. Find all the discontinuities and classify them.

$$f(x) = \begin{cases} \dfrac{1}{x^2} - 1, & \text{if } x < 1 \\ \dfrac{x^2 - 2x}{x - 2}, & \text{if } x \geq 1 \end{cases}$$

b. What is $\lim\limits_{x \to -1} f(x)$?

c. What is $\lim\limits_{x \to 3} f(x)$?

ISBN: 978-1-77149-223-2

⑬ The distance in kilometres a truck travels is described by $S(t) = 10t(t + 2)$, where t is the time in hours for $0 \le t \le 5$.

a. What is the average velocity of the truck?

b. Approximate the instantaneous velocity at $t = 3$.

c. What is the velocity at $t = 5$?

⑭ A balloon is dropped from a height of 80 m. After t seconds the balloon is S metres above the ground, where $S(t) = 80 - 0.2t^2$ and $0 \le t \le 20$.

a. What is the average velocity of the balloon?

b. What is the average velocity of the balloon between 1 s and 1.5 s?

c. What is the velocity at 2 s?

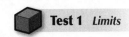

Communication

⑮ Given $f(x) = \dfrac{x-1}{\sqrt{x}-1}$, why is it necessary to rationalize the denominator to evaluate $\lim\limits_{x \to 1} f(x)$ but not for $\lim\limits_{x \to 4} f(x)$?

⑯ Describe the conditions required for $\lim\limits_{x \to a} f(x)$ to exist.

⑰ Explain why $\lim\limits_{x \to 2} \dfrac{x}{x-2}$ does not exist.

⑱ Describe 3 techniques to evaluate a limit algebraically.

 ISBN: 978-1-77149-223-2

⑲ Evaluate the limits algebraically. Show your work.

a. $\lim_{x \to 3} (5x^2 + 2x - 3)$

b. $\lim_{x \to -2} \dfrac{x^2 - 3x + 4}{3x^3 + 2x + 1}$

c. $\lim_{x \to -4} \sqrt{25 - x^2}$

d. $\lim_{x \to 12} \sqrt{\dfrac{4x^2}{x - 2}}$

e. $\lim_{x \to 4} \dfrac{x^2 - 6x + 8}{x - 4}$

f. $\lim_{x \to 0} \dfrac{\sqrt{x + 4} - 2}{x}$

g. $\lim_{x \to 0} \dfrac{(x + 81)^{\frac{1}{4}} - 3}{x}$

h. $\lim_{x \to 5} \dfrac{|x - 5|}{x - 5}$

Derivatives and Their Applications

TEST AREAS

- finding derivatives of polynomial functions
- understanding and applying derivative rules
- determining the maximum and minimum of a function
- solving optimization and other application problems

Knowledge and Understanding

Circle the correct answers.

① Which of the following is the notation of a derivative for $y = f(x)$?

A. $f'(x)$ 　　　　　 B. y'

C. $\dfrac{dy}{dx}$ 　　　　 D. all of the above

② Which is the definition of a derivative?

A. $\lim\limits_{h \to 0} \dfrac{f(a + h) - f(a)}{h}$

B. $\lim\limits_{x \to a} \dfrac{f(x) - f(a)}{x - a}$

C. $\lim\limits_{x \to 0} \dfrac{f(x + h) - f(x)}{x + h}$

D. A and B

③ If $f(x) = k$, where k is a constant, then

A. $f'(x) = k.$ 　　　 B. $f'(x) = 1.$
C. $f'(x) = 0.$ 　　　 D. $f'(x) = x.$

④ If $f(x) = x^n$, where n is a real number, then

A. $f'(x) = nx.$ 　　　 B. $f'(x) = nx^{-1}.$
C. $f'(x) = nx^n.$ 　　 D. $f'(x) = nx^{n-1}.$

⑤ The constant multiple rule states that if $f(x) = kg(x)$, where k is a constant, then

A. $f'(x) = kg(x).$ 　　 B. $f'(x) = kg'(x).$
C. $f'(x) = k + g(x).$ 　 D. $f'(x) = g(x)g'(x).$

⑥ Name the following rule: if $f(x) = p(x) - q(x)$, then $f'(x) = p'(x) - q'(x)$.

A. the sum rule 　　　 B. the difference rule
C. the product rule 　 D. the quotient rule

⑦ Which of the following is the product rule if $h(x) = f(x)g(x)$?

A. $h'(x) = f'(x)g'(x)$

B. $h'(x) = f'(x)g(x) + f(x)g'(x)$

C. $h'(x) = f'(x)g(x) - f(x)g'(x)$

D. $h'(x) = f'(x)g'(x) + f(x)g(x)$

⑧ Which of the following is the quotient rule if $h(x) = \dfrac{f(x)}{g(x)}$?

A. $h'(x) = \dfrac{f'(x)g(x) - f(x)g'(x)}{[g(x)]^2}$, $g(x) \neq 0$

B. $h'(x) = \dfrac{f(x)g'(x) - f'(x)g(x)}{[g(x)]^2}$, $g(x) \neq 0$

C. $h'(x) = \dfrac{f'(x)g(x) - f(x)g'(x)}{[f(x)]^2}$, $f(x) \neq 0$

D. $h'(x) = \dfrac{f(x)g'(x) - f'(x)g(x)}{[f(x)]^2}$, $f(x) \neq 0$

⑨ If $h(x) = (f \circ g)(x)$, then

A. $h'(x) = f'(g(x)).$ 　　　 B. $h'(x) = (f \circ g)(x)g'(x).$
C. $h'(x) = f'(g(x))g'(x).$ 　 D. $h'(x) = f(x)g(x)g'(x).$

⑩ Find the derivatives of each of the following functions.

a. $f(x) = 5x^2 + 2x$

b. $f(x) = 3x^3 - \frac{1}{2}x + 5$

c. $f(x) = x^6 + 7x^2 - 5x - 1$

d. $f(x) = 6\sqrt{x} + 3$

e. $f(x) = \frac{2}{x} - \frac{5}{x^2}$

f. $f(x) = 2\sqrt{x} - 6x + 7x^3$

g. $f(x) = x(x^2 + 1)$

h. $f(x) = (x + 3)(4x^4 - 2)$

i. $f(x) = \frac{1}{(x + 2)}$

j. $f(x) = \frac{(2x + 1)}{(x^2 - 1)}$

k. $f(x) = \frac{x^3}{(4 - x^2)}$

l. $f(x) = (x - 5)^2(x + 2)^3$

m. $f(x) = \sqrt{x^2 + 3x}$

n. $f(x) = 3(\sqrt{x} - 5)^2 + 1$

⑪ Determine the slope of the tangent to each of the curves at the given point.

a. $f(x) = \frac{x^3}{5 - 3x^2}$ (1, 0.5)

b. $f(x) = (x - 2)^2(x + 1)^3$ (-2, -16)

Calculus and Vectors

⑫ Complete the table with the derivatives.

$f(x) = x^2$ 　　　　$g(x) = 2x + 1$ 　　　　$h(x) = \sqrt{x - 3}$

	$y = f(x)h(x)$	$y = \dfrac{g(x)}{f(x)}$	$y = (h \circ g)(x)$
y'			
y''			

⑬ Find the point(s) where the tangent to the curve is horizontal.

a. $f(x) = -3x^2 + 108x - 722$ 　　　　　　b. $f(x) = (x^2 + x + 1)(x - 1)$

⑭ Find the absolute maximum and minimum for each function with the given interval.

a. $f(x) = (x^2 + 3)(x + 3)$, $-3 \le x \le 0$ 　　　　b. $g(x) = \dfrac{x^2 + 4}{x}$, $1 \le x \le 5$

⑮ A ball falls from a cliff at a height of 425 m. The ball's height, h, in metres above the ground after t seconds can be modelled by the function $h(t) = 425 - 4.9t^2$. How fast is the ball falling at 4 seconds?

⑯ A 6500-L swimming pool is drained in 20 minutes. The volume of the water that remains in the pool after t minutes is modelled by $V(t) = 6500(1 - \frac{t}{20})^2$, $0 \le t \le 20$. At what rate is the water flowing out of the pool when $t = 5$?

⑰ The position in metres of a car after t minutes can be modelled by $s(t) = (4 + 3t)^2\sqrt{t + 3}$. Determine the velocity of the car, $v(t)$. What is the velocity of the car at 6 minutes?

⑱ The volume of a balloon can be modelled by $V(r) = \frac{4}{3}\pi r^3$, where r is the radius in cm. Assume that the balloon is a perfect sphere. As the balloon is filled up, the radius is $r(t) = 0.5t^2$, $0 \le t \le 8$, where t is the time in seconds. At what rate will the volume of the balloon change with respect to time at 4 seconds?

⑲ The position of a subway train from a station in kilometres is $s(t) = 4t^2 - 2t^3$, $t \geq 0$, where t is the time in minutes.

a. What are the velocity $v(t)$ and acceleration $a(t)$ of the train at 1 minute?

b. When does the train stop?

c. When will the train return to the station?

d. Is the train moving toward or away from the station at 3 minutes?

⑳ Edward has 300 m of fencing to make a rectangular fence against a wall. What dimensions of fencing will enclose the largest possible area?

㉑ Franny wants to use 3600 m of fencing to enclose 2 identical rectangular stables. The stables have the same dimensions and 1 side in common. What dimensions will maximize the enclosed area?

㉒ A train between Ottawa and Toronto carries 8000 passengers daily when the fare is $50. For every $1 increase in fare, 125 fewer passengers will ride the train. If the number of passengers cannot fall below 6000, how much is the fare and how many passengers will there be when the revenue is maximized?

㉓ Anastasia is 28 km west of Rubin. Anastasia runs east at 6 km/h and Rubin runs north at 8 km/h. If they start running at the same time, after how many hours within 2 h will they be closest in distance?

㉔ A right triangle has a base of 24 cm and a height of 7 cm. What is the area of the largest rectangle that can be inscribed inside the right triangle?

㉕ Julia wants to build a square-based prism with a volume of 8000 cm³. She wants to use cardboard to cover all sides of the prism. What dimensions of the prism will use the least amount of cardboard?

Communication

㉖ Describe the three ways in which a derivative fails to exist.

㉗ Explain why $f(x) = |x - 1|$ is not differentiable at $x = 1$.

㉘ To find the derivative of a rational function, Laura says to use the quotient rule while Spencer says to use the product rule. Who is correct? Explain.

㉙ Describe the steps to solving an optimization problem.

㉚ Calculate the 4th derivative of each function.

a. $y = (1 - 5x^2)^2$

b. $y = (4x - 1)^3$

㉛ Find the equation of the tangent at the given point.

a. $f(x) = 3x^3 - 5x^{-2}$ at $x = -1$

b. $g(x) = \dfrac{(2x + 5)^2}{\sqrt{x - 1}}$ at $x = 2$

㉜ For each equation in Question 31, find the equation of the normal at the given point.

a. $f(x)$ at $x = -2$

b. $g(x)$ at $x = 5$

㉝ Find the equations of the lines that are tangent to both parabolas $f(x) = 2x^2 + 6$ and $g(x) = -x^2$. Let $(a, f(a))$ and $(b, g(b))$ represent the tangent points.

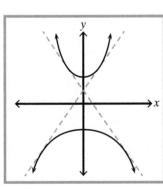

3 Curve Sketching

TEST AREAS

- analyzing functions to determine domains, intercepts, discontinuities, asymptotes, and end behaviours
- using the first derivative test to find critical numbers, intervals of increase and decrease, and local maxima and minima
- using the second derivative test to find points of inflection and intervals of concavity
- sketching the curve of a function

Knowledge and Understanding

Circle the correct answers.

① What are the x-intercepts of $f(x) = 2x^2 - 8x - 24$?

   A. (0,0), (2,0)　　B. (-2,0), (6,0)

   C. (-6,0), (2,0)　　D. (4,0), (6,0)

② What is the y-intercept of $f(x) = -3x^2 - 5$?

   A. (0,0)　　　　B. (0,-3)

   C. (-5,0)　　　D. (0,-5)

③ Which of the following does not guarantee an asymptote in $f(x)$?

   A. $\lim\limits_{x \to c^-} f(x) = +\infty$　　B. $\lim\limits_{x \to c^+} f(x) = -\infty$

   C. $\lim\limits_{x \to +\infty} f(x) = 0$　　D. $\lim\limits_{x \to -\infty} f(x) = \infty$

④ For $f(x)$, where the interval of $f'(x) < 0$, the function

   A. is increasing.　　B. is decreasing.

   C. is constant.　　D. does not exist.

⑤ The slope of the tangent at a point on a section of a curve that is increasing is always

   A. positive.　　B. negative.

   C. 0.　　　　D. undefined.

⑥ For $f(x)$, a local minimum occurs at c if

   A. $f'(x)$ changes from positive to negative at c.

   B. $f'(c) = 0$ and $f''(c) > 0$.

   C. $f''(c) = 0$.

   D. none of the above

⑦ For $f(x)$, a local maximum occurs at c if

   A. $f'(x)$ changes from negative to positive at c.

   B. $f'(x)$ changes from positive to negative at c.

   C. $f'(c) = 0$ and $f''(c) < 0$.

   D. B and C

⑧ A critical number occurs at

   A. $f(x) = 0$.　　　　B. $f'(x) = 0$.

   C. $f''(x) = 0$.　　　D. all of the above

⑨ For $f(x)$, where the interval of $f''(x) > 0$, the graph is

   A. concave up.　　　B. concave down.

   C. increasing.　　　D. decreasing.

⑩ The point where a graph changes from concave down to concave up is a

   A. local minima.　　B. y-intercept.

   C. point of inflection.　　D. vertical asymptote.

ISBN: 978-1-77149-223-2

⑪ Find the critical point(s) of each function. Then identify whether it is a local maximum, local minimum, or neither.

    a. $f(x) = -2x^2 + 3x + 2$

    b. $g(x) = \sqrt{4x^2 + 2x + 1}$

⑫ Check for discontinuities for each function. State the equation of the asymptotes, if any.

    a. $h(x) = \dfrac{x - 1}{x + 4}$

    b. $k(x) = \dfrac{3x + 6}{x^2 + 4x + 4}$

⑬ Find the local maximum or minimum values and asymptotes of each function, if applicable. Then put a checkmark to show the correct graph.

    a. $p(x) = x^3 - 3x^2$

    b. $q(x) = \dfrac{x^2}{x^2 + 2}$

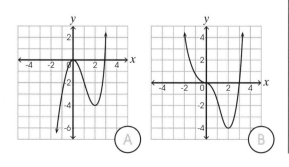

A   B

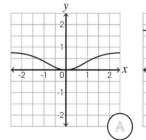

A

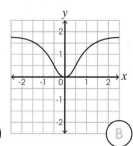

B

ISBN: 978-1-77149-223-2

Calculus and Vectors

⑭ Consider the functions below.

$f(x) = -(x + 1)(x - 6)$ $g(x) = -x^3 + 6x^2 + 8$ $p(x) = \dfrac{2x + 5}{x - 1}$ $q(x) = x(x - 3)^{\frac{1}{3}}$

a. Find the intervals of increase and decrease for each function, if applicable.

b. Determine where the graph is concave up and concave down for each function, if applicable.

⑮ Check and determine the key features that apply to each function. Then sketch its graph.

a. $f(x) = 3(x^3 - 3x^2)$

    Ⓐ x- and y-intercepts

    Ⓑ local maximum or local minimum

    Ⓒ vertical and/or horizontal asymptote(s)

    Ⓓ oblique asymptote

    Ⓔ concavity

    Ⓕ point of inflection

b. $f(x) = -\dfrac{2x^3 - 3x^2}{x^3}$

    Ⓐ x- and y-intercepts

    Ⓑ local maximum or local minimum

    Ⓒ vertical and/or horizontal asymptote(s)

    Ⓓ oblique asymptote

    Ⓔ concavity

    Ⓕ point of inflection

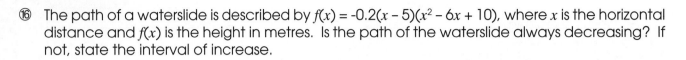

Application

⑯ The path of a waterslide is described by $f(x) = -0.2(x - 5)(x^2 - 6x + 10)$, where x is the horizontal distance and $f(x)$ is the height in metres. Is the path of the waterslide always decreasing? If not, state the interval of increase.

⑰ An experimental treatment is used to reduce algal blooms in a pond. The concentration of algae in the pond, in μg/L, is modelled by $C(t) = \dfrac{t^2 + 56}{4t + 2}$, where t is the time in months after the treatment. After how many months will the algae concentration increase?

Communication

⑱ Describe the steps to sketching the graph of a polynomial or rational function.

⑲ For any polynomial function of degree n, $f(x) = p^n$, describe how you would use derivatives to find the number of possible x-intercepts, critical numbers, and points of inflection.

ISBN: 978-1-77149-223-2

⑳ Find the equations of the oblique asymptotes.

a. $f(x) = \dfrac{x^2 + x - 3}{x - 1}$

b. $f(x) = \dfrac{-x^3 - x + 9}{x^2 - 3x}$

㉑ Find the values of the unknown variables in the equations that have the given properties.

a. $f(x) = x^2 + bx + c$
- local minimum at (1,6)

b. $f(x) = ax^3 + bx^2 + c$
- y-intercept at (0,12)
- point of inflection at (-2,4)

c. $f(x) = ax^3 + bx^2 + cx + d$
- local maximum at (2,8)
- point of inflection at (-1,-10)

Derivatives of Exponential and Trigonometric Functions

TEST AREAS

- understanding the natural number, e, and its properties
- determining the derivatives of exponential functions
- determining the derivatives of trigonometric functions
- solving rate of change and optimization problems

Knowledge and Understanding

Circle the correct answers.

① What is the derivative of $f(x) = e^x$?

A. x^e B. e^x

C. $\log x$ D. $\ln x$

② What is the derivative of $f(x) = b^x$?

A. b^x B. xb^x

C. $(\ln b)b^x$ D. $\ln b$

③ What is the derivative of $f(x) = e^{7x}$?

A. e^{7x} B. e^x

C. $7e^{7x}$ D. $7e^x$

④ What is the derivative of $f(x) = 4.8^x$?

A. $(\ln 4.8)4.8^x$ B. 23.04^x

C. $x4.8^x$ D. $(1.8)4.8^x$

⑤ What is the derivative of $f(x) = (9.2)^{5x-2}$?

A. $(\ln 9.2)9.2^x$ B. $(5)9.2^{5x-2}$

C. $(5 \ln 9.2)9.2^x$ D. $(5 \ln 9.2)9.2^{5x-2}$

⑥ What is the derivative of $f(x) = \sin x$?

A. $\cos x$ B. $\sin x$

C. $\tan x$ D. $\csc x$

⑦ What is the derivative of $f(x) = \cos x$?

A. $\sin x$ B. $-\sin x$

C. $\cos x$ D. $-\cos x$

⑧ What is the derivative of $f(x) = \tan x$?

A. $\sec x^2$ B. $\cot x$

C. $\csc^2 x$ D. $\sec^2 x$

⑨ $-5 \sin 5x$ is the derivative of

A. $f(x) = -\sin 5x$.

B. $f(x) = -\cos 5x$.

C. $f(x) = \cos 5x$.

D. $f(x) = \sin x^5$.

⑩ What is the derivative of $f(x) = x^2 \sin x$?

A. $x^2 \sin x - 2x \cos x$

B. $x(2 \sin x - x \cos x)$

C. $x^2 \cos x - 2x \sin x$

D. $x(x \cos x + 2 \sin x)$

⑪ What is the derivative of $f(x) = \cos (2 + x^2)$?

A. $-2x \sin (2 + x^2)$ B. $2 \cos (2x)$

C. $2x \cos x^2$ D. $-\sin (2 + x^2)$

ISBN: 978-1-77149-223-2

⑫ Differentiate each of the following functions.

a. $f(x) = -4e^{x^3}$

b. $f(x) = 2x^2e^{3x}$

c. $f(x) = \cos x^4$

d. $f(x) = 3 \sin^2 x$

⑬ Determine the slope of each curve at the given point.

a. $f(x) = e^{3x^2 - 2x - 5}$, $f'(-1)$

b. $f(x) = x^2 \tan x$, $f'(\pi)$

⑭ Find the equation of the tangent to each curve.

a. $f(x) = 5e^x$ at $x = \ln 5$

b. $f(x) = \dfrac{e^x}{2x^3}$ at $x = 3$

c. $f(x) = x^2 \cos 3x$ at $x = \dfrac{\pi}{6}$

d. $f(x) = \tan (3x - 1)$ at $x = \pi$

ISBN: 978-1-77149-223-2

Application

⑮ Cody purchased a new ant farm. The population of ants over time in t days is $P(t) = \dfrac{500}{1 + 9e^{-0.01t}}$. What is the largest possible population of the ant farm?

⑯ A clothing store finds that the sales of a piece of clothing relates to the number of days it had been on display for. The number of pieces sold can be modelled by $S(t) = 90te^{-\frac{t}{9}}$, where t is the number of days within 3 weeks. After how many days were the most pieces sold and how many were sold?

⑰ Max uses the equation $S(x) = -(x - 4)^2 \cdot 3^{-0.1x} + 38$ to predict the price of a stock in April, where x is the number of days into April. When will the stock have the highest and lowest prices?

⑱ The number of visitors to a park in hundreds is represented by $N(t) = 1.5^{\frac{t + 22}{5}} - 3^{\frac{t + 5}{10}}$, where t is the temperature above 0°C. At what temperature is the park empty? At what temperature is there a maximum number of visitors?

⑲ The area of a triangle can be found by $A = \dfrac{ab \sin c}{2}$, where a and b are the lengths of two of the arms and c is the size of the angle between the arms. If an isosceles triangle has 2 equal arms of 4 cm, what angle, θ, between the two arms will maximize the area of the triangle?

⑳ The height of a Ferris wheel in metres is given by $H(t) = 10 \cos (\dfrac{\pi}{15}t - \pi) + 13$, where t is the time in minutes. What are the maximum and minimum heights of the Ferris wheel in 30 minutes?

Communication

㉑ Describe the unique properties of the natural number, e.

㉒ Edwin is trying to find the maximum value for $f(x) = \tan \dfrac{x}{5}$ when $2 \le x \le 6$. He says, "There are no critical values from 2 to 6, so it is impossible to find the maximum value." Is he correct? Explain.

ISBN: 978-1-77149-223-2

Thinking

㉓ Find the derivatives.

a. $f(x) = \sqrt{x+1} \cdot e^x$

b. $g(x) = e^{x^3} + 4e^{-2x}$

c. $y = 3 \sin^5 x - 2 \cos^3 x$

d. $y = (\cos x + \tan x)^3$

e. $g(x) = \cos x \cdot 3 \sin x$

f. $y = \sin(e^{\tan x})$

㉔ Determine the maximum and minimum values of each function when $0 \le x \le 2\pi$.

a. $f(x) = \sin^2 x$

b. $f(x) = \cos(\sin x)$

ISBN: 978-1-77149-223-2

㉕ Do the differentiation using the derivative rules that you choose. Then match each pair of derivatives.

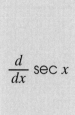

$\dfrac{d}{dx} \sec x$

$\dfrac{d}{dx} \csc x$

$\dfrac{d}{dx} \cot x$

- -csc x cot x

- -csc^2 x

- sec x tan x

㉖ Find the second derivatives.

a. $f(x) = xe^x$

b. $f(x) = \dfrac{e^x}{x}$

c. $y = \cot x$

d. $y = \sin^4 x$

e. $f(x) = e^{\sin x}$

f. $y = e^x \cos x$

ISBN: 978-1-77149-223-2

TEST AREAS

- understanding vectors, scalars, and magnitudes
- adding and subtracting vectors
- determining vectors in Cartesian coordinates
- performing operations with algebraic vectors in R^2 and R^3

Knowledge and Understanding

Circle the correct answers.

① A vector has

    A. magnitude only.

    B. direction only.

    C. both magnitude and direction.

    D. neither magnitude nor direction.

② The parallelogram is drawn using vectors.

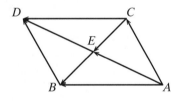

a. Which of the following is not equal to $\overrightarrow{AB}$?

    A. $-\overrightarrow{BA}$ B. $\overrightarrow{AE} + \overrightarrow{EB}$

    C. $\overrightarrow{CD}$ D. $\overrightarrow{AE} + -\overrightarrow{EB}$

b. Which of the following is equal to $\overrightarrow{AC}$?

    A. $\overrightarrow{AE} + \overrightarrow{CE}$ B. $-\overrightarrow{EB} + \overrightarrow{ED}$

    C. $\overrightarrow{CD} - \overrightarrow{ED}$ D. $\overrightarrow{CE} - \overrightarrow{AE}$

c. Which of the following is not a diagonal?

    A. $\overrightarrow{AB} + \overrightarrow{AC}$ B. $\overrightarrow{CD} - \overrightarrow{BD}$

    C. $\overrightarrow{BD} + \overrightarrow{CD}$ D. $\overrightarrow{AC} + \overrightarrow{DB}$

③ Which vector is in the opposite direction of $\vec{a}$?

    A. $2\vec{a}$ B. $\frac{1}{2}\vec{a}$ C. $-\frac{2}{3}\vec{a}$ D. $\frac{1}{|\vec{a}|}\vec{a}$

④ For vector $\vec{x}$, where $|\vec{x}| = 2$, the unit vector is

    A. $2\vec{x}$.   B. $-2\vec{x}$.   C. $\frac{1}{2}\vec{x}$.   D. $-\frac{1}{2}\vec{x}$.

⑤ Consider the vectors shown below.

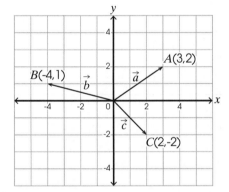

a. What is $\overrightarrow{AB}$?

    A. (7,1)   B. (-7,-1)   C. (-1,3)   D. (1,-3)

b. What is $\vec{a} - \vec{c}$?

    A. (1,4)   B. (-1,-4)   C. (5,0)   D. (-5,0)

c. What is $|\overrightarrow{AB}|$?

    A. $\sqrt{10}$ B. $\sqrt{13}$ C. $\sqrt{17}$ D. $\sqrt{50}$

d. What is $|\overrightarrow{CA}|$?

    A. $\sqrt{8}$ B. $\sqrt{13}$ C. $\sqrt{17}$ D. 5

⑥ Complete the table.

Vector	$\overrightarrow{OA}$	$\overrightarrow{OB}$	$\overrightarrow{AB}$
Component Form	(-3,5,2)		
Standard Unit Vectors		$2\vec{i} - 5\vec{j} - 3\vec{k}$	
Magnitude			
Unit Vector			

⑦

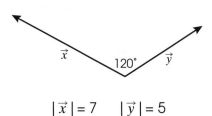

$|\vec{x}| = 7$ $|\vec{y}| = 5$

a. What is $|\vec{x} + \vec{y}|$?

b. What is the direction of $\vec{x} + \vec{y}$ relative to $\vec{x}$?

c. What is $|2\vec{x} - \vec{y}|$?

⑧

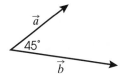

$|\vec{a}| = 2$ $|\vec{b}| = 3$

a. What is $|\vec{a} - \vec{b}|$?

b. What is the direction of $\vec{a} - \vec{b}$ relative to $\vec{b}$?

c. What is $|3\vec{a} + 2\vec{b}|$?

Calculus and Vectors

ISBN: 978-1-77149-223-2

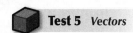

⑨ Given $\vec{a}$ = (-25,17) and $\vec{b}$ = (-25,-8), determine the following.

  a. $|\vec{a}|$

  b. $|\vec{b}|$

  c. $|\vec{a} + \vec{b}|$

  d. $|\vec{a} - \vec{b}|$

⑩ A(-4,2,-3) and B(5,8,2) are two points in R^2. Determine the following.

  a. $\overrightarrow{AB}$

  b. $|\overrightarrow{AB}|$

  c. a unit vector in the direction of $\overrightarrow{AB}$

  d. a unit vector in the direction of $\overrightarrow{BA}$

⑪ Given $\vec{a} = 2\vec{i} - \vec{j} - \vec{k}$, $\vec{b} = 3\vec{i} - 2\vec{j} + 4\vec{k}$, and $\vec{c} = \vec{i} + 5\vec{k}$, determine the following. Write the vectors using standard unit vectors.

  a. $\vec{a} + 2\vec{b}$

  b. $3\vec{b} - 2\vec{c}$

  c. $\vec{a} - \vec{b} + 2\vec{c}$

  d. $2(\vec{a} + \vec{b} - \vec{c})$

  ISBN: 978-1-77149-223-2

⑫ Find the unknowns.

    a. $2(a,2) - 3(1,b) = (7,-2)$
                                      b. $(a,3,c) + 4(-1,b,-2) = (6,-1,2c)$

⑬ Determine whether the vectors in each pair form a spanning set. Write R^2 or R^3. Otherwise, put a cross.

    a.
        $\vec{a} = (1,0)$ $\vec{b} = (0,1)$

    b.
        $\vec{c} = (0,1,0)$ $\vec{d} = (-1,0,-2)$

    c.
        $\vec{e} = (1,-2,-1)$ $\vec{f} = (-6,12,6)$

    d.
        $\vec{g} = (12,9)$ $\vec{h} = (-20,-15)$

⑭ Express each vector as a linear combination of the set of vectors.

    a. $\vec{a} = (8,1)$
       $\{(2,3), (-1,4)\}$

    b. $\vec{b} = (1,0)$
       $\{(2,-1), (-3,2)\}$

    c. $\vec{c} = (8,10,-9)$
       $\{(2,1,-1), (-1,-2,1), (1,2,-2)\}$

    d. $\vec{d} = (0,-7,8)$
       $\{(-1,2,1), (0,-1,2), (2,-1,-5)\}$

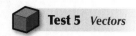

Application

⑮ An airplane is heading due N20°E at a speed of 350 km/h. It meets a wind from the west at 120 km/h. What is the resultant velocity of the airplane? Include a diagram.

⑯ Carla wants to swim across a river flowing at a speed of 4 km/h east. She can swim at a speed of 7 km/h. In what direction should she swim if she wants her resultant velocity to be due north? What will her resultant speed be?

Communication

⑰ Describe the properties of vector addition and scalar multiplication.

⑱ Compare collinear vectors and coplanar vectors in regard to forming a spanning set. Explain.

 ISBN: 978-1-77149-223-2

⑲ Show whether or not the vectors in each set lie on the same plane.

a. {(-5,8,13), (-4,2,3), (2,-1,4)}

b. {(3,15,3), (3,4,-2), (-2,1,3)}

c. {(-2,3,4), (3,1,-5), (-2,-8,15)}

d. {(8,9,31), (-1,2,3), (2,1,5)}

⑳ Determine the values of m and n such that $m\vec{a} + n\vec{b} = \vec{0}$ if

a. $\vec{a}$ and $\vec{b}$ are collinear in the same direction.

b. $\vec{a}$ and $\vec{b}$ are coplanar.

Applications of Vectors

TEST AREAS

- modelling real-life problems using vectors
- understanding and applying the dot product
- understanding and applying the cross product
- solving problems involving the dot product and cross product

Knowledge and Understanding

Circle the correct answers.

① What is the dot product of two vectors $\vec{a} = (a_1, a_2)$ and $\vec{b} = (b_1, b_2)$?

A. $\vec{a} \cdot \vec{b}$

B. $|\vec{a}| |\vec{b}| \cos \theta$

C. $a_1 b_1 + a_2 b_2$

D. all of the above

② What is the cross product, $\vec{a} \times \vec{b}$, of two vectors $\vec{a} = (a_1, a_2, a_3)$ and $\vec{b} = (b_1, b_2, b_3)$?

A. $(a_1 b_1 - a_2 b_2, a_2 b_2 - a_3 b_3, a_3 b_3 - a_1 b_1)$

B. $(a_2 b_3 - a_3 b_2, a_3 b_1 - a_1 b_3, a_1 b_2 - a_2 b_1)$

C. $(a_1 b_2 - a_2 b_1, a_2 b_3 - a_3 b_2, a_3 b_1 - a_1 b_2)$

D. $(a_3 b_1 - a_1 b_3, a_1 b_2 - a_2 b_1, a_2 b_1 - a_3 b_2)$

③ Which of the following is incorrect?

A. $\vec{p} \times \vec{q} = \vec{q} \times \vec{p}$

B. $\vec{p} \cdot \vec{q} = \vec{q} \cdot \vec{p}$

C. $\vec{p} \cdot \vec{p} = |\vec{p}|^2$

D. $|\vec{p} \times \vec{q}| = |\vec{p}| |\vec{q}| \sin \theta$

④ What is the scalar projection of $\vec{a}$ on $\vec{b}$?

A. $\dfrac{\vec{a} \cdot \vec{b}}{|\vec{a}|}$

B. $\dfrac{\vec{a} \cdot \vec{b}}{\vec{b} \cdot \vec{b}}$

C. $|\vec{a}| \cos \theta$

D. $\dfrac{\vec{a} \cdot \vec{b}}{|\vec{a}|^2} \vec{a}$

⑤ Given the vectors $\vec{a} = (-4, 2, 1)$, $\vec{b} = (3, 2, -1)$, and $\vec{c} = (6, 2, -3)$,

a. what is $\vec{a} \cdot \vec{b}$?

A. 3 B. 1

C. -9 D. -19

b. what is $\vec{b} \times \vec{c}$?

A. (3,0,-2) B. (9,4,-4)

C. (-4,3,-6) D. (-8,15,18)

c. what is $(\vec{a} \times \vec{b}) \times \vec{c}$?

A. (-4,-1,-14) B. (31,-96,-2)

C. (-21,52,20) D. (-15,-28,-4)

d. what is $\vec{a} \cdot (\vec{b} \times \vec{c})$?

A. -47 B. -8

C. 8 D. 16

e. what is the scalar projection of $\vec{a}$ on $\vec{b}$?

A. $\dfrac{-9}{\sqrt{21}}$ B. $\dfrac{-9}{\sqrt{14}}$ C. $\dfrac{-9}{14}$ D. $\dfrac{3}{7}$

f. what is the vector projection of $\vec{b}$ on $\vec{c}$?

A. $(\dfrac{75}{7}, \dfrac{25}{7}, -\dfrac{75}{14})$ B. $(\dfrac{75}{14}, \dfrac{25}{7}, -\dfrac{25}{14})$

C. $(\dfrac{150}{49}, \dfrac{50}{49}, -\dfrac{75}{49})$ D. $(\dfrac{75}{49}, \dfrac{50}{49}, -\dfrac{25}{49})$

ISBN: 978-1-77149-223-2

⑥ Two forces of 43 N and 55 N act at an angle of 80° to each other. Determine the resultant and equilibrant of these forces.

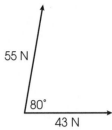

55 N

80°

43 N

⑦ A 45-kg mass is suspended from a ceiling by two cords. The cords make angles of 35° and 45° with the ceiling. Determine the tensions in the cords.

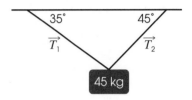

35°   45°

$\vec{T_1}$ $\vec{T_2}$

45 kg

⑧ A drone is flying at 7 km/h N47°E and the wind is blowing at 5 km/h N30°W. How long will it take the drone to fly 500 m north?

⑨ Davis pushed a shopping cart a distance of 150 m with a force of 90 N applied at an angle of 50° with the ground. How much work was done?

⑩ A force of 30 N is applied at the midpoint of a 20-cm wrench. The force makes a 75° angle with the wrench. What is the magnitude of the torque about the point of rotation?

Calculus and Vectors

Communication

⑪ Compare the dot product and cross product of the same two vectors. Explain the differences.

⑫ For any two vectors in R^3, how does the angle between them relate to their dot product? List the cases.

⑬ Consider vectors $\vec{a}$, $\vec{b}$, and $\vec{c}$ in R^3. Explain why $(\vec{a} \times \vec{b}) \cdot \vec{c}$ is possible while $(\vec{a} \cdot \vec{b}) \times \vec{c}$ is meaningless.

⑭ The vectors $\vec{a}$ and $\vec{b}$ are vectors in R^3. Explain why $\vec{a} \cdot (\vec{a} \times \vec{b}) = 0$ and $\vec{b} \cdot (\vec{a} \times \vec{b}) = 0$.

⑮ Using your knowledge of the torque and cross product, describe the criteria needed to maximize the torque for any fixed force.

ISBN: 978-1-77149-223-2

⑯ Consider the parallelogram shown with $A(2,5,3)$, $B(-3,2,1)$, and $C(2,0,-5)$.

a. What is the angle at A?

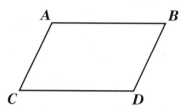

b. Find the area of the parallelogram using the cross product.

⑰ What are the angles, α, β, and γ, that the vector $\overrightarrow{OP} = (2,-3,3)$ makes with the x-, y-, and z-axes?

⑱ Find a unit vector perpendicular to both $\vec{a} = 3\vec{i} - 2\vec{j} + \vec{k}$ and $\vec{b} = 2\vec{i} - \vec{j} + 5\vec{k}$.

⑲ If $\vec{a}$ and $\vec{b}$ are unit vectors and $|\vec{a} + \vec{b}| = \sqrt{3}$, find $(\vec{a} - 2\vec{b}) \cdot (2\vec{a} + 3\vec{b})$.

ISBN: 978-1-77149-223-2

Test 7 Equations of Lines and Planes

TEST AREAS

- determining the vector, parametric, and Cartesian equations of a line in R^2
- determining the vector, parametric, and symmetric equations of a line in R^3
- determining the vector, parametric, and Cartesian equations of a plane in R^3
- understanding and sketching planes in R^3

Knowledge and Understanding

Circle the correct answers.

① Which of the following describes a line in R^3?

A. $\vec{r} = (0,-3) + s(2,-1)$

B. $\dfrac{x-3}{4} = \dfrac{y+4}{2} = \dfrac{z-3}{1}$

C. $x - 2y + 4z - 6 = 0$

D. $\vec{r} = (1,2,5) + s(2,3,1) + t(3,0,-2)$

② Which of the following is a normal to the vector $(2,-3,4)$?

A. $(-2,3,-4)$ B. $(3,2,0)$

C. $(4,3,-2)$ D. $(0,1,-1)$

③ Which of the following equations is not equal to $3x + y - 2z = 5$?

A. $\vec{r} = (0,5,0) + s(1,-3,0) + t(0,2,1)$

B. $x = s,\ y = t,\ z = \dfrac{3s + t - 5}{2}$

C. $\vec{r} = (5,3,0) + s(-1,3,0) + t(2,0,3)$

D. $x = \dfrac{5}{3} - s + 2t,\ y = 3s,\ z = 3t$

④ Which of the following is parallel to $2x - y + 3z - 1 = 0$?

A. $2x + 2y + 2z + 2 = 0$

B. $-2x + y + 3z + 1 = 0$

C. $6x - 3y + 9z + 1 = 0$

D. $x + y + z - 1 = 0$

⑤ Which of the following cannot describe a plane?

A. a line and a point not on the line

B. three collinear points

C. two intersecting lines

D. two parallel and non-coincident lines

⑥ If π_1 and π_2 are two perpendicular planes, with normals $\vec{n_1}$ and $\vec{n_2}$ respectively, then

A. $\vec{n_1} \cdot \vec{n_2} = 0$.   B. $\vec{n_1} = k\vec{n_2}$.

C. $\vec{n_1} \times \vec{n_2} = \vec{0}$.   D. $\vec{n_1} = \vec{n_2}$.

⑦ What equation does the xy-plane have?

A. $x = 0$ B. $y = 0$

C. $z = 0$ D. $x + y = 0$

⑧ Consider the plane π_1: $3x - y + 2z - 8 = 0$. What is the y-intercept?

A. $(\dfrac{8}{3},0,0)$ B. $(0,-8,0)$

C. $(0,0,4)$ D. $(0,0,0)$

⑨ Consider the plane π_2: $2x - 4z = 0$. Which of the following is true?

A. π_2 contains $(2,0,-4)$.

B. π_2 is parallel to the x-axis.

C. π_2 contains the y-axis.

D. π_2 cuts the yz-plane.

ISBN: 978-1-77149-223-2

⑩ Complete the chart.

Vector Form	$\vec{r} = (1,2) + s(2,-3)$, $s \in \mathbb{R}$		
Parametric Form			
Symmetric Form			
Cartesian Form		$4x + 2y - 6 = 0$	
Slope-y-intercept Form			$y = -\dfrac{1}{2}x + 3$

⑪ Convert each equation of a plane into the specified forms.

a. $x = 2 - s + 4t$, $y = 3 + 2s + 2t$, $z = 5 + s + 3t$, $s,t \in \mathbb{R}$

• vector form   • Cartesian form

b. $4x + 5y - 3z + 2 = 0$

• parametric form   • vector form

⑫ Determine if the points (9,-16) and (5,7) exist on the line $\vec{r} = (0,8) + s(3,-8)$.

⑬ Find three points that exist on the plane $\vec{r} = (2,3,5) + s(-1,2,1) + t(4,2,3)$, $s,t \in \mathbb{R}$.

ISBN: 978-1-77149-223-2

⑭ Determine the vector, parametric, and Cartesian equations for the line perpendicular to the line $\vec{r} = (-2,3) + s(1,-2)$ and passing through the point (-3,2).

⑮ Find the angle between the lines $L_1: \vec{a} = (-4,2,1) + s(1,5,-1)$ and $L_2: \vec{b} = (1,1,2) + s(2,3,-5)$.

⑯ Given the points $A(2,3,4)$, $B(1,0,2)$, and $C(1,1,1)$, determine the vector, parametric, and Cartesian equations for the plane that contains these three points.

⑰ The plane π intersects the x-, y-, and z-axes at (6,0,0), (0,2,0), and (0,0,-3). Determine the normal to this plane.

⑱ Determine the vector and Cartesian equations for a plane that contains the following vector equations of the two lines below:

$$L_1: = (2,-4,3) + t(3,0,-5),\ t \in \mathbb{R}$$
$$L_2: = (2,-4,3) + s(2,4,-2),\ s \in \mathbb{R}$$

⑲ Determine the angle between the two planes π_1: $x - y - z = 0$ and π_2: $x - y + z = 0$.

⑳ Sketch the planes defined by the following equations in R^3.

a. $3y - 2z + 1 = 0$

b. $x - 2y + 4z - 2 = 0$

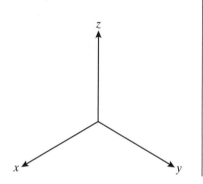
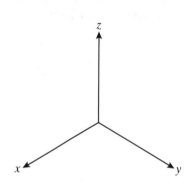

Application

㉑ The line $x = 16 - 4s$, $y = 5 + s$, $s \in \mathbb{R}$ intersects the x- and y-axis at $A(a,0)$ and $B(0,b)$ respectively. What is the area of $\triangle AOB$, where O is the origin?

㉒ A plane is given by $\vec{r} = (-2,1,5) + s(3,-2,0) + t(1,1,5)$, $s,t \in \mathbb{R}$. The plane cuts the x-, y-, and z-axes to form a triangular pyramid. What is the volume of the pyramid?

ISBN: 978-1-77149-223-2

Communication

㉓ What are the limits of the use of the symmetric and Cartesian equations in R^3?

㉔ Describe the method to determine whether two lines are parallel and coincident or parallel and non-coincident.

㉕ Describe how the dot product and the cross product can be used to find the relationship between two planes.

㉖ Describe the intersection of the plane in R^3 with the three coordinate axes for each case.

Case 1: The equation has 1 variable.

Case 2: The equation has 2 variables.

Case 3: The equation has 3 variables.

ISBN: 978-1-77149-223-2

㉗ The symmetric equation of a line is: $\dfrac{x-2}{4} = \dfrac{y-4}{-2} = z$. Determine the coordinates of the point where this line intersects the yz-plane.

㉘ Given the planes π_1: $4x - 2y + kz = 4$ and π_2: $kx - y + z = 7$,

   a. determine a value of k if these planes are parallel.

   b. determine a value of k if these planes are perpendicular.

㉙ Find the values of a, b, and c such that the two planes coincide.

$$\pi_1: (0,0,0) + s(-4,1,2) + t(-5,2,3),\ s,t \in \mathbb{R}$$
$$\pi_2: (a,0,1) + u(1,b,1) + v(2,1,c),\ u,v \in \mathbb{R}$$

㉚ Consider L_1: $\vec{r} = (2,1,0) + s(3,-2,2)$ and $A(2,2,-16)$. Find point B such that B lies on L_1 and $\overrightarrow{AB}$ is perpendicular to L_1.

Test 8 Points, Lines, and Planes

- understanding interactions among points, lines, and planes
- solving systems of equations to three equations and three unknowns
- identifying and determining intersections between lines and planes
- finding distances among points, lines, and planes

Knowledge and Understanding

Circle the correct answers.

① What are skew lines?

A. two parallel lines that intersect

B. two parallel lines that do not intersect

C. two non-parallel lines that intersect

D. two non-parallel lines that do not intersect

② Which scenario is not possible for a line and a plane?

A. intersecting at a point

B. the line being parallel to the plane

C. the line lying on the plane

D. intersecting at a plane

③ Which is not a possible case for two planes?

A. intersecting at a point

B. intersecting along a line

C. two parallel planes

D. two coincident planes

④ How many solutions does a system of equations have if it is consistent?

A. one   B. none

C. infinitely many   D. A and C

⑤ Which of the following is true if two planes with $\vec{n_1}$ and $\vec{n_2}$ as normals are parallel?

A. $\vec{n_1} = k\vec{n_2}$

B. $\vec{n_1} \neq k\vec{n_2}$

C. $\vec{n_1} \cdot \vec{n_2} = 0$

D. $\dfrac{\vec{n_1} \cdot \vec{n_2}}{|\vec{n_1}||\vec{n_2}|} = 0$

⑥ Which of the following cannot be an intersection of a consistent system of three equations?

A. three planes intersecting at a point

B. three planes intersecting along a line

C. three planes intersecting along a plane

D. three planes not intersecting

⑦ Which of the following is not an elementary operation used to solve a system of equations?

A. multiplying an equation by a non-zero constant

B. adding two equations

C. interchanging two equations

D. eliminating an equation

⑧ Which of the following is not equivalent to the given system?

$2x + y = 8$
$x - 3y = 4$

A. $2x + y = 8$
    $7y = 0$

B. $3x - 2y = 12$
    $x + 4y = 4$

C. $7x = 28$
    $x - 3y = 4$

D. $2x + y = 8$
    $4x + 2y = 16$

ISBN: 978-1-77149-223-2

⑨ Determine the intersection between each pair of line and plane. Match the pairs with the given cases.

A $L: \vec{r} = (1,-2,1) + s(4,-5,-1)$ $\pi: 2x + y + 3z - 3 = 0$

○

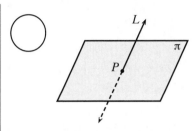

L intersects π at a point.

B $L: \vec{r} = (1,2,5) + s(2,-3,-5)$ $\pi: 3x + 2y - z - 7 = 0$

○

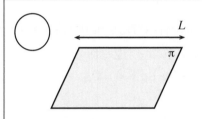

L is parallel to but not on π.

C $L: \vec{r} = (2,-2,-1) + s(7,-3,-2)$ $\pi: x + y + 2z - 3 = 0$

○

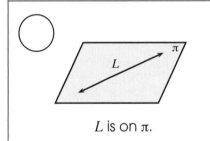

L is on π.

⑩ Determine the intersection between each pair of lines, if any exists.

$$\vec{a} = (-2,1,3) + s(-1,2,4) \qquad \vec{b} = (1,4,4) + t(-1,-1,3)$$
$$\vec{c} = (-1,5,11) + u(2,-4,-8) \qquad \vec{d} = (3,6,-2) + v(2,2,-6)$$

a. $\vec{a}$ and $\vec{c}$

b. $\vec{b}$ and $\vec{d}$

c. $\vec{b}$ and $\vec{c}$

d. $\vec{a}$ and $\vec{d}$

⑪ Match each set of parallel planes. Check the pairs that are coincident.

$x + 2y - z + 3 = 0$ •

• $x - 2y - z + 5 = 0$ ◯

$2x + y + 3z - 1 = 0$ •

• $-2x - 4y + 2z = 6$ ◯

$3x - 6y - 3z + 15 = 0$ •

• $\frac{1}{2}x + \frac{1}{4}y + \frac{3}{4}z - 4 = 0$ ◯

⑫ Determine the solution to each system of equations, if any exists.

a. $x + 3y - z + 2 = 0$
   $x - 3y + z - 4 = 0$

b. $2x - y + z - 3 = 0$
   $x - 3z + 7 = 0$

c. $x + 2y - 4z + 11 = 0$
   $-2x + 5y - z + 5 = 0$
   $3x - 6z + 15 = 0$

d. $3x + y - 2z - 7 = 0$
   $x - y + z + 2 = 0$
   $x + y + 3z = 0$

⑬ Determine the distance from the point (1,4) to the line $\vec{r} = (-2,5) + s(3,2)$, $s \in \mathbb{R}$.

⑭ Determine the distance from the point (1,4,6) to the plane π: $3x + 2y - 5z + 8 = 0$.

Application

⑮ A telephone cable's path can be described by $\vec{r} = (2,4,3) + s(-1,5,-2)$. Additional telephone cable is needed to connect the existing telephone cable to a new telephone pole at (3,1,6). What is the least amount of cable required? (Units are given in kilometres.)

⑯ Two ski lifts have paths described by L_1: $\vec{r} = (1,5,8) + s(2,1,2)$, $s \in \mathbb{R}$ and L_2: $\vec{r} = (3,-2,0) + t(3,-5,2)$. What is the least distance between the ski lifts? (Units are given in metres.)

Communication

⑰ Describe the possible scenarios, in R^3, for the intersections of

    a. a line and a plane.   b. two lines.

    c. two planes.   d. three planes.

⑱ Explain the difference between a consistent system and an inconsistent system.

⑲ Explain why skew lines do not exist in R^2.

⑳ Is it possible to have "skew planes" in R^3? In other words, can non-parallel planes not intersect?

ISBN: 978-1-77149-223-2

Thinking

㉑ For the given system of equations, find p and q such that there is/are

   a. 1 solution.

$$x - 3y + z = 2$$
$$2x + y - z = -2$$
$$3x - 2y + pz = q$$

   b. no solutions.   c. infinitely many solutions.

㉒ Determine the equation of a line that passes through the point $P(2,-1,3)$ and is parallel to the line of intersection of the planes π_1: $3x + y - 2z = 3$ and π_2: $2y + z = 1$.

㉓ Determine the distance between each pair of planes.

   a. π_1: $x + 2y - z + 9 = 0$ b. π_1: $2x - y + z - 6 = 0$

      π_2: $x + 2y - z + 5 = 0$ π_2: $4x - 2y + 2z - 3 = 0$

Knowledge and Understanding

Circle the correct answers.

① Given $f(x) = (r \circ h)(x)$, what is $f'(x)$?

A. $f'(x) = r(x)h'(x) + h(x)r'(x)$

B. $f'(x) = h'(r(x))r'(x)$

C. $f'(x) = r'(h(x))h'(x)$

D. $f'(x) = r(x)h(x) + r'(x)h'(x)$

② Given the graph of $y = f(x)$, when is it concave up?

A. $f'(x) = 0$ B. $f''(x) > 0$ C. $f''(x) < 0$ D. $f''(x) = 0$

③ What is the instantaneous rate of change in $y = f(x)$ with respect to x when $x = a$?

A. $\lim\limits_{h \to 0} \dfrac{f(a + h) + f(a)}{h}$

B. $\lim\limits_{h \to 0} \dfrac{f(a + h) - f(a)}{h}$

C. $\lim\limits_{a \to 0} \dfrac{f(a + h) + f(a)}{a}$

D. $\lim\limits_{a \to 0} \dfrac{f(a + h) - f(a)}{a}$

④ Which of the following describes an interval upon which a function has a negative first derivative?

A. concave up   B. increasing   C. concave down   D. decreasing

⑤ Which of the following describes an interval upon which a function has a negative second derivative?

A. concave up   B. increasing   C. concave down   D. decreasing

⑥ Given the points $B(-5,2,1)$ and $C(3,-2,4)$, determine the vector $\overrightarrow{BC}$.

A. $(8,-4,3)$ B. $(-8,4,-3)$ C. $(-15,-4,4)$ D. $(-2,0,5)$

⑦ Given $|\vec{a}| = 7$, $|\vec{b}| = 6$, and that the angle between them is 60°, find $\vec{a} \cdot \vec{b}$.

A. 42   B. $21\sqrt{3}$ C. 21   D. -20.5

⑧ If $\vec{d} \times \vec{h} = (3,-5,2)$, find $\vec{h} \times \vec{d}$.

A. $(3,-5,2)$ B. $(-3,5,-2)$ C. $(-5,2,3)$ D. $(-3,-5,-2)$

⑨ If $\vec{a} = (1,2,1)$ and $\vec{b} = (-2,1,0)$, find $\vec{a} \times \vec{b}$.

A. $(-1,3,1)$ B. $(-1,2,5)$ C. $(-1,-2,5)$ D. $(2,-1,0)$

⑩ The resultant of $\vec{a}$ and $\vec{b}$ is $-\vec{c}$. Which of the following shows the vectors $\vec{a}$, $\vec{b}$, and $\vec{c}$ being in a state of equilibrium?

A. $\vec{a} + \vec{b} + \vec{c} = 0$ B. $\vec{a} + \vec{b} - \vec{c} = \vec{0}$ C. $\vec{a} = -\vec{b} + \vec{c}$ D. $\vec{b} = \vec{c} - \vec{a}$

⑪ Which of the following is the normal to the plane $3x + 2y - 4z - 1 = 0$?

A. $(2,-4,-1)$ B. $(3,2,-4)$ C. $(3,2,-1)$ D. $(-4,2,3)$

⑫ Evaluate the limits algebraically.

a. $\lim\limits_{x \to 2} (4x - 1)$

b. $\lim\limits_{x \to -1} (x + 3)(x - 2)$

⑬ Find the derivatives.

a. $f(x) = 2x^3 - x^2 + x + 1$

b. $y = x^2(2x - 1)$

c. $f(x) = 2\sqrt{x} - 3$

d. $y = \dfrac{x^2}{x^2 - 1}$

e. $f(x) = \sqrt{x^2 - x + 1}$

f. $f(x) = e^{5x}$

g. $f(x) = x \cdot 3^x$

h. $y = -\tan 3x$

⑭ Find the second derivatives.

a. $f(x) = \dfrac{3x}{x - 1}$

b. $y = (2x + 1)(x - 3)$

c. $f(x) = \sin (x^2 - x)$

d. $y = 2 \cos^2 x$

⑮ Determine the slope of the tangent to each curve at the given point.

a. $f(x) = \dfrac{x+2}{x-1}$ at $(2,4)$

b. $f(x) = 2^{\sin x}$ at $(0,1)$

⑯ Find the point where the tangent to each curve is horizontal.

a. $f(x) = 5x^2 - 2x$

b. $f(x) = \dfrac{x-1}{x^2}$

⑰ Find the critical numbers for each function. Then identify whether it is a local maximum, local minimum, or neither.

a. $f(x) = -3x^4 + 5$

b. $f(x) = -5e^{2x+1}$

⑱ Determine the key features of the function $f(x) = x^3 + x^2 - 5x + 3$. Then sketch its graph.

ISBN: 978-1-77149-223-2

⑲ Given the vectors $\vec{a}$, $\vec{b}$, and $\vec{c}$, construct each of the following, starting at the given point.

$$\vec{a} + \vec{c} - \vec{b} \qquad\qquad 2\vec{a} - 3\vec{b} + \vec{c}$$

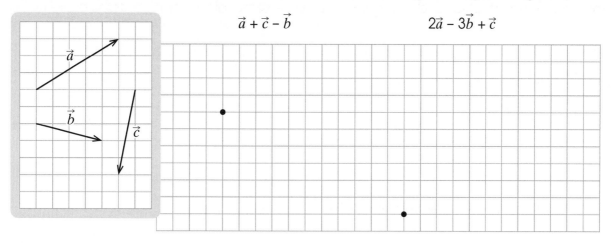

⑳ Write the vector (-16,-3,39) as a linear combination of the vectors (1,-2,5) and (-3,1,2).

㉑ Find the angles between the vectors (2,3,-5) and (1,9,-3).

㉒ Find the parametric and symmetric equations for the line that goes through the points (7,0,5) and (-2,4,3).

㉓ Find the vector and Cartesian equations for the plane that contains the points (4,-2,3), (2,-4,1), and (6,1,5).

㉔ Given the lines L_1: $\vec{r} = (4,7,-1) + s(4,8,-4)$ and L_2: $\vec{r} = (1,5,4) + t(1,-2,-3)$, where $s, t \in \mathbb{R}$. Determine the vector, parametric, and Cartesian equations of the plane that contains these two lines.

㉕ Find the distance between the point $(2,1,-2)$ and the plane $-x + 2y - 5z = 1$.

㉖ Solve the system of equations. Interpret what the system represents in R^3.

$x + 3y + 3z - 8 = 0$
$x - y - z - 4 = 0$
$2x + 6y + 6z - 16 = 0$

㉗ Determine the intersection between each pair of lines or planes.

a. L_1: $\vec{r} = (0,2,1) + s(2,5,-1)$
   L_2: $\vec{r} = (1,-3,2) + t(3,1,-1)$

b. π_1: $x - y + 3z - 4 = 0$
   π_2: $-x - 2y + 8z = 5$

     ISBN: 978-1-77149-223-2

㉘ The cat population in hundreds in an area is modelled for the next 8 years by the function $P(t) = -2t^2 + 16t + 5$, where t is the time in years.

a. What is the average rate of change between $t = 0$ and $t = 3$?

b. What is the instantaneous rate of change of the population at 2 years?

㉙ A transportation company sells 2000 bus tickets per day when the price is $10 per ticket. They believe that for every $1 increase in ticket price, they will sell 100 fewer tickets. Determine what price the company should charge to maximize their revenue.

㉚ The population of bugs in an area is given by $P(t) = 30\,000e^{-\frac{2t}{5}}$, where t is the time in weeks.

a. What is the average rate of change between $t = 0$ and $t = 1$?

b. What is the instantaneous rate of change of the population at 5 weeks?

③ A basketball player finds that the percent of baskets he makes is dependent on the number of consecutive hours he practises for. This is given by $P(t) = 15te^{-\frac{t^2}{4}}$, where t is the time practised in hours and $P(t)$ is the percent of successful baskets. If the player competing in a challenge can practise a maximum of 5 hours, how long should the player practise prior to the challenge to maximize his success? What is the maximum percent of successful baskets possible?

③ A soup manufacturer is redesigning their soup cans so that they can minimize the material cost. If the new soup can holds 375 mL, what dimensions should the new can be?

③ An 80-kg wheel is hanging from two ropes suspended from the ceiling. The ropes make angles of 35° and 50° with the ceiling. Determine the tension in each rope.

③ Mike pulls an object with a force of 120 N in the direction of N15°E. Henry pulls the object with a force of 150 N in the direction of S85°E. In what direction and with how much force should Irene pull the object so that the three are in a state of equilibrium?

ISBN: 978-1-77149-223-2

㉟ For the polynomial function $ax^n + bx^{n-1} + ... + c$, what is the nth derivative if $n > 0$ and $a > 0$? Explain.

㊱ For the function $f(x) = \sin x$, at what value of n will the nth derivative be equivalent to $f(x)$?

㊲ What are the possible cases for the intersections of three lines in R^2?

㊳ If a system of three planes have an infinite number of solutions, what are the possible cases of intersections?

Thinking

㊷ Find the derivatives.

a. $f(x) = (3x^2 - 5x + 1)^4$

b. $f(x) = e^{2x-1} \sin x$

c. $f(x) = x^3(3^x) - 4$

d. $f(x) = \cos^2(2x^2 - 5x + 3)$

㊸ Consider the piecewise function defined below. Find the values of the constants a and b so that the function $f(x)$ is continuous at any number.

$$f(x) = \begin{cases} \sqrt{bx + 1}, \text{ if } x \le -2 \\ 3, \text{ if } -2 < x < 2 \\ x^2 + a, \text{ if } x \ge 2 \end{cases}$$

㊹ Determine the maximum and minimum values for each function when $0 \le x \le \pi$.

a. $f(x) = \cos^2(x) + 3$

b. $f(x) = \sin x - \cos x$

㊺ Find the values of a, b, and c in $f(x) = ax^3 + bx^2 + c$ that has its x-intercept at $(-1,0)$ and point of inflection at $(1,4)$.

ISBN: 978-1-77149-223-2

43. Make a sketch of the planes in R^3.

a. $3x - y + 2z = 0$

b. π: $(1,0,2) + s(2,-1,2) + t(-1,1,-3)$, $s, t \in \mathbb{R}$

44. Find the distance between each pair.

a. $P(1,0,-3)$
$\vec{r} = (2,2,3) + s(0,1,3)$, $s \in \mathbb{R}$

b. L_1: $\vec{r} = (4,1,3) + s(2,0,-1)$, $s \in \mathbb{R}$
L_2: $\vec{r} = (5,-1,-2) + t(-1,1,-1)$, $t \in \mathbb{R}$

c. $P(6,2,1)$
π: $(1,2,-4) + s(1,7,-1) + t(2,4,-1)$

d. π_1: $2x - y + z + 3 = 0$
π_2: $6x - 3y + 3z - 3 = 0$

45. Find the area of the triangle with the vertices $A(1,0,9)$, $B(2,-4,3)$, and $C(4,5,-2)$.

ISBN: 978-1-77149-223-2

Complete MathSmart 12

Mathematics of Data Management

One-variable Statistics

TEST AREAS

- organizing and interpreting data
- calculating measures of central tendency (mean, median, and mode)
- evaluating measures of spread (standard deviation, variance, quartiles, interquartile ranges, percentiles, and z-scores)
- understanding samples and bias

Knowledge and Understanding

Circle the correct answers.

① Consider the following graph.

Rolling an 8-sided Dice

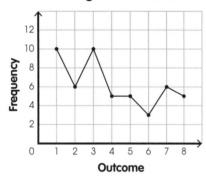

a. How many times was the die rolled?

   A. 8   B. 10   C. 50   D. 100

b. What was the relative frequency of rolling a 6?

   A. 0.03 B. 0.06 C. 0.1   D. 0.2

c. What was the cumulative frequency of rolling a 4?

   A. 0.1   B. 0.26 C. 0.5   D. 0.62

d. What was the mean outcome?

   A. 1.97 B. 3.25 C. 3.94 D. 4.5

e. What was the median outcome?

   A. 1   B. 3   C. 3.5   D. 4

② Which of the following sets of data has a mean of 13, a median of 12, a mode of 16, and a range of 6?

   A. 14, 9, 16, 10, 16   B. 12, 15, 16, 10, 12

   C. 16, 10, 10, 12, 16   D. 16, 12, 11, 10, 16

③ Which one represents the fiftieth percentile?

   A. mean   B. median C. Q_1 D. Q_3

④ Which one is the standard deviation of a sample?

   A. $\sqrt{\dfrac{\Sigma(x+\mu)^2}{N}}$ B. $\sqrt{\dfrac{\Sigma(x-\bar{x})^2}{n-1}}$

   C. $\dfrac{\Sigma(x+\mu)^2}{N}$ D. $\dfrac{\Sigma(x-\bar{x})^2}{n-1}$

⑤ If Q_1 and Q_3 of a set of data are 21 and 69 respectively, what is the semi-interquartile range?

   A. 24   B. 45   C. 48   D. 90

⑥ What type of sampling technique is interviewing baseball fans after they exit the stadium an example of?

   A. convenience   B. stratified

   C. multi-stage   D. simple random

⑦ A police officer asks a group of drivers, "Do you always follow the speed limit?" What type of bias might be present?

   A. sampling bias   B. non-response bias

   C. response bias   D. none of the above

⑧ Two sets of data are given.

a. Find the mean, median, and mode for each set of data.

Set A	Set B
21	23
17	18
22	20
18	24
18	19
19	18
20	24
21	17
22	23
20	24

b. Find the population standard deviation for each set of data. Which set of data is more consistent? Explain.

c. What are the z-scores of 17 and 24 for each set of data?

⑨ The following set of data has been arranged in order.

2	5	6	9	10	11	13	15	17	19
2	6	7	10	10	12	13	15	17	19
4	6	9	10	11	12	14	16	18	20

a. Find each quartile and create a box-and-whisker plot. (Assume that there are no outliers.)

- Q_1: _____   - Q_2: _____

- Q_3: _____

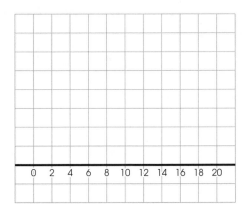

b. State which quartile each datum belongs to.

- 5: _____   - 10: _____

- 16: _____   - 20: _____

c. What is the data value that represents the

- 25th percentile?   _____

- 75th percentile?   _____

- 90th percentile?   _____

d. State which percentile each datum belongs to.

- 4: _____   - 14: _____

- 16: _____   - 18: _____

ISBN: 978-1-77149-223-2

Mathematics of Data Management

Application

⑩ The scores of a recent quiz are recorded.

Quiz Scores

7	11	15	9	14	6	10	10	12	5	4	13	11	12	15
8	6	5	7	9	15	13	9	7	1	10	12	15	10	9

a. Find the bin width that will form 8 intervals for the set of data. Complete the frequency distribution table and draw the resulting histogram.

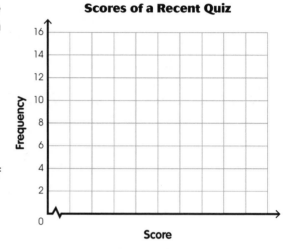

Scores of a Recent Quiz

b. What is the population variance for this set of data?

⑪ The ages of the musicians in an orchestra are shown. What are the mean and median ages?

Ages	Frequency
25 – 29	16
30 – 34	14
35 – 39	12
40 – 44	13
45 – 49	11
50 – 54	13
55 – 59	6
60 – 64	4
65 – 69	2

⑫ Melody measured the volumes of the sounds playing in her classmates' headphones. She recorded the volumes in decibels. Melody intends to create a box-and-whisker plot. Are there any outliers? Explain.

Volumes (in decibels)

61	84	75	28
92	105	61	145
90	42	82	78

ISBN: 978-1-77149-223-2

⑬ Mr. Soares collected the test scores of his class and intends to organize the data into a graph. Consider each type of graph and state its advantage.

a. frequency graph

b. cumulative-frequency graph

c. relative-frequency graph

⑭ Describe the characteristics of an index. Give an example.

⑮ Why are the formulas for calculating population standard deviation and sample standard deviation different? Explain the rationale of the difference.

⑯ Describe what a z-score represents.

⑰ Compare the standard deviation and semi-interquartile range as measures of spread. What are the advantages and disadvantages of each?

⑱ Bill wants to find the average number of hours of television students at his high school watch each week. For each type of sample, describe how Bill could select a sample.

a. convenience sample

b. systematic sample

c. stratified sample

d. cluster sample

e. multi-stage sample

f. voluntary-response sample

⑲ For each scenario, describe the type of bias present and suggest a way to avoid bias.

a. Wayne surveyed 300 Ontarians and found that the most popular hockey team in Canada is the Toronto Maple Leafs.

b. Owen asks, "Which is the best Canadian province: Nova Scotia or New Brunswick?"

c. A restaurant wants to survey a large proportion of its customers. A 10% discount is offered to each customer who completes the survey.

ISBN: 978-1-77149-223-2

⑳ Find the unknowns.

a. $\mu = ?$ $\sigma = 4.5$
   $x = 120$ $z = 3.2$

b. $\bar{x} = 75$ $s = ?$
   $x = 65.25$ $z = -1.95$

㉑ The table below shows a set of data that has a median of 53 and a mode of 52. What are the possible values of x?

Value	Frequency
51	5
52	10
53	x
54	6
55	2

㉒ A set of data has a semi-interquartile range of 15. In the data set, both 14 and 138 are outliers. Find the possible values of Q_1 and Q_3.

㉓ The cumulative-frequency graph for the heights of 200 students is given. Estimate the median and the interquartile range.

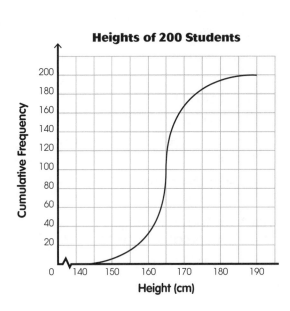

Heights of 200 Students

Two-variable Statistics

- identifying the relationship between two variables
- calculating and interpreting correlation
- applying linear and non-linear regressions
- understanding how statistical summaries can misinterpret two-variable data

Knowledge and Understanding

Circle the correct answers.

①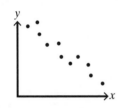

What is the correlation between x and y that the scatter plot shows?

A. weak positive linear correlation

B. strong negative linear correlation

C. no linear correlation

D. weak negative linear correlation

② Which of the following is true about outliers?

A. They have less effect on smaller samples.

B. They can always be ignored for a regression analysis.

C. They can skew a regression analysis.

D. none of the above

③ Which of the following is not a possible correlation coefficient?

A. 2　　　　　　　B. 0

C. -1　　　　　　D. 0.05

④ What does it mean for a set of data to have small residual values?

A. The correlation coefficient is close to zero.

B. There is no correlation.

C. There is a negative correlation.

D. There is a strong correlation.

⑤ Which of the following regressions does the coefficient of determination not apply?

A. linear　　　　　　B. exponential

C. polynomial　　　　D. none of the above

⑥ Which of the following is not a possible coefficient of determination?

A. 0　　　B. 1　　　C. 0.5　　　D. -1

⑦ Which of the following can cause a graph to be misleading?

A. inconsistent scales　　B. suggestive captions

C. small sample sizes　　D. all of the above

⑧ A regression analysis of price, x, in dollars, and sales, y, in $1000, resulted in the equation $y = 30\,000 - 7x$. The equation implies that an increase of $1 in price is associated with _____ in sales.

A. a decrease of $7　　　B. an increase of $7000

C. a decrease of $7000　　D. an increase of $7

⑨ Match each scatter plot with the type of regression and its value of r or r^2.

Types of Regressions

    linear   quadratic   cubic   exponential

Values of r or r^2

   -1   -0.5   0   0.2   0.8   1

a.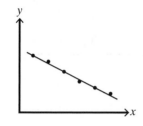

_____ $r =$ _____
type   value

b.

_____   _____
type   value

c.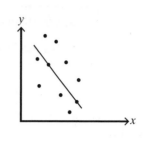

_____   _____
type   value

d.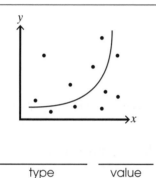

_____   _____
type   value

e.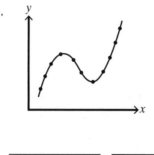

_____   _____
type   value

f.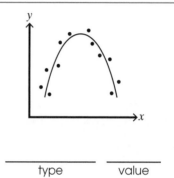

_____   _____
type   value

⑩ Check the correct formulas. Then find the unknowns using the given information.

a. Correlation coefficient:

Ⓐ $r = \dfrac{n(\Sigma x)(\Sigma y) - (\Sigma xy)}{\sqrt{(n\Sigma x - \Sigma x)^2(n\Sigma y - \Sigma y)^2}}$

Ⓑ $r = \dfrac{n(\Sigma xy) - (\Sigma x)(\Sigma y)}{\sqrt{(n\Sigma x^2 - (\Sigma x)^2)(n\Sigma y^2 - (\Sigma y)^2)}}$

$r =$ _____

b. Line of best fit:

Ⓐ $a = \dfrac{n(\Sigma xy) - (\Sigma x)(\Sigma y)}{n(\Sigma x^2) - (\Sigma x)^2}$

Ⓑ $a = \dfrac{n(\Sigma x)(\Sigma y) - (\Sigma xy)}{n(\Sigma x)^2 - (\Sigma x^2)}$

Ⓐ $b = \bar{y} - a\bar{x}$

Ⓑ $b = \bar{x} - a\bar{y}$

$n = 3$

$\Sigma x = 24$

$\Sigma y = 72$

$\Sigma x^2 = 210$

$\Sigma y^2 = 2274$

$\Sigma xy = 477$

$\bar{x} = 8$

$\bar{y} = 24$

$a =$ _____ $b =$ _____ $y =$ _____$x +$ _____

Mathematics of Data Management

Application

⑪ The following table shows the percent of adult population that smoke and the percent of adult population that has heart diseases in some cities.

Smoking Rate (x)	20	19	20	20	18	16	21	20	20	14
Heart Disease Rate (y)	6.3	5.5	6.4	4.7	5.4	5	4.7	5	3.3	3.9

The equation of its linear line of best fit is $y = 0.12x + 2.76$ and the r value is 0.27.

a. State the slope of the line and interpret its meaning.

b. Interpret the meaning of the r value.

⑫ A scientist wants to determine if there is a relationship between the number of minutes spent on a treadmill and the amount of calories burned.

a. Complete the table and find the linear correlation coefficient.

Time x	Calories y	x^2	y^2	xy
14	71			
19	107			
25	142			
23	113			
10	67			
18	91			
29	159			
34	176			
Sum:				

c. Complete the scatter plot.

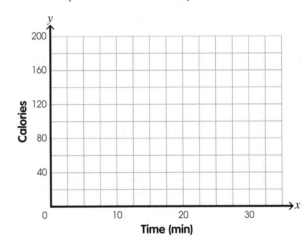

d. Find the equation of the line of best fit. Draw it in the graph.

b. What can you conclude about the relationship between the two variables?

e. Use the equation to estimate the calories burned at 20 minutes and at 45 minutes. Are the results reasonable?

ISBN: 978-1-77149-223-2

⑬ Identify the type of causal relationship present (cause-and-effect, common-cause, reverse cause-and-effect, accidental, or presumed) in each scenario. Justify your answer.

a. The sales of yoga mats and the number of traffic tickets have both increased.

b. Toxic waste dumping increases and the fish population decreases.

c. Researchers found that as the sales of ice cream increases, the temperature increases.

d. The number of cyclists increases and the number of pedestrians also increases.

e. As the viewership of a basketball game increases, the number of people at a beach decreases.

⑭ Tommy draws the curve of best fit shown and concludes that "the cost and efficiency of airlines are strongly correlated." Do you agree? Explain.

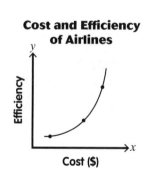

Cost and Efficiency of Airlines

⑮ Explain how a control group can be used to account for extraneous variables.

⑯ Compare the correlation coefficient and the correlation of determination.

⑰ Describe possible errors when using a regression equation to extrapolate information from a set of data.

⑱ For each scenario, describe why the statistical claim is invalid.

a. Tommy surveyed 5 drivers and concluded that as the number of cups of coffee consumed increases, the average driving speed also increases.

b. By analyzing the bestselling books of the year, Sally concludes that as the number of pages of a book increases, the sales of the book decreases.

c. Cody conducted an experiment and found that players with longer fingers score better in a video game.

⑲ What is a hidden variable and how does it affect correlation? How can hidden variables be detected?

ISBN: 978-1-77149-223-2

⑳ In his experiment, Jason recorded the temperature of a freshly brewed cup of tea as it cooled. The initial temperature was 84°C.

a. Using a graphing calculator, find the following regression models along with their r^2 values.

Time (min)	Temp. (°C)
0	84
5	76
8	70
11	65
15	61
18	57
22	52
25	51
30	47
34	45
38	43
42	41
45	39
50	38

	equation	r^2
linear	_____	_____
quadratic	_____	_____
cubic	_____	_____
exponential	_____	_____

b. Using the values of r^2, determine the regression model that provides the best fit for the set of data.

c. For each regression model, consider the initial value. Which regression models the initial value the best?

d. For each regression model, extrapolate the temperature when the time is 100 min. Which regression model is the best for extrapolation?

e. In your opinion, which regression models the data the best? Explain.

ISBN: 978-1-77149-223-2

Mathematics of Data Management

Test 3

Permutations and Counting

TEST AREAS

- solving counting problems using the additive and multiplicative counting principles
- understanding factorials and permutations
- evaluating permutations with identical items
- identifying Pascal's triangle and its properties

Knowledge and Understanding

Circle the correct answers.

① A restaurant's menu has 3 appetizers, 3 mains, and 2 desserts.

a. In how many ways can a 3-course meal be ordered?

A. 8   B. 12   C. 18   D. 20

b. A customer only ordered 1 main and 1 dessert. In how many ways can they be ordered?

A. 5   B. 6   C. 8   D. 12

c. A customer can order up to 3 appetizers. In how many ways can appetizers be ordered without repeating?

A. 3   B. 7   C. 8   D. 9

② What is the value of 5!?

A. 5   B. 20

C. 60   D. 120

③ What is $_nP_r$?

A. $n! - r!$ B. $\dfrac{n!}{(n-r)!}$

C. $\dfrac{n!}{r!}$ D. $n!\,r!$

④ What is the value of $_6P_2$?

A. 30   B. 120

C. 360   D. 720

⑤ Which word has the fewest permutations?

A. DOLLY   B. STORY

C. LOCCO   D. GLOOM

⑥ How many permutations of the letters in the name "LALA" are there?

A. 4   B. 6   C. 12   D. 24

⑦ Which of the following expressions is not equal to the others?

A. $_{23}P_2$ B. $\dfrac{23!}{21!}$ C. 506   D. 253

⑧ What is the value of the term $t_{6,2}$ in Pascal's triangle?

A. 6   B. 10   C. 15   D. 20

⑨ Which row of Pascal's triangle has a sum of 2048?

A. 8   B. 9   C. 10   D. 11

⑩ A random number generator picks three different two-digit numbers. In how many ways can this be done?

A. $100 \times 99 \times 98$ B. $90 \times 89 \times 88$

C. $90! \times 89! \times 88!$ D. $90! \times 3$

⑪ a. Complete the first 8 rows of Pascal's triangle.

```
            1
          1   1
```

b. Evaluate each using Pascal's triangle.

- $t_{3,1} =$ _____
- $t_{4,3} =$ _____
- $t_{6,0} =$ _____

c. Express each term as a sum of two terms of Pascal's triangle.

- $t_{6,2} = t_{5,1} +$ _____
- $t_{9,5} =$ _____
- $t_{15,10} =$ _____

⑫ Fill in the blanks using Pascal's method.

_____   __28__   _____   _____

_____   __53__   __27__

__87__   _____

_____

⑬ Evaluate without a calculator. Show your work.

a. $_5P_0$ b. $P(8,2)$

c. $\dfrac{7!\,5!}{4!\,3!}$ d. $_3P_3$

⑭ Express each using factorials.

a. $8 \times 7 \times 6 \times 5$ _____

b. $\dfrac{8 \times 7 \times 6}{3 \times 2 \times 1}$ _____

c. $\dfrac{10 \times 9 \times 8 \times 7 \times 6}{7(6!)}$ _____

d. $9 \times 8 \times 3 \times 2 \times 1$ _____

e. $\dfrac{10 \times 9 \times 8 \times 4(3!)}{5 \times 4 \times 3 \times 2 \times 1}$ _____

⑮ Solve for n.

a. $\dfrac{(n + 1)!}{n!} = 12$

b. $_{n+1}P_3 = 12(_{n-1}P_2)$

Application

⑯ Sam is 5 blocks east and 3 blocks south of his house. How many possible routes back home are there if he walks only west and north?

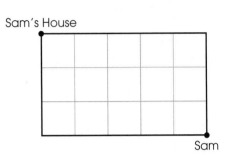

Sam's House

Sam

⑰ You flip a coin six times. In how many different orders can four heads and two tails occur?

⑱ How many five-digit numbers can be made with the digits 5, 6, 7, 8, and 9 if

a. the 5 and 6 cannot be beside each other?

b. the number must be greater than 79 999?

c. the number is even?

d. the number is odd and less than 80 000

⑲ How many arrangements can be made with the letters in "SUCCESSFUL" if

a. there are no restrictions?

b. it must start with a consonant?

c. it contains "LESS" in the arrangement?

d. it begins and ends with a "U"?

ISBN: 978-1-77149-223-2

⑳ Determine how many paths will spell "CHARACTER" if you start at the top and proceed to the next row by moving diagonally down to the left or right.

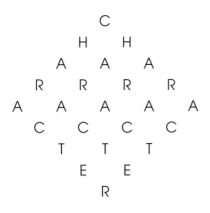

```
              C
           H     H
        A     A     A
     R     R     R     R
  A     A     A     A     A
     C     C     C     C
        T     T     T
           E     E
              R
```

㉑ In a game of checkers, the checker can only move forward diagonally left or right. How many different possible paths exist if the checker cannot move through the "✗"?

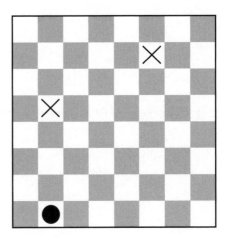

㉒ The written test for a driver's license has 40 multiple choice questions. Each question has 5 choices for an answer. In how many ways can the test be answered?

㉓ Six volleyball players stand in a line. How many different formations are there if

a. there are no restrictions?

b. Natalie and Una must stand together?

c. Hannah must not stand beside either Jen or Anna?

㉔ How many possible pathways are there if John travels from A to B and he can only travel south and east from point A?

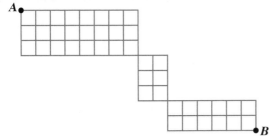

ISBN: 978-1-77149-223-2

Communication

㉕ Are all permutations $_nP_r$ whole numbers? Assume that $n > r$ and n and r are positive integers.

㉖ What is the value of 0!? Use $_nP_r$ to show your reasoning.

㉗ Describe the patterns of Pascal's triangle by relating it to
   • powers of 2.

   • triangular numbers.

   • perfect squares.

㉘ Describe the benefit of using an indirect method to solving a problem. Give an example.

ISBN: 978-1-77149-223-2

㉙ Determine the number of possible routes from A to B if you can only move south and east.

a.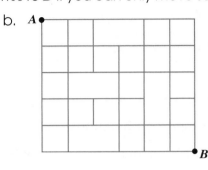

b.

㉚ How many four-digit numbers that are divisible by 5 can be formed from the digits 0, 1, 3, 4, 5, 6, 8, and 9 if each digit can only be used once?

㉛ A freight train must carry 10 cargo cars. There are two food cargo cars that must be placed in the first 5 cars and two furniture cargo cars that must not be placed in the last 4 cars. In how many ways can the cargo cars be arranged if they are all different?

㉜ At a wedding, 8 guests are to be seated around a circular table. Assume that arrangements that are rotations of one another are considered the same.

a. In how many ways can the guests be seated?

b. If the guests are all couples and must sit next to each other, in how many ways can the guests be seated?

Test 4 Combinations and Binomial Theorem

TEST AREAS

- applying set theory and Venn diagram as tools for counting problems
- understanding combinations
- solving problems involving combinations and subsets
- identifying patterns in Pascal's triangle and its relation to the expansion of binomials

Knowledge and Understanding

Circle the correct answers.

① If A and B are two sets, $A \cup B$ represents
A. all elements in both A and B.
B. all sets that include A and B.
C. all elements in either A or B.
D. all elements in B but not in A.

② There are 46 students. 22 of them play rugby and 34 of them play softball. How many students play both?
A. 8   B. 10   C. 46   D. 56

③ How many subsets does a set with six different elements have?
A. 64   B. 63   C. 12   D. 6!

④ What can the combination of eight items taken three at a time be written as?
A. $C(3,8)$ B. $P(8,3)$
C. $C(8,3)$ D. $C(8 - 3)$

⑤ Which of the following is equal to $_{17}C_6$?
A. $\dfrac{17!}{6!}$ B. $17!6!$
C. $\dfrac{17!}{(17 - 6)!17!}$ D. $\dfrac{17!}{6!(17 - 6)!}$

⑥ Which of the following is not equivalent to the others?
A. $_nC_r$ B. $C(n,r)$
C. $\dbinom{r}{n}$ D. $\dfrac{n!}{(n - r)!r!}$

⑦ Kenny can buy up to 3 muffins, 5 doughnuts, and 2 cupcakes. How many different purchases can Kenny make?
A. 29   B. 30
C. 71   D. 72

⑧ Consider $(a + b)^{12}$.
a. What is the coefficient of the 5th term?
A. 5   B. 495
C. 792   D. 924

b. What is the term number of the term containing a^6?
A. 6   B. 7
C. 8   D. 9

⑨ Which of the following is equal to $t_{7,4}$ in Pascal's triangle?
A. $_7C_5$ B. $_7C_4$ C. $_6C_3$ D. $_6C_4$

ISBN: 978-1-77149-223-2

⑩ Complete the Venn diagrams and find the answers.

a.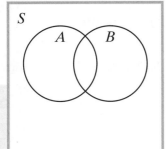

$n(S) = 100$
$n(A) = 56$
$n(B) = 29$
$n(A \cap B) = 7$

• $n(A \cup B)$ _____

• $n(S \cap A)$ _____

• $n(S \cup B)$ _____

b.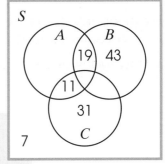

$n(A) = 61$
$n(B \cup C) = 115$
$n(A \cup B \cup C) = 143$

• $n(B \cap C)$ _____

• $n(A \cap B \cap C)$ _____

• $n(S)$ _____

⑪ Evaluate without using a calculator.

a. $_{10}C_3$

b. $_9C_7$

c. $_{12}C_4$

d. $_8C_8$

e. $_6C_0$

f. $_{10}C_7$

⑫ Complete the table using Pascal's formula.

Single Term	$_{16}C_4$		
Addition		$_{21}C_{13} + {_{21}}C_{14}$	
Subtraction			$_{18}C_3 - {_{17}}C_2$

⑬ In the expression of $(x + y)^n$, what is the value of a in the following terms?

a. $C(13,a)x^7y^a$

b. $\binom{a}{8}x^9y^8$

c. $a(x^6y^2)$

Application

⑭ The given results are obtained from a survey of 203 students. Draw a Venn diagram.

- 125 have Math classes
- 97 have Science classes
- 149 have English classes
- 98 have both Math and English classes
- 65 have both Science and English classes
- 50 have both Math and Science classes
- 38 have all three classes

a. How many students have exactly one of the three classes?

b. How many students have at least one of the three classes?

c. How many students have fewer than two classes?

⑮ There are 21 boys and 30 girls in a class. 7 students will be chosen to represent the class. How many ways are there to choose the students if

a. exactly three girls must be chosen?

b. at least 1 boy and 1 girl must be chosen?

⑯ There are eight clubs at a school and each student can join up to three clubs. In how many ways can a student choose?

⑰ Ariel is going to her soccer game. On her kitchen table, there are 3 granola bars, 3 bananas, and 4 muffins. In how many ways can she get some snacks for her game?

⑱ Describe the difference between permutations and combinations. Give an example of each.

⑲ Consider the following formulas.

- $(p + 1)(q + 1)(r + 1)... - 1$
- $2^n - 1$

Describe the type of problem that requires each formula to solve. Give an example of each.

⑳ Create a combination problem where you have to select r items from a group of n items and some of the items to be selected may be identical. Then describe your approach to solving the problem.

㉑ Describe how the Binomial Theorem relates to Pascal's triangle.

Mathematics of Data Management

Thinking

㉒ Consider four sets of integers: W, X, Y, and Z.

Set W
{1, 2, 3, 5, 7, 11, 13, 17, 19, 23, 29, 31}

Set X
{1, 3, 6, 10, 15, 21, 28, 36, 45, 55, 66}

Set Y
{1, 2, 3, 5, 8, 13, 21, 34, 55, 89}

Set Z
{1, 4, 9, 16, 25, 36, 49, 64, 81}

a. Complete the Venn diagram to show the number of integers in each subset.

b. Find the values.
  • $n(W \cup X)$

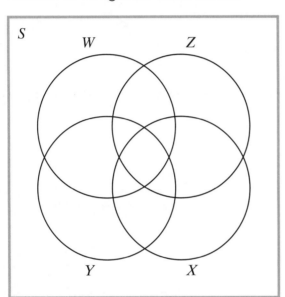

  • $n(X \cap Y \cap Z)$

  • $n(W \cup X \cup Y \cup Z)$

㉓ Thirteen students volunteered to run a lemonade stand over three days. There will be three students on Friday, five students on Saturday, and five students on Sunday. Jessie and Mitch requested to be scheduled on the same day. In how many ways can the students be scheduled?

㉔ Five cards are drawn from a regular 52-card deck of cards. How many ways are there for each of the following to be drawn?

a. a flush, where all 5 cards have the same suit

b. four of a kind, where there are 4 cards with the same number/letter, plus an extra card

ISBN: 978-1-77149-223-2

㉕ Expand and fully simplify.

a. $(2x - \frac{2}{x^2})^4$

b. $(4y + \frac{3}{\sqrt{y}})^6$

㉖ For $(6x - \frac{1}{3x})^{20}$, what is the

a. 11th term?

b. 19th term?

㉗ Find the first 5 terms of each polynomial.

a. $[(x + y)(x - y)]^{20}$

b. $(2x + y)^{10}(2x - y)^{10}$

㉘ Evaluate $\binom{199}{102} + \binom{199}{103} - \binom{200}{97}$ without a calculator.

ISBN: 978-1-77149-223-2

Probability

TEST AREAS

- understanding types of probabilities and the concept of complements
- evaluating odds
- identifying independent, dependent, and mutually exclusive events
- solving problems using permutations, combinations, and counting strategies

Knowledge and Understanding

Circle the correct answers.

① "Shark Team has about a 75% chance of winning the championship this year because they won it last year." This statement is an example of

A. classical probability. B. theoretical probability.

C. empirical probability. D. subjective probability.

② The odds against Ashley winning a tennis game on a clay court are 3 to 4. Her odds against winning on a hard court are 7 to 3. Which of the following statements is false?

A. Her chance of winning on a clay court is 57.1%.

B. Her chance of winning on a clay court is greater.

C. Her chance of winning on a hard court is greater.

D. Her chance of winning on a hard court is 30%.

③ If Event X is rolling a three on a standard die and Event Y is tossing a tail on a coin, then Events X and Y are

A. mutually exclusive events. B. independent events.

C. dependent events. D. both A and B

④ A box contains 3 red marbles and 4 green marbles. If two marbles are picked randomly at the same time, what is the probability that both marbles are green?

A. $\frac{2}{7}$ B. $\frac{3}{7}$ C. $\frac{4}{7}$ D. $\frac{5}{7}$

⑤ A coin is tossed three times. What is the probability of tossing exactly two heads?

A. $\frac{3}{8}$ B. $\frac{1}{4}$ C. $\frac{1}{36}$ D. $\frac{5}{36}$

⑥ Two cards are randomly drawn from a standard deck of cards with replacement. What is the probability that both of them are hearts?

A. $\frac{1}{26}$ B. $\frac{11}{51}$

C. $\frac{1}{16}$ D. $\frac{1}{17}$

⑦ If the odds in favour of raining tomorrow are 3:8, what is the probability of not raining tomorrow?

A. $\frac{3}{8}$ B. $\frac{5}{8}$

C. $\frac{3}{11}$ D. $\frac{8}{11}$

⑧ Thirteen kindergarten children line up for a picture. What is the probability that they will line up in order from shortest to tallest from the entrance?

A. $\frac{1}{13!}$ B. $\frac{2}{13!}$

C. $\frac{1}{13}$ D. $\frac{13}{13!}$

⑨ Consider A as an event in a sample space.

a. What is the sum of $P(A)$ and $P(A')$? Explain.

_____

_____

_____

_____

_____

b. Complete the table.

$P(A)$	0.3				
$P(A')$		25%			$\frac{7}{10}$
odds in favour of A			$\frac{3}{5}$		
odds against A				1:4	

⑩ Two standard six-sided dice are rolled.

a. Complete the table to show their sums.

+	1	2	3	4	5	6
1						
2						
3						
4						
5						
6						

b. What is the probability of rolling a sum of 7?

c. What is the probability of rolling a sum greater than 7?

d. What is the probability that a sum greater than 7 is not rolled?

⑪ When drawing 2 cards simultaneously from a standard deck of cards, what is the probability of

a. getting a pair of kings?

b. getting a black jack and a ten?

⑫ There is a 30% chance that Sophie likes a song on the radio and a 45% chance that Luke likes a song on the radio. What is the chance that a song on the radio is disliked by both Sophie and Luke if

a. the songs Sophie and Luke like are mutually exclusive?

b. the chance that Sophie and Luke both like a song on the radio is 10%?

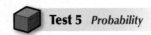

Application

⑬ Four coins are tossed. Draw a tree diagram to show all the possible outcomes.

    a. What are the odds in favour of tossing at least three tails?

    b. What is the probability of tossing heads on the fourth coin if the first three coins were heads?

    c. Given that heads were tossed on the first two coins, what is the probability that at least three heads will be tossed?

⑭ Mike always places his loose socks in the drawer without pairing them. He has five white socks, six black socks, and four grey socks. What is the probability that he randomly picks two socks of the same colour?

⑮ A locker combination consists of three numbers from 0 to 39. What is the probability that a locker combination contains exactly one "24"?

⑯ Kenneth is going to select 5 letters from the given letters and then arrange them. He picks the letters at random without repeats. What is the probability of having two vowels next to each other?

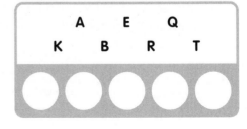

   ISBN: 978-1-77149-223-2

⑰ Three marbles are taken out at random from a bag of six green marbles and three yellow marbles. What is the probability that there are exactly two green marbles and one yellow marble if

a. there is no replacement?

b. each marble is replaced after it is taken out?

⑱ The school hockey team only loses 15% of the time when Chris plays. When Chris does not play, the team loses 45% of the time. Chris plays 6 out of 7 games.

a. What is the probability that Chris does not play a game and the team loses?

b. What is the probability that the team loses a game?

⑲ A weather report says there is a 60% chance of having sunny skies and a 40% chance of having cloudy skies tomorrow. If the sky is sunny, there is a 5% chance of rain, and if the sky is cloudy, there is an 80% chance of rain. What is the chance of rain tomorrow?

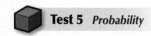

Test 5 *Probability*

Communication

⑳ What are theoretical, empirical, and subjective probabilities?

㉑ Compare the probability and the odds of an event.

㉒ Describe the difference between the probabilities of independent and dependent events.

㉓ Are an event and its complement mutually exclusive? Explain.

ISBN: 978-1-77149-223-2

Thinking

㉔ Shanna predicts that the odds of her winning a game are 7:11, the odds of losing are 5:13, and the odds of having a draw are 1:2. Are Shanna's predictions possible?

㉕ If all the letters in the word "TRIGONOMETRY" are rearranged, what is the probability that the word starts with a "T" and ends with an "O"?

㉖ A spinner is divided equally into five colours. If orange is spun, then a number is randomly selected from a bag containing the numbers 1, 2, 3, 4, and 5. If orange is not spun, a 10-sided die (numbers 1 to 10) is rolled. If an outcome has an even number, what is the probability that orange was spun?

㉗ Students in a class have the options between regular milk and chocolate milk. On Monday, 60% of the students chose regular milk. On each subsequent day, 40% of the students who chose regular milk will choose regular milk again, while 80% of the students who chose chocolate milk will choose chocolate milk again. What is the probability of a student choosing chocolate milk on Friday?

Probability Distribution

TEST AREAS

- identifying discrete random variables
- understanding types of probability distributions (uniform, binomial, geometric, hypergeometric)
- calculating the expected value for a given probability distribution
- solving real-life problems involving discrete probability distribution

Knowledge and Understanding

Circle the correct answers.

① Which of the following is a discrete random variable?

A. length of the classroom

B. number of birds inside the nest

C. length of time practising the piano

D. volume of water in the aquarium

② Which of the following describes successive trials in binomial distributions?

A. independent

B. dependent

C. mutually exclusive

D. equally likely

③ In which distribution does the probability of success change from trial to trial?

A. uniform distribution

B. binomial distribution

C. geometric distribution

D. hypergeometric distribution

④ What is the expected value of a fair game?

A. 1

B. more than 0

C. 0

D. between 0 and 1

⑤ What is the random variable in a geometric distribution?

A. total number of trials

B. waiting time

C. number of successful trials

D. a single value for each outcome

⑥ What is the expected value of a binomial distribution?

A. $\dfrac{ra}{n}$ 　　B. np 　　C. $\dfrac{q}{p}$ 　　D. $\sum\limits_{i=1}^{n} x_i P(x_i)$

⑦ What is the probability of any outcome, x, in a uniform probability distribution involving m possible outcomes?

A. $\dfrac{1}{m}$ 　　B. 1 　　C. $\dfrac{1}{x}$ 　　D. $_mC_x(\dfrac{1}{m})^x$

⑧ What is the probability of getting 3 heads when flipping 5 coins?

A. $(\dfrac{1}{2})^3(\dfrac{1}{2})^2$ 　　　　B. $_5C_2(\dfrac{1}{2})^2$

C. $_5C_3(\dfrac{1}{2})^3$ 　　　　D. $_5C_3(\dfrac{1}{2})^3(\dfrac{1}{2})^2$

⑨ A game is won 30% of the time. What is the probability of winning the game on the third try?

A. 0.7 　　B. 0.3(0.7) 　　C. $0.3(0.7)^2$ 　　D. $0.7(0.3)^2$

⑩ What is the expected number of roses picked if 5 flowers are picked randomly from 8 roses and 6 lilies?

A. $\dfrac{5}{8}$ 　　B. $\dfrac{5 \times 6}{8}$ 　　C. $\dfrac{5 \times 8}{14}$ 　　D. $\dfrac{5 \times 6}{14}$

⑪ For each scenario, identify the type of distribution needed to solve it.

a. A basketball player makes 65% of his basket throws. How many throws can he make before he misses? _____

b. A lottery has a $1000 prize. If 2000 tickets were sold, how much should each ticket cost to make the lottery fair? _____

c. In a group of 30 students, 6 of them speak French. If a study surveys 10 students at random, what is the probability that 3 French speaking students are surveyed? _____

d. A 3-D printer can make parts with a 5% chance of failure. If the printer makes 100 parts, what is the probability of having 3 defects? _____

⑫ Consider the following distribution.

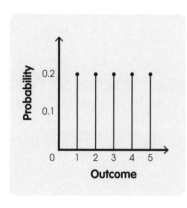

a. Find the probabilities.

- $P(x = 2)$ _____
- $P(x < 2)$ _____
- $P(x \geq 1)$ _____
- $P(1 < x < 5)$ _____

b. What is the expected outcome?

⑬ Consider the probability distribution, $P(x) = {}_{20}C_x(\frac{2}{7})^x(\frac{5}{7})^{20-x}$. Identify the following.

a. number of trials: _____   b. probability of success: _____

c. probability of failure: _____   d. $P(9)$: _____

⑭ A 4-number PIN code is randomly generated.

a. Complete the probability table.

Number of Digits that are 2 or 5	Probability
0	
1	
2	
3	
4	

b. What is the probability of generating at least 2 digits that are 2 or 5?

c. What is the probability of generating fewer than 3 digits that are 2 or 5?

ISBN: 978-1-77149-223-2

Mathematics of Data Management

Application

⑮ If 8% of Canadians are vegetarians, what is the probability that in a group of 12 people, 5 of them are vegetarians?

⑯ Five cards are dealt from a standard 52-card deck. What is the expected number of cards that are hearts?

⑰ What is the expected number of trials needed to get a double when rolling a pair of standard 6-sided dice?

⑱ Matthew is an archer and 75% of his arrows hit the target.

   a. What is the probability that Matthew misses his arrow for the first time on his fifth attempt?

   b. What is the probability that Matthew hits the target within 5 arrows?

⑲ George surveyed 50 students on the number of stop signs they encounter on their way to school. Based on the data, what is the expected number of stop signs a student will encounter on their way to school?

Number of Stop Signs	Number of Students
0	2
1	11
2	23
3	9
4	4
5	1

⑳ A vending machine contains 50 toys and 5 of them are toy cars. The machine dispenses the toys at random. Thomas got 6 toys.

a. What is the probability that he got 3 toy cars?

b. What is the probability that he got fewer than 3 toy cars?

㉑ An online company has 6 servers that each has a failure rate of 10%. As long as one server remains online, the network is functional.

a. What is the probability that the network is functional?

b. To maintain optimal network speed, at least 3 servers must remain online. What is the probability that the network operates at optimal speed?

Communication

㉒ What is the difference between discrete random variables and continuous random variables?

㉓ For each type of distribution, describe its key characteristics.
   a. uniform distribution

   b. binomial distribution

   c. geometric distribution

   d. hypergeometric distribution

㉔ Define a Bernoulli trial. Give an example.

ISBN: 978-1-77149-223-2

㉕ A lottery has a prize of $1 000 000. The winner must match a 6-digit code exactly. If each lottery ticket costs $2, what is the expected profit for playing the lottery.

㉖ When rolling a pair of standard 6-sided dice, what is the probability of rolling doubles for the first time within the first 4 rolls?

㉗ A lollipop can be either lemon- or apple-flavoured. Assuming a Bernoulli trial, the probability of picking 6 lollipops randomly and getting 3 lemon-flavoured lollipops is 0.18522. What is the probability of a lollipop being apple-flavoured if it is more likely to get an apple-flavoured lollipop?

㉘ A card collection is sold at random, with each card having a 15% chance of being rare. Joanne wants to purchase a number of cards so that the probability of her getting her first rare card within her purchases is greater than 50%. How many cards should Joanne purchase?

Mathematics of Data Management

Normal Distribution

TEST AREAS

- understanding continuous probability distribution
- identifying the properties of normal distribution
- applying the normal distribution to approximate binomial distribution
- solving real-life problems involving normal distribution

Knowledge and Understanding

For the Z-score Table, go to page 196.

Circle the correct answers.

① Which of the following describes this distribution?

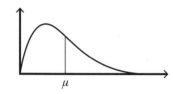

A. positively-skewed

B. bimodal

C. negatively-skewed

D. bell-shaped

② Which of the following is true for a standard normal distribution?

A. $\mu = 1, \sigma = -1$

B. $\mu = 1, \sigma = 0$

C. $\mu = 0, \sigma = -1$

D. $\mu = 0, \sigma = 1$

③ In a normal distribution, what percent of the data will fall within $\mu \pm 2\sigma$?

A. 65% B. 90%

C. 95% D. 99%

④ What is $P(z < 1.52)$?

A. 0.0643 B. 0.9222

C. 0.9332 D. 0.9357

⑤ What is the population of data with a z-score between 0 and 2 in a normal distribution?

A. 0.4772 B. 0.6844

C. 0.7517 D. 0.9505

⑥ Which of the following must be met to use normal approximation of a binomial distribution?

A. $np > 5$ B. $nq > 5$

C. $\sqrt{npq} < 5$ D. A and B

⑦ Which of the following is used to approximate the mean and standard deviation of a binomial distribution?

A. $\mu = np, \sigma = npq$ B. $\mu = np, \sigma = \sqrt{npq}$

C. $\mu = npq, \sigma = \sqrt{np}$ D. $\mu = npq, \sigma = \sqrt{npq}$

⑧ Which of the following is equivalent to $P(-0.5 < z < 1.2)$?

A. $1 - P(z < 1.2)$ B. $P(z < 1.2) - P(z < -0.5)$

C. $1 - P(z < -0.5)$ D. $P(z > 1.2) + P(z < -0.5)$

⑨ Which of the following is necessary when modelling discrete data with a continuous distribution?

A. continuity correction B. repeated sampling

C. confidence intervals D. large sample size

⑩ What is the tail size, $\frac{\alpha}{2}$, for a 90% confidence level?

A. 0.45 B. 0.9

C. 0.05 D. 0.1

ISBN: 978-1-77149-223-2

⑪ Convert the following discrete probabilities into continuous probabilities using continuity correction.

Discrete	$P(x = 7)$	$P(x < 18)$	$P(x \geq 35)$	$P(5 \leq x < 13)$
Continuous				

⑫ Consider a normal distribution with a mean of 29 and a standard deviation of 7. Find the following discrete probabilities and fill in the corresponding area under the curve.

a. $P(x < 32)$

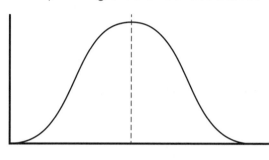

b. $P(31 < x < 39)$

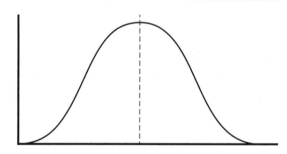

c. $P(x > 25)$

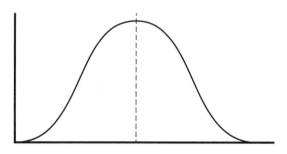

⑬ In a binomial distribution, the probability of success is 35%. If 250 trials are conducted, what is the probability of getting

a. at least 70 successes?   b. exactly 90 successes?

ISBN: 978-1-77149-223-2

Mathematics of Data Management

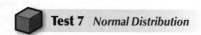

Application

⑭ The thickness of automobile brake pads are normally distributed. If automobile brake pads have an average thickness of 12.4 mm and a standard deviation of 0.03 mm, without using *z*-scores, predict what percent of brake pads have a thickness

a. between 12.31 mm and 12.4 mm.

b. of more than 12.46 mm.

⑮ Georgina is 167 cm tall. At school, girls' heights are normally distributed with a mean of 158 cm and a standard deviation of 7 cm.

a. What is the probability that the first girl Georgina meets at school tomorrow will be taller than her?

b. What percentile of heights does Georgina fall into?

⑯ A recent report shows that North American homes have an average of 7 electronic devices, with a standard deviation of 2.3. Assuming the number of devices is normally distributed, how many households have at least 6 electronic devices in a city if it has approximately 370 000 households?

⑰ For international air flights to Europe, an airline has four different meal choices: chicken, beef, salmon, and vegetarian. From past records, 12% of passengers chose vegetarian meals. If there are 450 passengers on a flight from Toronto to Copenhagen, what is the probability that no more than 65 passengers will choose vegetarian meals?

⑱ Steve is performing an experiment where he measures the lengths of worms he grows. He assumes that the lengths of worms are normally distributed. He measured and recorded the lengths of 10 worms.

Worm	Length (mm)
1	27
2	29
3	24
4	20
5	25
6	20
7	29
8	21
9	28
10	27

a. What is the probability that a worm's length is greater than 26 mm?

b. What is the probability that a worm's length is between 23 mm and 28 mm?

c. If Steve measures 10 more worms, how many worms should he expect to be longer than 20.5 mm?

⑲ Assume that the weights of muffins have a standard deviation of 10 g. How large of a sample is needed to be 95% confident that the mean weight is 140 g ± 3 g?

ISBN: 978-1-77149-223-2

Communication

⑳ Explain why the probability that a continuous random variable taking any single value is zero.

㉑ Describe the curve of a bimodal distribution. When does this type of distribution occur? Give an example.

㉒ Explain why when $np < 5$ or $nq < 5$, the normal distribution does not approximate a binomial distribution.

㉓ What is the reasoning for using continuity correction?

㉔ Two teachers have classes of similar sizes. After final exams, the mean grades in both classes are 75. However, Class A has a standard deviation of 3 while Class B's is 9. Why might you consider one student who receives 80 in one class to be better than another student who receives the same grade in another class? Explain your reasoning using concepts of normal distribution.

 ISBN: 978-1-77149-223-2

㉕ For the month of June, there is always a 75% chance that there will be less than 4.1 cm of rain and a 95% chance that there will be less than 5.2 cm of rain. If the amount of rain fallen is normally distributed, what is the probability that there will be between 2.5 cm and 3.5 cm of rain in June?

㉖ There are some passengers on a bus. The probability of each passenger getting off the bus at a stop is the same. There is a 68% chance that fewer than 9 passengers will get off and a 36% chance that fewer than 7 passengers will get off. How many passengers are there on the bus?

㉗ At a chicken egg farm, 95% of the eggs weigh between 45 g and 53 g. What is the probability of an egg weighing between 50 g and 52.5 g, assuming that the weights are normally distributed?

Knowledge and Understanding

Circle the correct answers.

① The odds in favour of the Montreal Canadiens beating the New York Islanders are 9:5. What is the probability that the Montreal Canadiens will win?

A. $\frac{9}{5}$ B. $\frac{5}{9}$ C. $\frac{9}{14}$ D. $\frac{5}{14}$

② In the cafeteria, Mia has a choice of 4 salads, 4 burgers, and 2 desserts. In how many ways can Mia choose her meal if she has a salad, a burger, and a dessert?

A. 32   B. 10   C. 4   D. 3

③ Which of the following is not equal to $P(151,2)$?

A. $\frac{151!}{2!149!}$ B. 22 650   C. $\frac{151!}{149!}$ D. $_{151}P_2$

④ Seven picture frames are to be arranged from a collection of twelve frames. In how many ways can they be arranged?

A. $_{12}C_7$ B. $7!$ C. 12^7 D. $_{12}P_7$

⑤ Brandon bought a new karaoke sound mixer which has nine function knobs. Each knob has four levels of intensity. In how many ways can Brandon adjust his karaoke sound mixer?

A. 9^4 B. 9×4 C. 4^9 D. $9 + 4$

⑥ If $P(x) = 0.2$ and $P(y) = 0.5$, where x and y are mutually exclusive events, which one of the following statements is true?

A. $P(x \text{ and } y) = 0.7$ B. $P(x \text{ and } y) = 0$ C. $P(x \text{ or } y) = 0.01$ D. $P(x \text{ or } y) = 0.5$

⑦ What is the value of the term $t_{6,2}$ in Pascal's triangle?

A. 5   B. 6   C. 10   D. 15

⑧ Inman passes out a survey at the library entrance to determine the number of pairs of sneakers a student owns on average. What sampling technique does Inman use?

A. stratified   B. simple random   C. cluster   D. convenience

⑨ Which of the binomial distributions listed below should not be modelled by a normal distribution?

A. $n = 38, p = 0.1$ B. $n = 100, p = 0.09$ C. $n = 46, p = 0.23$ D. $n = 17, p = 0.45$

⑩ The age distribution of students enrolled in a first year community college program is shown. What is the median age of the students?

A. 18   B. 19   C. 20   D. 21

Age	Frequency
18	13
19	25
20	24
21	22

ISBN: 978-1-77149-223-2

⑪ A set of data shows that as more people are vaccinated for a specific illness, fewer cases of that illness are reported. If the correlation coefficient is -0.832, the scatter plot for the data will have

A. an array of dots with no noticeable pattern to them.

B. dots clustered around a line sloping down to the right.

C. dots tightly clustered around a line sloping down to the left.

D. a cluster of dots in the middle of the graph.

⑫ An outlier is a data point that

A. should sometimes be left out of a statistical analysis.

B. may be an abnormal result.

C. may significantly affect the calculation of the correlation coefficient.

D. all of the above

⑬ Which of the following predictions can be calculated using binomial distribution?

A. surveying 500 people to find how many of them watched the news today

B. tossing a coin 50 times to see how many heads occur

C. both of the above

D. none of the above

⑭ Which of the following questions is biased?

A. Which health centre are you most likely to go to when you are sick?

B. Do you think the government should spend more on health care?

C. Which flavour do you prefer, vanilla or chocolate?

D. Do you find the school's clear and timely communications helpful?

⑮ Which of the following demonstrates a cause-and-effect relationship?

A. The costs of almonds and computers increase over time.

B. The median household income is strongly correlated with the number of gas stations in an area.

C. Oxygen availability decreases as altitude increases.

D. The number of rabbit sightings and the cost of carrots have both increased.

⑯ Which of the following is an example of dependent trials in a hypergeometric distribution?

A. asking a group of people whether or not they wear glasses

B. the number of prime digits in a phone number

C. the number of trials required to roll doubles with a pair of dice

D. the number of heart cards dealt from a deck

Mathematics of Data Management

⑰ The weights of a number of bowling balls are given. Find each of the following.

Weights of Bowling Balls

6	10	12	13
7	10	12	13
8	11	12	14
8	11	12	14
9	12	13	15

a. mean

_____

b. median

_____

c. mode

_____

d. standard deviation

_____

e. Q_1

_____

f. Q_3

_____

g. cumulative-frequency graph

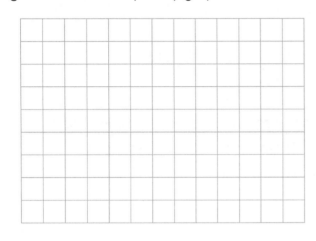

h. box-and-whisker plot

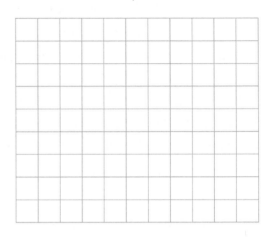

⑱ Henry collected the following data about the number of hours of television watched weekly and the recent math test scores of a group of students.

Hours Watched	Math Score
25	73
24	80
21	69
19	82
18	87
21	91
37	64
23	85
45	54
30	63

a. Find the correlation coefficient.

b. Find the line of best fit.

c. Graph the data and its regression.

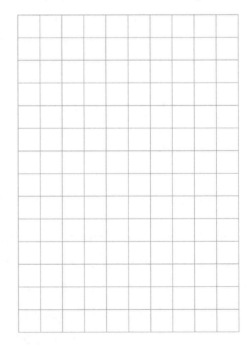

ISBN: 978-1-77149-223-2

⑲ Simplify each into a factorial. Then evaluate.

a. $\dfrac{7!}{5!3!}$

b. $\dfrac{6!3!}{5!}$

c. $_7P_4$

d. $P(4,1)$

e. $_8C_1$

f. $\dbinom{5}{3}$

⑳ Complete the table with terms in Pascal's triangle.

$t_{n,r}$	Sum of Terms	Difference of Terms	Value
$t_{3,1}$			
	$t_{4,2} + t_{4,3}$		
		$t_{5,1} - t_{4,0}$ or $t_{5,2} - t_{4,2}$	
			70

㉑ Expand $(3y - \dfrac{1}{4})^7$.

㉒ If the probability of Event A is 0.4, what is

a. $P(A')$?

b. the odds in favour of A?

c. the odds against A?

㉓ Find the expected values.

a. the number rolled with a 10-sided die

b. the number of doubles rolled from a pair of 6-sided dice after 4 rolls

c. the number of trials before failure if the probability of success is 80%

d. the number of oranges chosen from a fruit basket containing 10 oranges and 8 apples, when 5 fruits are chosen

ISBN: 978-1-77149-223-2

Mathematics of Data Management

Cumulative Test

Application

㉔ A school has 9 Math teachers, 7 English teachers, 5 Business teachers, 3 Chemistry teachers, and 4 Gym teachers. If David takes all 5 courses, how many different sets of teachers are possible?

㉕ In how many ways can a 3, a 10, or an ace be chosen from a deck of 52 cards?

㉖ In how many ways can 7 people line up for a photo if Millie and Billy must be next to each other?

㉗ In how many ways can the letters in the word "MATHEMATICS" be arranged?

㉘ How many triangles can be formed using 11 noncollinear points on a Cartesian plane?

㉙ If four coins are tossed, what is the probability of tossing at least one head?

㉚ A pizza can have 3 types of meat, 4 types of vegetables, and 2 types of cheese. In how many ways can a pizza be ordered?

ISBN: 978-1-77149-223-2

③¹ After surveying 100 students on their after-school activities, the following information is collected.

After-school Activity	Number of Students
Extra-curricular	48
Part-time job	47
Volunteering	44
Extra-curricular and part-time job	21
Extra-curricular and volunteering	18
Part-time job and volunteering	22
Extra-curricular, part-time job, and volunteering	8

a. Create a Venn diagram.

b. How many students participate in at least one after-school activity?

c. How many students do not have after-school activities?

③² A committee of 8 teachers is to be chosen at random from 11 Math teachers and 8 English teachers. What is the probability that there will be more English teachers than Math teachers?

③³ In a group of 20 guinea pigs, 7 of them have grey fur. If 8 guinea pigs are randomly selected, is it more probable to get more than 5 guinea pigs with grey fur or fewer than 3 guinea pigs with grey fur?

ISBN: 978-1-77149-223-2

㉞ In a game of mini-golf, the probability of Gina hitting the ball into the hole is 35%.

a. What is the probability that Gina will get the ball into the hole within 5 strokes?

b. In a game with 18 holes, how many strokes should Gina expect to need?

㉟ Suppose that 75% of adults with allergies report symptomatic relief with a specific medication. If the medication is given to 24 new patients with allergies,

a. what is the probability that it is effective in exactly 18 patients?

b. what is the probability that it is effective in at least 15 patients?

㊱ Suppose the lengths of adults' hand span are normally distributed. If the average length of an adult's hand span is 18 cm with a standard deviation of 2.2 cm,

a. what is the z-score for a hand span of 15 cm?

b. what is the probability that the hand span is less than 17 cm?

c. what is the probability that the hand span is greater than 21 cm?

ISBN: 978-1-77149-223-2

㊲ Would you conduct a census or use a sample to collect the following information? Explain.

a. the number of defective speakers in a batch of 1000

b. the weights of a dozen rabbits

c. the students' test score improvement after a practice test

㊳ The owner of a company wants to convince people that his products are effective. Describe three possible methods the owner can use to deliberately influence the outcome of a set of data.

㊴ Explain the advantages and disadvantages of using a normal distribution to approximate a binomial distribution.

㊵ Describe a scenario where a strong correlation between two variables does not imply a cause-and-effect relationship.

㊶ Describe the criteria when deciding the regression model to be adopted for a set of data.

Mathematics of Data Management

Thinking

㊷ How many different paths are there from point A to point B if moving only east or south is permitted?

a.

b.

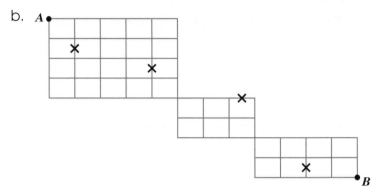

㊸ Capsule A contains 6 white balls and 4 black balls. Capsule B contains 2 white balls and 2 black balls. Two balls are selected randomly from Capsule A and transferred to Capsule B. From Capsule B, two balls are then randomly taken out together. What is the probability that exactly one of the two balls is white?

㊹ A game comes with 30 jelly beans. Each bean has a 35% chance of being sour, 15% chance of being spicy, 5% chance of being bitter, and the remaining chances of being sweet.

a. If Raymond eats 8 jelly beans, what is the probability that fewer than 3 are sweet or sour?

b. If Linda eats jelly beans until she gets a bitter one, what is the probability that she eats more than 4 jelly beans?

c. Which is more likely, eating 5 jelly beans that are all sweet or getting one of each flavour from 4 jelly beans?

ISBN: 978-1-77149-223-2

㊺ IQ testing scores are normally distributed among a population.

a. If the middle 68% of the population have scores between 86 and 114, what are the mean and standard deviation for the scores?

b. What percent of the population will score between 90 and 120?

c. What percentile corresponds to an IQ score of over 123?

d. Sasha's IQ score placed her in the 99th percentile. What is her IQ score?

㊻ Ivan recorded the number of Popsicles sold each day and found that there is a 23.6% chance that fewer than 35 Popsicles are sold in a day and a 11.5% chance that more than 62 Popsicles are sold in a day.

a. What are the mean and standard deviation of the set of data?

b. Ivan found two outliers in the set of data: 4 and 90. What is the semi-interquartile range?

c. Based on the given information, what is the maximum probability that the Popsicles sold is within the Q_1 to Q_3 range?

ISBN: 978-1-77149-223-2

Mathematics of Data Management

ISBN: 978-1-77149-223-2

Handy Reference

Advanced Functions

Polynomial Functions

— leading coefficient

Standard Form: $ax^3 + bx^2 + cx + d$

Factored Form: $a(x - p)(x - q)(x - r)$

Factor Theorem: $x - a$ is a factor of $f(x)$ if and only if $f(a) = 0$

	$x \in (-\infty, 0)$	$x \in [1,5)$
Interval Notation		
Set Notation	$\{x \in \mathbb{R} \mid x < 0\}$	$\{x \in \mathbb{R} \mid 1 \leq x < 5\}$

Degree of a Function
- the highest exponent in an expression
- the shape of a graph depends on the degree, n, of the function

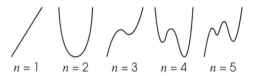

$n = 1 \quad n = 2 \quad n = 3 \quad n = 4 \quad n = 5$

End Behaviours
- odd-degree functions
  - leading coefficient < 0
    - $x \to -\infty, y \to \infty$
    - $x \to \infty, y \to -\infty$
  - leading coefficient > 0
    - $x \to -\infty, y \to -\infty$
    - $x \to \infty, y \to \infty$
- even-degree functions
  - leading coefficient < 0
    - $x \to \pm\infty, y \to -\infty$
  - leading coefficient > 0
    - $x \to \pm\infty, y \to \infty$

Symmetry
- even function where $f(-x) = f(x)$: symmetrical in the y-axis
- odd function where $f(-x) = -f(x)$: have rotational symmetry about the origin

Factoring
- sum of cubes
  $A^3 + B^3 = (A + B)(A^2 - AB + B^2)$
- difference of cubes
  $A^3 - B^3 = (A - B)(A^2 + AB + B^2)$

Rational Functions

Rational Function

$f(x) = \dfrac{p(x)}{q(x)}$, $q(x) \neq 0$

Reciprocal Function

$f(x) = \dfrac{1}{p(x)}$, $p(x) \neq 0$

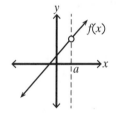

point discontinuity:
$p(x)$ and $q(x)$ have a common factor of $x - a$

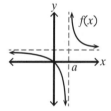

vertical asymptote:
when $q(a) = 0$
horizontal asymptote:
when the degree of $p(x)$ is less than or equal to the degree of $q(x)$

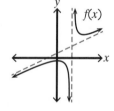

oblique asymptote:
when the degree of $p(x)$ is exactly 1 more than the degree of $q(x)$

Trigonometric Functions

Conversions
- **degrees to radians:** multiply by $\dfrac{\pi}{180°}$
- **radians to degrees:** multiply by $\dfrac{180°}{\pi}$

CAST Rule
- quadrant 1: all (A) ratios are positive
- quadrant 2: only sine (S) is positive
- quadrant 3: only tangent (T) is positive
- quadrant 4: only cosine (C) is positive

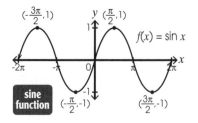

sine function

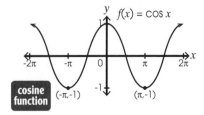

cosine function

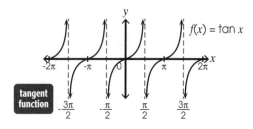

tangent function

Exponential and Logarithmic Functions

Consider $f(x) = a^x$ and $g(x) = \log_a x$.

- $a > 1$

  functions are increasing

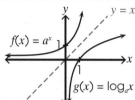

$y = x$

$f(x) = a^x$

$g(x) = \log_a x$

- $0 < a < 1$

  functions are decreasing

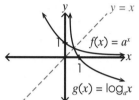

$y = x$

$f(x) = a^x$

$g(x) = \log_a x$

Properties and Laws of Logarithm

$\log_a 1 = 0$

$\log_a a^x = x$

$a^{\log_a x} = x$

$a > 0, a \neq 1$
$x > 0$
$y > 0$

$\log_a xy = \log_a x + \log_a y$

$\log_a \left(\dfrac{x}{y}\right) = \log_a x - \log_a y$

$\log_a x^r = r \log_a x$

Transformations

Quadratic Functions	Sine/Cosine Functions	Logarithmic Functions
$f(x) = a(k(x - d))^2 + c$	$f(x) = a \sin(k(x - d)) + c$ $f(x) = a \cos(k(x - d)) + c$	$f(x) = a \log_{10}(k(x - d)) + c$

Vertical Stretch/Compression and Reflection

- $|a| > 1$: vertical stretch by a factor of $|a|$
- $0 < |a| < 1$: vertical compression by a factor of $|a|$
- $a < 0$: reflection in the x-axis
- $|a|$ is an amplitude for sine and cosine functions.

Horizontal Stretch/Compression and Reflection

- $|k| > 1$: horizontal compression by a factor of $\left|\dfrac{1}{k}\right|$
- $0 < |k| < 1$: horizontal stretch by a factor of $\left|\dfrac{1}{k}\right|$
- $k < 0$: reflection in the y-axis
- $\dfrac{2\pi}{k}$ gives the period for sine and cosine functions.

Horizontal Translation

- $d > 0$: translation to the right
- $d < 0$: translation to the left

Vertical Translation

- $c > 0$: translation up
- $c < 0$: translation down

Trigonometric Identities

Reciprocal Identities

$\csc x = \dfrac{1}{\sin x}$

$\sec x = \dfrac{1}{\cos x}$

$\cot x = \dfrac{1}{\tan x}$

Equivalent Trigonometric Functions

$\sin x = \cos\left(x - \dfrac{\pi}{2}\right)$

$\sin\left(x + \dfrac{\pi}{2}\right) = \cos x$

$\cos x = \cos(-x)$

$\sin(-x) = -\sin x$

$\tan(-x) = -\tan x$

Pythagorean Identities

$\sin^2 x + \cos^2 x = 1$

$1 + \tan^2 x = \sec^2 x$

$1 + \cot^2 x = \csc^2 x$

Addition and Subtraction Formulas

$\sin(x + y) = \sin x \cos y + \cos x \sin y$

$\sin(x - y) = \sin x \cos y - \cos x \sin y$

$\cos(x + y) = \cos x \cos y - \sin x \sin y$

$\cos(x - y) = \cos x \cos y + \sin x \sin y$

$\tan(x + y) = \dfrac{\tan x + \tan y}{1 - \tan x \tan y}$

$\tan(x - y) = \dfrac{\tan x - \tan y}{1 + \tan x \tan y}$

Quotient Identities

$\tan x = \dfrac{\sin x}{\cos x}$

$\cot x = \dfrac{\cos x}{\sin x}$

Double Angle Formulas

$\sin 2x = 2 \sin x \cos x$

$\cos 2x = \cos^2 x - \sin^2 x$

$\cos 2x = 2 \cos^2 x - 1$

$\cos 2x = 1 - 2 \sin^2 x$

$\tan 2x = \dfrac{2 \tan x}{1 - \tan^2 x}$

Rates of Change

average rate of change $= \dfrac{f(x_2) - f(x_1)}{x_2 - x_1}$ ← slope of secant line

instantaneous rate of change $= \dfrac{f(a + h) - f(a)}{h}$ ← slope of tangent line

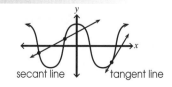

secant line   tangent line

ISBN: 978-1-77149-223-2

Handy Reference

Calculus

Limits

Properties of Limits

Suppose that $f(x)$ and $g(x)$ both have limits that exist at $x = a$, for any real number a.

- $\lim\limits_{x \to a} k = k$, for any constant k

- $\lim\limits_{x \to a} x = a$

- $\lim\limits_{x \to a} [f(x) \pm g(x)] = \lim\limits_{x \to a} f(x) \pm \lim\limits_{x \to a} g(x)$

- $\lim\limits_{x \to a} [kf(x)] = k[\lim\limits_{x \to a} f(x)]$, for any constant k

- $\lim\limits_{x \to a} [f(x)g(x)] = [\lim\limits_{x \to a} f(x)][\lim\limits_{x \to a} g(x)]$

- $\lim\limits_{x \to a} \dfrac{f(x)}{g(x)} = \dfrac{\lim\limits_{x \to a} f(x)}{\lim\limits_{x \to a} g(x)}$, for $\lim\limits_{x \to a} g(x) \neq 0$

- $\lim\limits_{x \to a} [f(x)]^n = [\lim\limits_{x \to a} f(x)]^n$, for any rational number n

Derivatives

Definition of Derivatives: $f'(x) = \lim\limits_{h \to 0} \dfrac{f(x + h) - f(x)}{h}$ or $f'(a) = \lim\limits_{x \to a} \dfrac{f(x) - f(a)}{x - a}$

Rule	Derivative
Constant	For $f(x) = k$, $f'(x) = 0$
Linear	For $f(x) = kx$, $f'(x) = k$
Constant Multiple	For $f(x) = kg(x)$, $f'(x) = kg'(x)$
Power	For $f(x) = x^n$, $f'(x) = nx^{n-1}$
Power of a Function	For $f(x) = [g(x)]^n$, $f'(x) = n[g(x)]^{n-1} g'(x)$
Sum	For $f(x) = p(x) + q(x)$, $f'(x) = p'(x) + q'(x)$
Difference	For $f(x) = p(x) - q(x)$, $f'(x) = p'(x) - q'(x)$

Rule	Derivative
Product	For $h(x) = f(x)g(x)$, $h'(x) = f'(x)g(x) + f(x)g'(x)$
Quotient	For $h(x) = \dfrac{f(x)}{g(x)}$, $h'(x) = \dfrac{f'(x)g(x) - f(x)g'(x)}{[g(x)]^2}$
Chain	For $h(x) = f(g(x))$, $h'(x) = f'(g(x))g'(x)$
Trigonometric	For $f(x) = \sin x$, $f'(x) = \cos x$ For $f(x) = \cos x$, $f'(x) = -\sin x$ For $f(x) = \tan x$, $f'(x) = \sec^2 x$
Exponential	For $f(x) = e^x$, $f'(x) = e^x$ For $f(x) = b^x$, $f'(x) = b^x \ln b$

Curve Sketching

Determine the following information for curve sketching.

- domain, including point discontinuities and/or asymptotes
- x- and y-intercepts
- end behaviours
  - vertical asymptote if $\lim\limits_{x \to c^\pm} f(x) = \pm\infty$
  - horizontal asymptote if $\lim\limits_{x \to \pm\infty} f(x) = L$

- applying first derivative test
  - critical numbers at $f'(x) = 0$
  - local minimum when $f'(x)$ changes from negative to positive
  - local maximum when $f'(x)$ changes from positive to negative
  - intervals of increase and decrease
- applying second derivative test
  - points of inflection at $f''(x) = 0$
  - local minimum when $f''(c) > 0$
  - local maximum when $f''(c) < 0$
  - intervals of concavity

Handy Reference

Vectors

Vectors in R^2 and R^3

- **Magnitude:**

  for $\overrightarrow{OP} = (a,b)$, $|\overrightarrow{OP}| = \sqrt{a^2 + b^2}$

  for $\overrightarrow{OP} = (a,b,c)$, $|\overrightarrow{OP}| = \sqrt{a^2 + b^2 + c^2}$

- **Unit Vector:** $\dfrac{1}{|\vec{a}|}\vec{a}$

- **Properties:**

$$\vec{a} + \vec{b} = \vec{b} + \vec{a} \qquad\qquad \vec{a} + \vec{0} = \vec{a}$$

$$(\vec{a} + \vec{b}) + \vec{c} = \vec{a} + (\vec{b} + \vec{c}) \qquad m(n\vec{a}) = mn\vec{a}$$

$$k(\vec{a} + \vec{b}) = k\vec{a} + k\vec{b} \qquad (m + n)\vec{a} = m\vec{a} + n\vec{a}$$

Projections

- **Scalar Projection of $\vec{a}$ on $\vec{b}$:**

$$\frac{\vec{a} \cdot \vec{b}}{|\vec{b}|} = |\vec{a}| \cos \theta$$

- **Vector Projection of $\vec{a}$ on $\vec{b}$:**

$$\left(\frac{\vec{a} \cdot \vec{b}}{\vec{b} \cdot \vec{b}}\right)\vec{b}, \ \vec{b} \neq 0$$

- **Direction Cosines for $\overrightarrow{OP} = (a,b,c)$:**

$$\cos \alpha = \frac{a}{\sqrt{a^2 + b^2 + c^2}}$$

$$\cos \beta = \frac{b}{\sqrt{a^2 + b^2 + c^2}}$$

$$\cos \gamma = \frac{c}{\sqrt{a^2 + b^2 + c^2}}$$

Applications

- **Dot Product**

$$\vec{a} \cdot \vec{b} = |\vec{a}||\vec{b}| \cos \theta \longleftarrow$$

$$\cos \theta = \frac{\vec{a} \cdot \vec{b}}{|\vec{a}||\vec{b}|}$$

If $\theta = 90°$, then $\vec{a} \cdot \vec{b} = 0$

$$\vec{a} \cdot \vec{b} = \vec{b} \cdot \vec{a}$$

$$\vec{a} \cdot (\vec{b} + \vec{c}) = \vec{a} \cdot \vec{b} + \vec{a} \cdot \vec{c}$$

$$\vec{a} \cdot \vec{a} = |\vec{a}|^2$$

$$(k\vec{a}) \cdot \vec{b} = \vec{a} \cdot (k\vec{b}) = k(\vec{a} \cdot \vec{b})$$

In R^2, $\vec{a} \cdot \vec{b} = a_1b_1 + a_2b_2$

In R^3, $\vec{a} \cdot \vec{b} = a_1b_1 + a_2b_2 + a_3b_3$

- **Cross Product**

$$\vec{a} \times \vec{b} = (a_2b_3 - a_3b_2,\ a_3b_1 - a_1b_3,\ a_1b_2 - a_2b_1)$$

$$\vec{a} \times \vec{b} = -\vec{b} \times \vec{a}$$

$$\vec{a} \times (\vec{b} + \vec{c}) = \vec{a} \times \vec{b} + \vec{a} \times \vec{c}$$

$$(k\vec{a}) \times \vec{b} = \vec{a} \times (k\vec{b}) = k(\vec{a} \times \vec{b})$$

$$|\vec{a} \times \vec{b}| = |\vec{a}||\vec{b}| \sin \theta$$

work: $\vec{w} = \vec{f} \cdot \vec{s}$ \qquad torque: $\vec{r} \times \vec{f} = |\vec{r}||\vec{f}| \sin \theta$

area of parallelogram with sides $\vec{a}$ and $\vec{b}$: $|\vec{a} \times \vec{b}|$

Equations of Lines and Planes

Form	Line in R^2	Line in R^3	Plane in R^3
Vector	$(x,y) = (x_0,y_0) + t(a,b)$	$(x,y,z) = (x_0,y_0,z_0) + t(a,b,c)$	$(x,y,z) = (x_0,y_0,z_0) + s(a_1,a_2,a_3) + t(b_1,b_2,b_3)$
Parametric	$x = x_0 + at,\ y = y_0 + bt$	$x = x_0 + at,\ y = y_0 + bt,\ z = z_0 + ct$	$x = x_0 + sa_1 + tb_1,\ y = y_0 + sa_2 + tb_2,\ z = z_0 + sa_3 + tb_3$
Symmetric	$\dfrac{x - x_0}{a} = \dfrac{y - y_0}{b}$	$\dfrac{x - x_0}{a} = \dfrac{y - y_0}{b} = \dfrac{z - z_0}{c}$	N/A
Cartesian	$Ax + By + C = 0,\ \vec{n} = (A,B)$	N/A	$Ax + By + Cz + D = 0,\ \vec{n} = (A,B,C)$

Distances between Points, Lines, and Planes

A Point and a Line in R^2:

$$d = \frac{|Ax_0 + By_0 + C|}{\sqrt{A^2 + B^2}}$$

Point: (x_0, y_0)
Line: $Ax + By + C = 0$

A Point and a Line in R^3:

$$d = \frac{|\vec{m} \times \overrightarrow{QP}|}{|\vec{m}|}$$

where Q is a point on the line, P is any point, and $\vec{m}$ is the direction vector of the line

A Point and a Plane in R^3:

$$d = \frac{|Ax_0 + By_0 + Cz_0 + D|}{\sqrt{A^2 + B^2 + C^2}}$$

Point: (x_0, y_0, z_0)
Plane: $Ax + By + Cz + D = 0$

ISBN: 978-1-77149-223-2

Mathematics of Data Management

Statistics

mean: the sum of all values divided by the number of ← values

Population Mean
$$\mu = \frac{\Sigma x}{N}$$

Sample Mean
$$\bar{x} = \frac{\Sigma x}{n}$$

median: the middle value when the values are ranked in order

mode: the most frequently occurring value

standard deviation: a measure of how closely a set ← of data clusters around its mean

Population Standard Deviation
$$\sigma = \sqrt{\frac{\Sigma(x - \mu)^2}{N}}$$

Sample Standard Deviation
$$s = \sqrt{\frac{\Sigma(x - \bar{x})^2}{n - 1}}$$

correlation coefficient: a quantitative measure of ← the correlation between two variables

$$r = \frac{n(\Sigma xy) - \Sigma x \Sigma y}{\sqrt{n\Sigma x^2 - (\Sigma x)^2}\sqrt{n\Sigma y^2 - (\Sigma y)^2}}$$

line of best fit: the straight line that best represents ← the data on a scatter plot

$$y = ax + b$$
where $a = \dfrac{n(\Sigma xy) - \Sigma x \Sigma y}{n\Sigma x^2 - (\Sigma x)^2}$ and $b = \bar{y} - a\bar{x}$

Permutations and Combinations

Factorial:

the multiplication of consecutive natural numbers

$$n! = n \times (n - 1) \times (n - 2)... \times 2 \times 1$$

Permutation:

the number of permutations of r items taken from n distinct items

$$_nP_r = \frac{n!}{(n - r)!}$$

Combination:

the number of combinations of r items chosen from n distinct items

$$_nC_r = \frac{n!}{(n - r)!\, r!}$$

Pascal's Formula
$$_nC_r = {_{n-1}C_{r-1}} + {_{n-1}C_r}$$

Binomial Theorem
$$(a + b)^n = \sum_{r=0}^{n} {_nC_r}\, a^{n-r}b^r$$

Probability

$$P(A) = \frac{n(A)}{n(s)} \begin{array}{l}\leftarrow \text{no. of outcomes in } A \\ \leftarrow \text{total no. of outcomes}\end{array}$$

$$P(A) = 1 - P(A')$$

odds in favour of $A = \dfrac{P(A)}{P(A')}$

odds against $A = \dfrac{P(A')}{P(A)}$

$P(A \text{ and } B) = P(A) \times P(B)$
if A and B are independent

$P(A \text{ or } B) = P(A) + P(B)$
if A and B are
mutually exclusive

$P(A \text{ and } B) = P(A) \times P(B|A)$
if B is dependent on A

$P(A \text{ or } B) = P(A) + P(B) - P(A \cap B)$
if A and B are
non-mutually exclusive

Distributions

Distribution	Uniform	Binomial	Geometric	Hypergeometric
Probability	$P(x) = \dfrac{1}{n}$ x – random variable n – no. of possible outcomes	$P(x) = {_nC_x}p^x q^{n-x}$ x – no. of successes n – no. of independent trials p – probability of success q – probability of failure	$P(x) = q^x p$ x – no. of failures q – probability of failure p – probability of success	$P(x) = \dfrac{{_aC_x} \times {_{n-a}C_{r-x}}}{_nC_r}$ x – no. of successes n – no. of possible outcomes a – no. of successes in n r – no. of dependent trials
Expected Value	$E(x) = \sum\limits_{i=1}^{n} x_i P(x_i)$	$E(x) = np$	$E(x) = \dfrac{q}{p}$	$E(x) = \dfrac{ra}{n}$

Z-score $\quad z = \dfrac{x - \mu}{\sigma}$

Normal Approximation to Binomial Distribution
$\mu = np \qquad \sigma = \sqrt{npq}$
if $np > 5$ and $nq > 5$

ISBN: 978-1-77149-223-2

Z-score Table

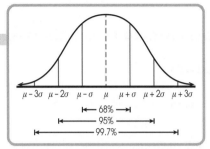

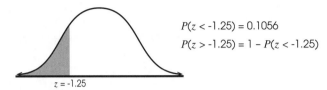

$P(z < -1.25) = 0.1056$

$P(z > -1.25) = 1 - P(z < -1.25)$

$z = -1.25$

$\mu - 3\sigma \quad \mu - 2\sigma \quad \mu - \sigma \quad \mu \quad \mu + \sigma \quad \mu + 2\sigma \quad \mu + 3\sigma$

68%
95%
99.7%

z	0.00	0.01	0.02	0.03	0.04	0.05	0.06	0.07	0.08	0.09
-2.9	0.0019	0.0018	0.0018	0.0017	0.0016	0.0016	0.0015	0.0015	0.0014	0.0014
-2.8	0.0026	0.0025	0.0024	0.0023	0.0023	0.0022	0.0021	0.0021	0.0020	0.0019
-2.7	0.0035	0.0034	0.0033	0.0032	0.0031	0.0030	0.0029	0.0028	0.0027	0.0026
-2.6	0.0047	0.0045	0.0044	0.0043	0.0041	0.0040	0.0039	0.0038	0.0037	0.0036
-2.5	0.0062	0.0060	0.0059	0.0057	0.0055	0.0054	0.0052	0.0051	0.0049	0.0048
-2.4	0.0082	0.0080	0.0078	0.0075	0.0073	0.0071	0.0069	0.0068	0.0066	0.0064
-2.3	0.0107	0.0104	0.0102	0.0099	0.0096	0.0094	0.0091	0.0089	0.0087	0.0084
-2.2	0.0139	0.0136	0.0132	0.0129	0.0125	0.0122	0.0119	0.0116	0.0113	0.0110
-2.1	0.0179	0.0174	0.0170	0.0166	0.0162	0.0158	0.0154	0.0150	0.0146	0.0143
-2.0	0.0228	0.0222	0.0217	0.0212	0.0207	0.0202	0.0197	0.0192	0.0188	0.0183
-1.9	0.0287	0.0281	0.0274	0.0268	0.0262	0.0256	0.0250	0.0244	0.0239	0.0233
-1.8	0.0359	0.0351	0.0344	0.0336	0.0329	0.0322	0.0314	0.0307	0.0301	0.0294
-1.7	0.0446	0.0436	0.0427	0.0418	0.0409	0.0401	0.0392	0.0384	0.0375	0.0367
-1.6	0.0548	0.0537	0.0526	0.0516	0.0505	0.0495	0.0485	0.0475	0.0465	0.0455
-1.5	0.0668	0.0655	0.0643	0.0630	0.0618	0.0606	0.0594	0.0582	0.0571	0.0559
-1.4	0.0808	0.0793	0.0778	0.0764	0.0749	0.0735	0.0721	0.0708	0.0694	0.0681
-1.3	0.0968	0.0951	0.0934	0.0918	0.0901	0.0885	0.0869	0.0853	0.0838	0.0823
-1.2	0.1151	0.1131	0.1112	0.1093	0.1075	0.1056	0.1038	0.1020	0.1003	0.0985
-1.1	0.1357	0.1335	0.1314	0.1292	0.1271	0.1251	0.1230	0.1210	0.1190	0.1170
-1.0	0.1587	0.1562	0.1539	0.1515	0.1492	0.1469	0.1446	0.1423	0.1401	0.1379
-0.9	0.1841	0.1814	0.1788	0.1762	0.1736	0.1711	0.1685	0.1660	0.1635	0.1611
-0.8	0.2119	0.2090	0.2061	0.2033	0.2005	0.1977	0.1949	0.1922	0.1894	0.1867
-0.7	0.2420	0.2389	0.2358	0.2327	0.2296	0.2266	0.2236	0.2206	0.2177	0.2148
-0.6	0.2743	0.2709	0.2676	0.2643	0.2611	0.2578	0.2546	0.2514	0.2483	0.2451
-0.5	0.3085	0.3050	0.3015	0.2981	0.2946	0.2912	0.2877	0.2843	0.2810	0.2776
-0.4	0.3446	0.3409	0.3372	0.3336	0.3300	0.3264	0.3228	0.3192	0.3156	0.3121
-0.3	0.3821	0.3783	0.3745	0.3707	0.3669	0.3632	0.3594	0.3557	0.3520	0.3483
-0.2	0.4207	0.4168	0.4129	0.4090	0.4052	0.4013	0.3974	0.3936	0.3897	0.3859
-0.1	0.4602	0.4562	0.4522	0.4483	0.4443	0.4404	0.4364	0.4325	0.4286	0.4247
-0.0	0.5000	0.4960	0.4920	0.4880	0.4840	0.4801	0.4761	0.4721	0.4681	0.4641
0.0	0.5000	0.5040	0.5080	0.5120	0.5160	0.5199	0.5239	0.5279	0.5319	0.5359
0.1	0.5398	0.5438	0.5478	0.5517	0.5557	0.5596	0.5636	0.5675	0.5714	0.5753
0.2	0.5793	0.5832	0.5871	0.5910	0.5948	0.5987	0.6026	0.6064	0.6103	0.6141
0.3	0.6179	0.6217	0.6255	0.6293	0.6331	0.6368	0.6406	0.6443	0.6480	0.6517
0.4	0.6554	0.6591	0.6628	0.6664	0.6700	0.6736	0.6772	0.6808	0.6844	0.6879
0.5	0.6915	0.6950	0.6985	0.7019	0.7054	0.7088	0.7123	0.7157	0.7190	0.7224
0.6	0.7257	0.7291	0.7324	0.7357	0.7389	0.7422	0.7454	0.7486	0.7517	0.7549
0.7	0.7580	0.7611	0.7642	0.7673	0.7704	0.7734	0.7764	0.7794	0.7823	0.7852
0.8	0.7881	0.7910	0.7939	0.7967	0.7995	0.8023	0.8051	0.8078	0.8106	0.8133
0.9	0.8159	0.8186	0.8212	0.8238	0.8264	0.8289	0.8315	0.8340	0.8365	0.8389
1.0	0.8413	0.8438	0.8461	0.8485	0.8508	0.8531	0.8554	0.8577	0.8599	0.8621
1.1	0.8643	0.8665	0.8686	0.8708	0.8729	0.8749	0.8770	0.8790	0.8810	0.8830
1.2	0.8849	0.8869	0.8888	0.8907	0.8925	0.8944	0.8962	0.8980	0.8997	0.9015
1.3	0.9032	0.9049	0.9066	0.9082	0.9099	0.9115	0.9131	0.9147	0.9162	0.9177
1.4	0.9192	0.9207	0.9222	0.9236	0.9251	0.9265	0.9279	0.9292	0.9306	0.9319
1.5	0.9332	0.9345	0.9357	0.9370	0.9382	0.9394	0.9406	0.9418	0.9429	0.9441
1.6	0.9452	0.9463	0.9474	0.9484	0.9495	0.9505	0.9515	0.9525	0.9535	0.9545
1.7	0.9554	0.9564	0.9573	0.9582	0.9591	0.9599	0.9608	0.9616	0.9625	0.9633
1.8	0.9641	0.9649	0.9656	0.9664	0.9671	0.9678	0.9686	0.9693	0.9699	0.9706
1.9	0.9713	0.9719	0.9726	0.9732	0.9738	0.9744	0.9750	0.9756	0.9761	0.9767
2.0	0.9772	0.9778	0.9783	0.9788	0.9793	0.9798	0.9803	0.9808	0.9812	0.9817
2.1	0.9821	0.9826	0.9830	0.9834	0.9838	0.9842	0.9846	0.9850	0.9854	0.9857
2.2	0.9861	0.9864	0.9868	0.9871	0.9875	0.9878	0.9881	0.9884	0.9887	0.9890
2.3	0.9893	0.9896	0.9898	0.9901	0.9904	0.9906	0.9909	0.9911	0.9913	0.9916
2.4	0.9918	0.9920	0.9922	0.9925	0.9927	0.9929	0.9931	0.9932	0.9934	0.9936
2.5	0.9938	0.9940	0.9941	0.9943	0.9945	0.9946	0.9948	0.9949	0.9951	0.9952
2.6	0.9953	0.9955	0.9956	0.9957	0.9959	0.9960	0.9961	0.9962	0.9963	0.9964
2.7	0.9965	0.9966	0.9967	0.9968	0.9969	0.9970	0.9971	0.9972	0.9973	0.9974
2.8	0.9974	0.9975	0.9976	0.9977	0.9977	0.9978	0.9979	0.9979	0.9980	0.9981
2.9	0.9981	0.9982	0.9982	0.9983	0.9984	0.9984	0.9985	0.9985	0.9986	0.9986

ISBN: 978-1-77149-223-2

ANSWERS

Advanced Functions

1 Polynomial Functions

1. C
2. B
3. A
4. B
5. C
6. D
7. C

8a. $\{x \in \mathbb{R} \mid -6 < x \le 10\}$; $(-6, 10]$

b.

Domain: $\{x \in \mathbb{R}\}$; $(-\infty, \infty)$
Range: $\{y \in \mathbb{R} \mid y \ge -9\}$; $[-9, \infty)$

c. Domain: $\{x \in \mathbb{R}\}$; $(-\infty, \infty)$
Range: $\{y \in \mathbb{R}\}$; $(-\infty, \infty)$

9a. $y = 2^2(-3)(1) = -12$
$(0, -12)$

b. $y = 4(3)^2(-4) = -144$
$(0, -144)$

c. $y = 5$
$(0, 5)$

d. $y = -2(1)(-3)(2)(-5)(-1) = 60$
$(0, 60)$

10a.
x	y
-2	5
-1	0
0	-3
1	-4
2	-3

-5 ⟩2
-3 ⟩2
-1 ⟩2
1

quadratic

b.
x	y
2	6
3	0
4	0
5	12
6	42

-6 ⟩6
0 ⟩6
12 ⟩12 ⟩6
30 ⟩18

cubic

11a.
root	1	0	-3
multiplicity	2	2	1

b.
root	1	-2	-3
multiplicity	1	3	2

c. $y = (x - 4)(x + 3)(x - 2)^5$

root	4	2	-3
multiplicity	1	5	1

12. $f(x) = a(x + 4)^2(x - 2)^2$
$-8 = a(4)^2(-2)^2$
$-8 = a(64)$
$a = -\dfrac{1}{8}$
$f(x) = -\dfrac{1}{8}(x + 4)^2(x - 2)^2$

13a. $= (x^2 + 4x + 4)(x - 3)$
$= x^3 - 3x^2 + 4x^2 - 12x + 4x - 12$
$= x^3 + x^2 - 8x - 12$

b. $= 1 - \dfrac{1}{2}(x^2 + 6x + 9)(2 + x)$
$= 1 - \dfrac{1}{2}(2x^2 + x^3 + 12x + 6x^2 + 18 + 9x)$
$= 1 - \dfrac{1}{2}(x^3 + 8x^2 + 21x + 18)$
$= 1 - \dfrac{1}{2}x^3 - 4x^2 - \dfrac{21}{2}x - 9$
$= -\dfrac{1}{2}x^3 - 4x^2 - \dfrac{21}{2}x - 8$

14.
$x \to \infty,\ y \to \infty$ $x \to -\infty,\ y \to \infty$	$x \to \infty,\ y \to -\infty$ $x \to -\infty,\ y \to -\infty$
$x \to \infty,\ y \to \infty$ $x \to -\infty,\ y \to -\infty$	$x \to \infty,\ y \to -\infty$ $x \to -\infty,\ y \to \infty$
$x \to \infty,\ y \to \infty$ $x \to -\infty,\ y \to \infty$	$x \to \infty,\ y \to -\infty$ $x \to -\infty,\ y \to -\infty$
$x \to \infty,\ y \to \infty$ $x \to -\infty,\ y \to -\infty$	$x \to \infty,\ y \to -\infty$ $x \to -\infty,\ y \to \infty$

15A:
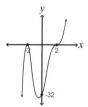

B:
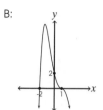

C:
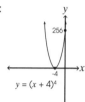
$y = (x + 4)^4$

D:
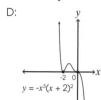
$y = -x^3(x + 2)^2$

16.
$y = 4(x - 1)^3 - 32$	$y = -(x + 2)^3 + 8$	$y = (2x)^3 - 27$
$y = 4x^3 - 12x^2 + 12x - 36$	$y = -x^3 - 6x^2 - 12x$	$y = 8x^3 - 27$
$y = 4(x - 3)(x^2 + 3)$	$y = -x(x^2 + 6x + 12)$	$y = (2x - 3)(4x^2 + 6x + 9)$
$(3, 0)$	$(0, 0)$	$(\frac{3}{2}, 0)$
$(0, -36)$	$(0, 0)$	$(0, -27)$

17a. $y = a(x + 5)(x + 2)(x - 2)(x - 5)$

b. $y = ax(x + 3)(x + 2)(x - 1)(x - 4)$

18. $y = a(x - 3)^2(x - 1)$
$9 = a(-3)^2(-1)$
$9 = a(-9)$
$a = -1$
$\therefore f(x) = -(x - 3)^2(x - 1)$

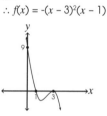

19. degree: 4
roots: 0, 2, and -3
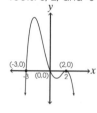

20. $P(x) = -2x^2 + 7x - 3$
$= (-2x + 1)(x - 3)$
roots: $\dfrac{1}{2}$ and 3
max: $(\dfrac{1}{2} + 3) \div 2 = 1.75$
$P(1.75) = 3.125$
Ezra can maximize the profit to the amount of \$3125 by selling 175 burgers.

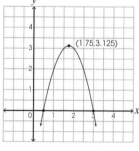

21. $d(x) = 2x^3 - 22x^2 + 78x - 90$
$= 2(x^3 - 11x^2 + 39x - 45)$
$= 2(x^2 - 6x + 9)(x - 5)$
$= 2(x - 3)^2(x - 5)$

x	y
2	-6
3	0
4	-2
5	0
6	18

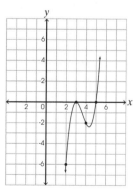

The ship will have travelled 600 km east when it travelled 1800 km north.

22. $y = -\frac{1}{3}(2x + 10)^3 + 4$

$y = -\frac{1}{3}(2(x + 5))^3 + 4$

• vertically compressed by a factor of $\frac{1}{3}$ and reflected in the x-axis
• horizontally compressed by a factor of $\frac{1}{2}$
• translated 5 units left and 4 units up

23. $f(x) = ax^5 + bx^4 + cx^3 + dx^2 + ex + f$ ⟵ an odd function
A quintic function has a degree of 5. A function of odd degree has opposite end behaviours.
e.g.

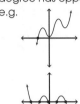

The minimum number of real roots is 1 because the function must cross the x-axis at least once.

The maximum is 5 real roots.

24. An even function is any function that is symmetric about the y-axis; it has the property $f(-x) = f(x)$.
e.g. $f(x) = x^2$
$f(-x) = (-x)^2 = x^2 = f(x)$
An odd function is any function that has rotational symmetry about the origin; it has the property $f(-x) = -f(x)$.
e.g. $f(x) = x^3$
$f(-x) = (-x)^3 = -x^3 = -f(x)$
Neither: $f(x) = x^2 + x + 1$

25. $f(1) = 1^4 + 2(1)^2 + 1 = 4$
$f(-1) = (-1)^4 + 2(-1)^2 + 1 = 4$
Since no values of x can satisfy $f(x) = 0$, according to the factor theorem, where $(x - a)$ is a factor of $f(x)$ if and only if $f(a) = 0$, the polynomial has no factors and cannot be factored.

26a.

x	y
0	3
1	6
2	13
3	24
4	39
5	58

3, 7, 11, 15, 19
4, 4, 4, 4

The second differences are constant, so the function is quadratic. The general equation is:
$Ax^2 + Bx + C = y$

$C = 3$
$A + B + C = 6$
$4A + 2B + C = 13$
$9A + 3B + C = 24$
$16A + 4B + C = 39$
$25A + 5B + C = 58$

$A + B = 3$
$3A + B = 7$
$5A + B = 11$
$7A + B = 15$
$9A + B = 19$

$2A = 4$
$2A = 4$
$2A = 4$
$2A = 4$

$A = 2, B = 1, C = 3$
$\therefore f(x) = 2x^2 + x + 3$

b.

x	y
0	1
1	4
2	1
3	-20
4	-71
5	-164

3, -3, -21, -51, -93
-6, -18, -30, -42
-12, -12, -12

The third differences are constant, so the function is cubic. The general equation is:
$Ax^3 + Bx^2 + Cx + D = y$

$A = -2, B = 3, C = 2, D = 1$
$\therefore f(x) = -2x^3 + 3x^2 + 2x + 1$

27. 6
16
1
As $x \to \infty$, $y \to \infty$ and
as $x \to -\infty$, $y \to \infty$.
$x = 4$ (mult: 1),
$x = 1$ (mult: 3),
$x = -2$ (mult: 2)

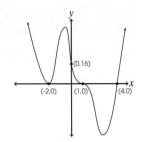

28. (Suggested answers)
a. $y = 3(x - 2)^2(x - 7)$
$y = -(x - 2)^2(x - 7)$
b. $y = -(x + 7)^2(x - 7)^2$
$y = -5(x + 7)^2(x - 7)^2$
c. $y = -x(x - 2)^2(x + 5)^2$
$y = -2(x + 1)(x - 2)^2(x + 5)^2$
d. $y = -2x^2(x + 1)$
$y = -2x^2(x - 4)$

29.

x	y		x	y
-3	-27		-8	-9.5
-2	-8		-6	0
-1	-1		-4	3.5
0	0		-2	4
1	1		0	4.5
2	8		2	8
3	27		4	17.5

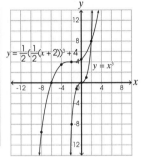

The original function and the transformed function intersect at (2,8).

2 Polynomial Equations and Inequalities

1. C 2. C 3. D
4. B 5. B 6. D

7a.

3 | 2 -15 -12 12
  | 6 -27 -117
  | 2   -9 -39 -105

$= (x - 3)(2x^2 - 9x - 39) - 105$

b.

-2 | 3   1   -4   -6
   | -6   10 -12
   | 3 -5   6 -18

$= (x + 2)(3x^2 - 5x + 6) - 18$

8a. $4x^3 - 20x^2 + 25x = 0$
$x(4x^2 - 20x + 25) = 0$
$x(2x - 5)(2x - 5) = 0$
$x(2x - 5)^2 = 0$
$x = 0$ or $x = \frac{5}{2}$

c.

$$
\begin{array}{r}
x^2 - x - 6 \\
x - 4 \overline{\smash{)}\ x^3 - 5x^2 - 2x + 24} \\
\underline{x^3 - 4x^2} \\
-x^2 - 2x \\
\underline{-x^2 + 4x} \\
-6x + 24 \\
\underline{-6x + 24}
\end{array}
$$

b.

-3 | 1   2   -5   -6
   | -3   3   6
 2 | 1 -1   -2   0
   | 2   2
-1 | 1   1   0
   | -1
   | 1   0

$$
\begin{array}{r}
x + 2 \\
x - 3 \overline{\smash{)}\ x^2 - x - 6} \\
\underline{x^2 - 3x} \\
2x - 6 \\
\underline{2x - 6}
\end{array}
$$

$(x + 3)(x - 2)(x + 1) = 0$
$x = -3$ or $x = 2$ or $x = -1$

$(x - 4)(x - 3)(x + 2) = 0$
$x = 4$ or $x = 3$ or $x = -2$

9. $(x + 2)(2x - 1)(x - 5) > 0$

The x-intercepts are at -2, $\frac{1}{2}$, and 5.
The graph is above 0 when $-2 < x < \frac{1}{2}$ or $x > 5$.
$\therefore -2 < x < \frac{1}{2}$ or $x > 5$

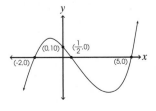

10. $(t + 3)(t - 4)(t - 7) < 0$
The roots are -3, 4, and 7.

Intervals	$t < -3$	$-3 < t < 4$	$4 < t < 7$	$t > 7$
$(t + 3)$	–	+	+	+
$(t - 4)$	–	–	+	+
$(t - 7)$	–	–	–	+
product	–	+	–	+

∴ $t < -3$ or $4 < t < 7$

11. $P(x) = a(x + 2)(x + 1)(2x - 1)$ ⟵ $x = \frac{1}{2}$
$12 = a(1 + 2)(1 + 1)(2(1) - 1)$
$12 = 6a$
$a = 2$
$P(x) = 2(x + 2)(x + 1)(2x - 1)$

12a. $m(1)^4 + (2m + 1)(1)^3 + (3 + m) = 0$
$4m + 4 = 0$
$m = -1$

b. $3m(1)^3 - (4 - m)(1) - 2m = 0$
$2m - 4 = 0$
$m = 2$

13. $(2x - 7)(2x + 3)(x - 2) = 117$
$4x^3 - 16x^2 - 5x + 42 = 117$
$4x^3 - 16x^2 - 5x - 75 = 0$
$(x - 5)(4x^2 + 4x + 15) = 0$
$x = 5$ no real roots
Width: $2(5) - 7 = 3$
Length: $2(5) + 3 = 13$
Height: $5 - 2 = 3$
The dimensions of the cargo are 3 m by 13 m by 3 m.

14. $(32 - 2x)(28 - 2x)(x) = 1920$
$4x^3 - 120x^2 + 896x = 1920$
$4x^3 - 120x^2 + 896x - 1920 = 0$
$4(x - 4)(x - 6)(x - 20) = 0$
$x = 4$ or $x = 6$ or $x = 20$ (too large)
If $x = 4$, length = $32 - 2(4) = 24$
width = $28 - 2(4) = 20$
height = 4
If $x = 6$, length = $32 - 2(6) = 20$
width = $28 - 2(6) = 16$
height = 6
The possible dimensions are 24 cm by 20 cm by 4 cm and 20 cm by 16 cm by 6 cm.

15. $V(x) = (2x - 1)(x + 1)(x + 3)$
When $x = 2$, $2(2) - 1 = 3$
$2 + 1 = 3$
$2 + 3 = 5$
The dimensions of the cage are $(2x - 1)$ by $(x + 1)$ by $(x + 3)$.
When $x = 2$, the dimensions are 3 m by 3 m by 5 m.

16. $-25t^3 + 25t^2 + t > 1$
$-25t^3 + 25t^2 + t - 1 > 0$
$-(t - 1)(5t - 1)(5t + 1) > 0$
The x-intercepts are at -0.2, 0.2, and 1.
The graph is above the x-axis when $t < -0.2$ and $0.2 < t < 1$.
Since time cannot be negative, the ball's height will be greater than 1 m between 0.2 s and 1 s.

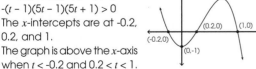

17. They make a profit when the revenue is greater than the cost.
$28 - 2x < 9x - x^2$
$x^2 - 11x + 28 < 0$
$(x - 4)(x - 7) < 0$
The x-intercepts are at 4 and 7.
The graph is below the x-axis when $4 < x < 7$.
They can sell the cookies between $4 and $7 to make a profit.

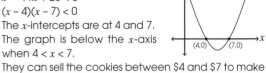

18. $112t - 16t^2 \geq 160$
$-16t^2 + 112t - 160 \geq 0$
$-16(t - 2)(t - 5) \geq 0$
The x-intercepts are at 2 and 5.
When $t = 2$ or $t = 5$, $h(t) = 160$.
The helicopter is 160 m above the ground or higher when $2 \leq t \leq 5$.

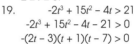

19. $-2t^3 + 15t^2 - 4t > 21$
$-2t^3 + 15t^2 - 4t - 21 > 0$
$-(2t - 3)(t + 1)(t - 7) > 0$
The x-intercepts are at -1, $\frac{3}{2}$, and 7.
The graph is above the x-axis when $t < -1$ and $\frac{3}{2} < t < 7$.
Since time cannot be negative, Adrian was over 21 km from the warehouse when $\frac{3}{2} < t < 7$.

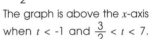

20. $-d^4 + 8d^3 - 16d^2 + 16 > 7$
$-d^4 + 8d^3 - 16d^2 + 9 > 0$
$-(d - 1)(d - 3)(d^2 - 4d - 3) > 0$
$d = 1$ or $d = 3$ or $d = 2 \pm \sqrt{7}$
$\doteq 4.65$ or -0.65
The x-intercepts are at -0.65, 1, 3, and 4.65.
The graph is above the x-axis when $-0.65 < d < 1$ and $3 < d < 4.65$. Since the distance cannot be negative, the ball is greater than 7 dm above the ground when $0 \leq d < 1$ and $3 < d < 4.65$.

21. - Find $f(\frac{b}{a}) = 0$ where b is a factor of -6 and a is a factor of 2.
- Divide $f(x)$ by $(ax - b)$ and repeat until it is fully factorized.
- Solve the inequality graphically or using a factor table.

22.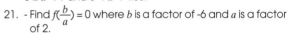
5 intervals need to be tested. The intervals are:
$x < a$, $a < x < b$, $b < x < c$, $c < x < d$, and $x > d$.

23. $f(x) > g(x)$
$x^3 - 2x^2 > 3x + 2$
$x^3 - 2x^2 - 3x - 2 > 0$
$h(x) > 0$
The inequality $f(x) > g(x)$ is the same as $h(x) > 0$ when rearranged, and thus they have the same solution.

24. Polynomial division would be used because synthetic division can only be used when the divisor is linear.

25. $= \dfrac{4x^3 + 12x^2 + 3x + 3}{x^2 + 2x + 1}$

```
                    4x + 4
x² + 2x + 1 ) 4x³ + 12x² + 3x + 3
              4x³ +  8x² + 4x
                     4x² -  x + 3
                     4x² + 8x + 4
                         -9x - 1
```

∴ $(x^2 + 2x + 1)(4x + 4) - 9x - 1$

26. $(x - 1)$: $a(1)^4 + 3(1)^3 - b(1)^2 + 2 = 4$

$a - b = -1$ ①

$(x + 3)$: $a(-3)^4 + 3(-3)^3 - b(-3)^2 + 2 = 56$

$81a - 9b = 135$ ②

$$81a - 9b = 135 \quad ②$$
$$-) \quad 9a - 9b = -9 \quad ① \times 9$$
$$72a = 144$$

$a = 2$

$b = 2 + 1 = 3$

$\therefore a = 2$ and $b = 3$

27. $4x^4 - 12x^3 - x^2 + 3x \le 0$

$x(x - 3)(2x - 1)(2x + 1) \le 0$

Intervals	$x < -\frac{1}{2}$	$-\frac{1}{2} < x < 0$	$0 < x < \frac{1}{2}$	$\frac{1}{2} < x < 3$	$x > 3$
x	−	−	+	+	+
$(x - 3)$	−	−	−	−	+
$(2x - 1)$	−	−	−	+	+
$(2x + 1)$	−	+	+	+	+
product	+	−	+	−	+

$\therefore -\frac{1}{2} \le x \le 0$ or $\frac{1}{2} \le x \le 3$

28. $2x^4 + x^3 - 13x^2 + 6x > 0$

$x(2x - 1)(x - 2)(x + 3) > 0$

The x-intercepts are at -3, 0, $\frac{1}{2}$, and 2.

The graph is above the x-axis when $x < -3$, $0 < x < \frac{1}{2}$, and $x > 2$.

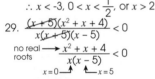

$\therefore x < -3$, $0 < x < \frac{1}{2}$, or $x > 2$

29. $\dfrac{(x + 5)(x^2 + x + 4)}{x(x + 5)(x - 5)} < 0$

no real roots ⟶ $\dfrac{x^2 + x + 4}{x(x - 5)} < 0$

$x = 0$↗ ↖$x = 5$

Intervals	$x < 0$	$0 < x < 5$	$x > 5$
$(x^2 + x + 4)$	+	+	+
x	−	+	+
$(x - 5)$	−	−	+
quotient	+	−	+

$\therefore 0 < x < 5$

30. (Suggested answer)

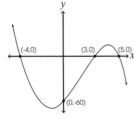

$-(x + 4)(x - 3)(x - 5) > 0$

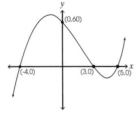

$(x + 4)(x - 3)(x - 5) < 0$

31. Divide into 2 cases:

$-3x^3 + 5x^2 + x + 8 < 3x^3 - 2x + 10$

$0 < 6x^3 - 5x^2 - 3x + 2$

$0 < (3x + 2)(2x - 1)(x - 1)$

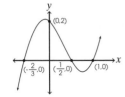

$-\frac{2}{3} < x < \frac{1}{2}$ or $x > 1$

$3x^3 - 2x + 10 < -2x^3 + 6x^2 + 97x - 10$

$5x^3 - 6x^2 - 99x + 20 < 0$

$(x + 4)(5x - 1)(x - 5) < 0$

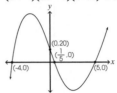

$x < -4$ or $\frac{1}{5} < x < 5$

Combine the cases:

$\therefore \frac{1}{5} < x < \frac{1}{2}$ or $1 < x < 5$

3 Rational Functions

1. B	2. C	3. B
4. B	5. D	6. B

7a.

	✔	
✔		✔
		✔
✔		

b. Point discontinuity: fully factor the numerator and denominator of the rational function and determine if any common factors exist

Vertical asymptote: if x is present in the denominator after factoring and simplifying

Horizontal asymptote: if the degree of the numerator is equal to or less than the degree of the denominator

Oblique asymptote: if the degree of the numerator is exactly 1 more than the degree of the denominator

8. D ; C

B ; A

9a. $= \dfrac{(3x + 5)(x - 1)}{x(x - 1)}$

Point discontinuity at $x = 1$

Vertical asymptote at $x = 0$

Horizontal asymptote at $y = 3$

b. $= \dfrac{2x^2 + 1}{(x + 5)(x - 4)}$

Vertical asymptotes at $x = -5$ and $x = 4$

Horizontal asymptote at $y = 2$

10a.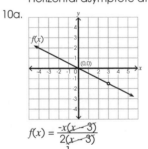

b.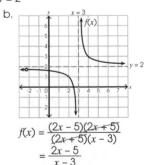

$f(x) = \dfrac{-x(x - 3)}{2(x - 3)}$

$= -\dfrac{1}{2}x$

$f(x) = \dfrac{(2x - 5)(2x + 5)}{(2x + 5)(x - 3)}$

$= \dfrac{2x - 5}{x - 3}$

			positive: $(-\infty, 0)$ negative: $(0, 3), (3, \infty)$	
$\{x \in \mathbb{R} \mid x \ne 3\}$	$\{y \in \mathbb{R} \mid y \ne -\frac{3}{2}\}$	none	positive: $(-\infty, 0)$ negative: $(0, 3), (3, \infty)$	decrease: $(-\infty, 3), (3, \infty)$
$\{x \in \mathbb{R} \mid x \ne 3\}$	$\{y \in \mathbb{R} \mid y \ne 2\}$	$x = 3$ $y = 2$	positive: $(-\infty, 2.5), (3, \infty)$ negative: $(2.5, 3)$	decrease: $(-\infty, 3), (3, \infty)$

ISBN: 978-1-77149-223-2

11a. $3(x + 5) = 2(x - 3)$
 $3x + 15 = 2x - 6$
 $x = -21$

b. $(3x + 2)(1 - 4x) = 7(4x - 1)$
 $-12x^2 - 5x + 2 = 28x - 7$
 $-12x^2 - 33x + 9 = 0$
 $-3(4x^2 + 11x - 3) = 0$
 $-3(4x - 1)(x + 3) = 0$
 $x = \dfrac{1}{4}$ or $x = -3$

12a. $\dfrac{(x + 3)(x + 1)}{(x + 2)^2} > 0$
 $\therefore x < -3$ or $x > -1$

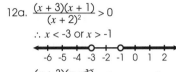

b. $\dfrac{(x + 3)(x - 1)}{(x + 4)(x - 1)} < 0 \qquad x \neq 1$
 $\dfrac{(x + 3)}{(x + 4)} < 0$
 $\therefore -4 < x < -3$

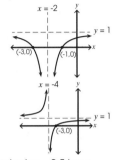

13a. $f(0) = \dfrac{20}{0 + 5} = 4$
 The heating pack can generate heat for 4 hours when it is brand new.

b. 30 minutes = 0.5 hour
 $0.5 = \dfrac{20}{x + 5}$
 $0.5(x + 5) = 20$
 $0.5x + 2.5 = 20$
 $0.5x = 17.5$
 $x = 35$
 It will generate heat for only 30 min after 35 uses.

14a. $w(0) = \dfrac{56(1 + 0.5(0))}{8 + 0.04(0)} = \dfrac{56}{8} = 7$
 There were 7 weeds when $x = 0$.

b. $w(10) = \dfrac{56(1 + 0.5(10))}{8 + 0.04(10)} = \dfrac{336}{8.4} = 40$
 There will be 40 weeds after 10 weeks.

c. $100 = \dfrac{56(1 + 0.5x)}{8 + 0.04x}$
 $100(8 + 0.04x) = 56(1 + 0.5x)$
 $800 + 4x = 56 + 28x$
 $24x = 744$
 $x = 31$
 There will be 100 weeds after 31 weeks.

15.

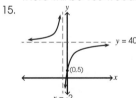

Since the cost of printing must be greater than 0, the price range of the textbook is $5 < x < \$40$.

16.
$$H(x) > C(x)$$
$$\dfrac{x^2 - 9}{-4x - 3} > \dfrac{-x + 7}{5x + 1}$$
$$\dfrac{x^2 - 9}{-4x - 3} - \dfrac{-x + 7}{5x + 1} > 0$$
$$\dfrac{(x^2 - 9)(5x + 1) - (-x + 7)(-4x - 3)}{(-4x - 3)(5x + 1)} > 0$$
$$\dfrac{(5x^3 + x^2 - 45x - 9) - (4x^2 + 3x - 28x - 21)}{(-4x - 3)(5x + 1)} > 0$$
$$\dfrac{5x^3 - 3x^2 - 20x + 12}{(-4x - 3)(5x + 1)} > 0$$
$$\dfrac{(5x - 3)(x - 2)(x + 2)}{(-4x - 3)(5x + 1)} > 0$$

	$0 < x < \frac{3}{5}$	$\frac{3}{5} < x < 2$	$x > 2$
$(5x - 3)$	−	+	+
$(x - 2)$	−	−	+
$(x + 2)$	+	+	+
$(-4x - 3)$	−	−	−
$(5x + 1)$	+	+	+
quotient	−	+	−

← Ignore the intervals when $x < 0$ because time must be positive.
$\therefore \dfrac{3}{5} < x < 2$

It will have more battery charge when $\dfrac{3}{5} < x < 2$.

17. Lisa is incorrect. In an inequality, you cannot move the denominator with a variable in it because the value of the denominator can be 0. Instead, she should have moved the "2" by subtracting it on both sides because it is a constant.

18. A point discontinuity is a hole in a graph. When a graph approaches a point discontinuity, it converges to the same value from both sides but is undefined at that point. When a graph approaches an asymptote from both sides, it goes to infinity but does not touch the asymptote.

19. - If the degree of $p(x)$ is less than that of $q(x)$, then the horizontal asymptote is $y = 0$.
 - If the degree of $p(x)$ is equal to that of $q(x)$, then the horizontal asymptote is $y = \dfrac{a}{b}$, where a and b are the leading coefficients of $p(x)$ and $q(x)$ respectively.
 - If the degree of $p(x)$ is greater than that of $q(x)$ by exactly 1, then there is an oblique asymptote.

20. $f(x) = \dfrac{(x + 3)(x + 2)}{(x + 3)(x + 4)} = \dfrac{(x + 2)}{(x + 4)} \qquad x \neq -3$
 $f(x)$ and $g(x)$ both have a horizontal asymptote at $y = 1$ and a vertical asymptote at $x = -4$. The difference is that $f(x)$ has a point discontinuity at $x = -3$ and $g(x)$ does not.

21a. Point discontinuity: $x = -2$
 Vertical asymptote: $x = 2$
 Horizontal asymptote: $y = 0$
 Point: $(3, 1)$
 $f(x) = \dfrac{a(x + 2)}{(x + 2)(x - 2)}$
 $f(3) = \dfrac{a(3 + 2)}{(3 + 2)(3 - 2)}$
 $a = 1$
 $\therefore f(x) = \dfrac{(x + 2)}{(x + 2)(x - 2)}$

b. Point discontinuities: $x = -2, 1$
 y-intercept: $(0, 1)$
 $g(x) = \dfrac{(x + b)(x + 2)(x - 1)}{(x + 2)(x - 1)}$
 $g(0) = 0 + b$
 $b = 1$
 $\therefore g(x) = \dfrac{(x + 1)(x + 2)(x - 1)}{(x + 2)(x - 1)}$

22. (Suggested answers)
 a. $f(x) = \dfrac{1}{(x - 2)(x - 1)}$
 b. $g(x) = \dfrac{x - 2}{3x + 1}$
 c. $h(x) = \dfrac{3x(2x - 1)}{(x - 1)(2x - 1)}$
 d. $k(x) = \dfrac{1}{4(x + 2)}$

23. (Suggested answer)
 - no point discontinuities or vertical asymptotes: the denominator has no real roots
 - horizontal asymptote at $y = 0$: the degree of the numerator is less than the denominator
 - $f(0) = 2$
 $\therefore f(x) = \dfrac{2}{x^2 + x + 1}$

24a. $g(x) = \dfrac{x^2}{x + 2}$
 $$\dfrac{x + 2}{x^2} = \dfrac{x^2}{x + 2}$$
 $$(x + 2)^2 = x^4$$
 $$x^4 - x^2 - 4x - 4 = 0$$
 $$(x + 1)(x - 2)(x^2 + x + 2) = 0$$
 $x = -1$ or $x = 2$ ← no real roots
 $f(-1) = 1 \qquad f(2) = 1$
 The points of intersection are $(-1, 1)$ and $(2, 1)$.

b.
$$\frac{x+2}{x^2} > \frac{x^2}{x+2}$$
$$\frac{x+2}{x^2} - \frac{x^2}{x+2} > 0$$
$$\frac{(x+2)^2 - x^4}{x^2(x+2)} > 0$$
$$\frac{-1(x^4 - x^2 - 4x - 4)}{x^2(x+2)} > 0$$
$$\frac{-1(x+1)(x-2)(x^2+x+2)}{x^2(x+2)} > 0$$

	$x<-2$	$-2<x<-1$	$-1<x<0$	$0<x<2$	$x>2$
x^2	+	+	+	+	+
$(x+2)$	−	+	+	+	+
$(x+1)$	−	−	+	+	+
$(x-2)$	−	−	−	−	+
(x^2+x+2)	+	+	+	+	+
-1	−	−	−	−	−
quotient	+	−	+	+	−

$\therefore x < -2$ or $-1 < x < 2$

25. $f(x) = \dfrac{2x}{x+1}$

Reciprocal: $g(x) = \dfrac{x+1}{2x}$

$$\frac{2x}{x+1} = \frac{x+1}{2x}$$
$$4x^2 = x^2 + 2x + 1$$
$$3x^2 - 2x - 1 = 0$$
$$(3x+1)(x-1) = 0$$
$$x = -\frac{1}{3} \text{ or } x = 1$$
$$f(-\frac{1}{3}) = -1 \quad f(1) = 1$$

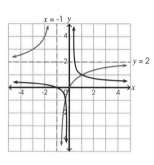

The points of intersection are $(-\frac{1}{3}, -1)$ and $(1,1)$.

4 Trigonometric Functions

1. B 2. C 3. B
4. D 5. D 6. C
7. C 8. D 9. B

10a. $\dfrac{\pi}{3}$

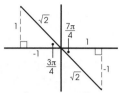

$\tan\theta$: $\tan\dfrac{\pi}{3} = \dfrac{\sqrt{3}}{1}$
$= \sqrt{3}$

$\csc\theta$: $\csc\dfrac{\pi}{3} = \dfrac{2}{\sqrt{3}}$

b. 135°

$\sin\theta$: $\sin 135° = \dfrac{\frac{\sqrt{2}}{2}}{1}$
$= \dfrac{\sqrt{2}}{2}$

$\cot\theta$: $\cot 135° = \dfrac{-\frac{\sqrt{2}}{2}}{\frac{\sqrt{2}}{2}}$
$= -1$

c. $\dfrac{17\pi}{3}$

$\sec\theta$: $\sec\dfrac{17\pi}{3} = \dfrac{1}{\frac{1}{2}}$
$= 2$

$\cos\theta$: $\cos\dfrac{17\pi}{3} = \dfrac{\frac{1}{2}}{1}$
$= \dfrac{1}{2}$

11a.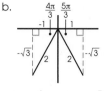

$\theta = \dfrac{3\pi}{4}$ and $\theta = \dfrac{7\pi}{4}$

b.

$\theta = \dfrac{4\pi}{3}$ and $\theta = \dfrac{5\pi}{3}$

c.

$\theta = \dfrac{3\pi}{4}$ and $\theta = \dfrac{5\pi}{4}$

12a.

(-2,3) is in Quadrant 2.
$\tan^{-1}(-\dfrac{3}{2}) \doteq -0.98$
$\theta \doteq \pi - 0.98$
$\theta \doteq 2.16$

b.

(7,-6) is in Quadrant 4.
$\tan^{-1}(-\dfrac{6}{7}) \doteq -0.71$
$\theta \doteq 2\pi - 0.71$
$\theta \doteq 5.57$

c.

(-4,-8) is in Quadrant 3.
$\tan^{-1}(\dfrac{-8}{-4}) = \tan^{-1}(2) \doteq 1.11$
$\theta \doteq \pi + 1.11$
$\theta \doteq 4.25$

13. Amplitude: 3   Vertical translation: -1
Maximum: $3 \times 1 - 1 = 2$
Minimum: $3 \times (-1) - 1 = -4$
The maximum value is 2 and the minimum value is -4.

14a. The period of
$y = \sin x$ is 2π.
$$\frac{2\pi}{\frac{\pi}{2}} = 4$$
The period is 4.

b. The period of
$y = \tan x$ is π.
$$\frac{\pi}{\frac{\pi}{6}} = 6$$
The period is 6.

15a. $\dfrac{10 - (-2)}{2} = 6$
The amplitude is 6.

b. $10 - 6 = 4$
The vertical translation is 4 units up.

16a. 2   b. $-\dfrac{\pi}{3}$ c. 2π d. -1

17a. $y = 2\sin(2(x - \dfrac{\pi}{2})) + 3$

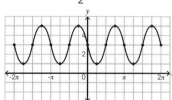

b. $y = -\dfrac{1}{2}\cos(\dfrac{1}{2}(x + \pi))$

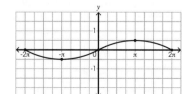

ISBN: 978-1-77149-223-2

18. $r^2 + r^2 = 18^2$
$2r^2 = 324$
$r^2 = 162$
$r \doteq 12.73$

$\theta = \dfrac{a}{r}$

$\dfrac{\pi}{2} = \dfrac{a}{12.73}$

$a \doteq 12.73 \times \dfrac{\pi}{2}$

$a \doteq 19.99$

The length of the arc is 19.99 cm.

19. $a = 28 \text{ km/h} \times \dfrac{1 \text{ h}}{3600 \text{ s}} \times 45 \text{ s} = 0.35 \text{ km}$

$\theta = \dfrac{a}{r} = \dfrac{0.35}{0.5} = 0.7$

The angle in radians is 0.7.

20. Amplitude: $\dfrac{2.25 - 0.85}{2} = 0.7$

Period: $6.2 \times 2 = 12.4$

$\dfrac{2\pi}{k} = 12.4$

$k = \dfrac{5\pi}{31}$

Vertical translation: $\dfrac{2.25 + 0.85}{2} = 1.55$

Horizontal translation: $6.2 \div 2 = 3.1$

$\therefore y = 0.7 \sin (\dfrac{5\pi}{31}(x - 3.1)) + 1.55$

21a. Amplitude: $\dfrac{15\,000 - 500}{2} = 7250$

Period: $6 \times 2 = 12$

$\dfrac{2\pi}{k} = 12$

$k = \dfrac{\pi}{6}$

Vertical translation: $\dfrac{15\,000 + 500}{2} = 7750$

Horizontal translation: 0

$\therefore P(n) = 7250 \cos (\dfrac{\pi}{6}x) + 7750$

$P(7) = 7250 \cos (\dfrac{\pi}{6} \times 7) + 7750$

$= 7250(-\dfrac{\sqrt{3}}{2}) + 7750$

$\doteq 1471$

The population at the end of July is about 1471.

b. $11\,375 = 7250 \cos (\dfrac{\pi}{6}x) + 7750$

$3625 = 7250 \cos (\dfrac{\pi}{6}x)$

$\dfrac{1}{2} = \cos (\dfrac{\pi}{6}x)$

$\dfrac{\pi}{6}x = \dfrac{\pi}{3}$ or $\dfrac{\pi}{6}x = \dfrac{5\pi}{3}$

$x = 2 \qquad\qquad x = 10$

The population will be around 11 375 at the end of February and October.

22. Similarities:
- They both have an amplitude of 1 and a period of 2π.

Differences:
- $y = \sin x$ has a y-intercept of $(0,0)$ and $y = \cos x$ has a y-intercept of $(0,1)$.
- $y = \sin x$ has x-intercepts at $n\pi$, where $n \in \mathbb{I}$, and $y = \cos x$ has x-intercepts at $\dfrac{(2n + 1)\pi}{2}$, where $n \in \mathbb{I}$.
- They are horizontal translations of each other.

23a. - vertical asymptotes in the reciprocals at the points where their primary trigonometric functions equal 0
- same periods as their primary trigonometric functions
- domains are $\{x \in \mathbb{R}\}$ except where the asymptotes exist
- ranges are $\{y \in \mathbb{R} \mid |y| \geq 1\}$ for cosecant and secant functions, and $\{y \in \mathbb{R}\}$ for cotangent functions

b. • $y = \csc \theta$:
Vertical asymptotes: $\theta = n\pi$, where $n \in \mathbb{I}$
Period: 2π
Domain: $\{\theta \in \mathbb{R} \mid \theta \neq n\pi$, where $n \in \mathbb{I}\}$
Range: $\{y \in \mathbb{R} \mid |y| \geq 1\}$

• $y = \sec \theta$:
Vertical asymptotes: $\theta = \dfrac{(2n + 1)\pi}{2}$, where $n \in \mathbb{I}$
Period: 2π
Domain: $\{\theta \in \mathbb{R} \mid \theta \neq \dfrac{(2n + 1)\pi}{2}$, where $n \in \mathbb{I}\}$
Range: $\{y \in \mathbb{R} \mid |y| \geq 1\}$

• $y = \cot \theta$:
Vertical asymptotes: $\theta = n\pi$, where $n \in \mathbb{I}$
Period: π
Domain: $\{\theta \in \mathbb{R} \mid \theta \neq n\pi$, where $n \in \mathbb{I}\}$
Range: $\{y \in \mathbb{R}\}$

24. When it is more convenient to express angles without units, radians would be used over degrees. For example, to apply the formula $\theta = \dfrac{a}{r}$, it is preferable to have the angle expressed in radians. Using radians also makes it possible to get exact answers without rounding when working with trigonometric functions.

25. (Suggested answers)

a. Amplitude: $\dfrac{4 - 0}{2} = 2$

Period: $\dfrac{11\pi}{4} - (-\dfrac{5\pi}{4}) = 4\pi$

$\dfrac{2\pi}{k} = 4\pi$

$k = \dfrac{1}{2}$

Vertical translation: $\dfrac{4 + 0}{2} = 2$

Horizontal translation: $-\dfrac{9\pi}{4}$

$\therefore y = 2 \sin (\dfrac{1}{2}(x + \dfrac{9\pi}{4})) + 2$

b. Horizontal translation: $-\dfrac{5\pi}{4}$

$\therefore y = 2 \cos (\dfrac{1}{2}(x + \dfrac{5\pi}{4})) + 2$

26. $\dfrac{2\pi}{k} = \pi$

$k = 2$

$y = 3 \sin (2(x - d)) + 1$

$1 = 3 \sin (2(\dfrac{\pi}{3} - d)) + 1$

$0 = 3 \sin (2(\dfrac{\pi}{3} - d))$

$0 = \sin (2(\dfrac{\pi}{3} - d))$

$2(\dfrac{\pi}{3} - d) = 0$ or $2(\dfrac{\pi}{3} - d) = \pi$

$d = \dfrac{\pi}{3} \qquad\qquad d = -\dfrac{\pi}{6}$

The horizontal translation is $\dfrac{\pi}{3}$ or $-\dfrac{\pi}{6}$. In general, it is $\dfrac{\pi}{3} + n\pi$ or $-\dfrac{\pi}{6} + n\pi$, where $n \in \mathbb{I}$.

27. $(\frac{\pi}{6},0)$:

$0 = a \cos(\frac{\pi}{6} + \frac{\pi}{6}) + c$

$0 = a \cos(\frac{\pi}{3}) + c$

$0 = \frac{a}{2} + c$

$a = -2c$

$-3 = -(-2c) + c$

$-3 = 3c$

$c = -1$

$a = 2$

a is 2 and c is -1.

$(\frac{5\pi}{6},-3)$:

$-3 = a \cos(\frac{5\pi}{6} + \frac{\pi}{6}) + c$

$-3 = a \cos \pi + c$

$-3 = -a + c$

5 Trigonometric Equations

1. B
2. B
3. B
4. D
5. C
6. D
7. A
8. D

9a. $= \sin \frac{\pi}{2} \cos \theta - \cos \frac{\pi}{2} \sin \theta$

$= (1) \cos \theta - (0) \sin \theta$

$= \cos \theta$

b. $= \cos(5\theta + 4\theta)$

$= \cos 9\theta$

c. $= \sin 2(\frac{\pi}{6})$

$= \sin \frac{\pi}{3}$

d. $= \cos 2(2\theta)$

$= \cos 4\theta$

10a. $= \dfrac{(\frac{\sqrt{3}}{2})(\frac{1}{\sqrt{3}})}{\sqrt{2}}$

$= \frac{1}{2} \times \frac{1}{\sqrt{2}}$

$= \frac{\sqrt{2}}{4}$

b. $= (2)(\sqrt{3}) - (-1)$

$= 2\sqrt{3} + 1$

c. $= \sin \frac{5\pi}{4} \cos \frac{2\pi}{3} - \cos \frac{5\pi}{4} \sin \frac{2\pi}{3}$

$= (-\frac{\sqrt{2}}{2})(-\frac{1}{2}) - (-\frac{\sqrt{2}}{2})(\frac{\sqrt{3}}{2})$

$= \frac{\sqrt{2}}{4} + \frac{\sqrt{6}}{4}$

$= \frac{\sqrt{2} + \sqrt{6}}{4}$

d. $= \tan(\frac{7\pi}{8} - \frac{5\pi}{8})$

$= \tan \frac{\pi}{4}$

$= 1$

e. $= (\sec(\frac{11\pi}{6}))^2 - (\csc(\frac{7\pi}{4}))^2$

$= (\frac{2}{\sqrt{3}})^2 - (-\sqrt{2})^2$

$= \frac{4}{3} - 2$

$= -\frac{2}{3}$

f. $= \cos(\frac{2\pi}{3} - \frac{\pi}{4}) + \cos(\frac{\pi}{3} - \frac{\pi}{4})$

$= \cos \frac{2\pi}{3} \cos \frac{\pi}{4} + \sin \frac{2\pi}{3} \sin \frac{\pi}{4} + \cos \frac{\pi}{3} \cos \frac{\pi}{4} + \sin \frac{\pi}{3} \sin \frac{\pi}{4}$

$= (-\frac{1}{2})(\frac{\sqrt{2}}{2}) + (\frac{\sqrt{3}}{2})(\frac{\sqrt{2}}{2}) + (\frac{1}{2})(\frac{\sqrt{2}}{2}) + (\frac{\sqrt{3}}{2})(\frac{\sqrt{2}}{2})$

$= -\frac{\sqrt{2}}{4} + \frac{\sqrt{6}}{4} + \frac{\sqrt{2}}{4} + \frac{\sqrt{6}}{4}$

$= \frac{\sqrt{6}}{2}$

11.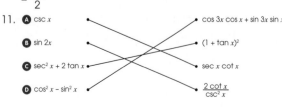

A: $\sec x \cot x$

$= \frac{1}{\cos x} \times \frac{\cos x}{\sin x}$

$= \frac{1}{\sin x}$

$= \csc x$

B: $\frac{2 \cot x}{\csc^2 x}$

$= \frac{2 \sin^2 x}{\tan x}$

$= \frac{2 \sin^2 x}{\frac{\sin x}{\cos x}}$

$= 2 \sin x \cos x$

$= \sin 2x$

C: $(1 + \tan x)^2$

$= 1 + 2 \tan x + \tan^2 x$

$= 1 + \tan^2 x + 2 \tan x$

$= \sec^2 x + 2 \tan x$

D: $\cos 3x \cos x + \sin 3x \sin x$

$= \cos(3x - x)$

$= \cos 2x$

$= \cos^2 x - \sin^2 x$

12a. $\cos \frac{\pi}{3} = \frac{1}{2}$ or $\cos \frac{5\pi}{3} = \frac{1}{2}$
(out of range)

$\therefore \theta = \frac{\pi}{3}$

b. $\sin \theta = \pm \frac{1}{2}$

$\sin \frac{\pi}{6} = \frac{1}{2}$ or $\sin \frac{5\pi}{6} = \frac{1}{2}$ or $\sin \frac{7\pi}{6} = -\frac{1}{2}$ or $\sin \frac{11\pi}{6} = -\frac{1}{2}$
(out of range)

$\therefore \theta = \frac{7\pi}{6}$ or $\frac{11\pi}{6}$

c. $\sqrt{3} \sec \theta = -2$

$\sec \theta = -\frac{2}{\sqrt{3}}$

$\sec \frac{5\pi}{6} = -\frac{2}{\sqrt{3}}$ or $\sec \frac{7\pi}{6} = -\frac{2}{\sqrt{3}}$
(out of range)

$\therefore \theta = \frac{7\pi}{6}$

d. $\csc^2 \theta = 2$

$\csc \theta = \pm \sqrt{2}$

$\csc \frac{\pi}{4} = \sqrt{2}$ or $\csc \frac{3\pi}{4} = \sqrt{2}$ or

$\csc \frac{5\pi}{4} = -\sqrt{2}$ or $\csc \frac{7\pi}{4} = -\sqrt{2}$
(out of range)

$\therefore \theta = \frac{\pi}{4}$ or $\frac{3\pi}{4}$

13. $\tan \theta = \frac{0.8}{L}$

$L = \frac{0.8}{\tan \theta}$

$\tan 2\theta = \frac{1 + 0.8}{L}$

$\frac{2 \tan \theta}{1 - \tan^2 \theta} = \frac{1.8}{L}$

$2 \tan \theta \times L = 1.8 - 1.8 \tan^2 \theta$

$2 \tan \theta (\frac{0.8}{\tan \theta}) = 1.8 - 1.8 \tan^2 \theta$

$1.6 = 1.8 - 1.8 \tan^2 \theta$

$\tan^2 \theta = \frac{1}{9}$

$\tan \theta = \pm \frac{1}{3}$

$L = \frac{0.8}{\frac{1}{3}}$ (must be positive)

$L = 2.4$

The distance is 2.4 m.

14. $20 = -24 \cos(\frac{2\pi}{52}w) + 8$

$-\frac{1}{2} = \cos(\frac{2\pi}{52}w)$

$\frac{2\pi}{52}w = \frac{2\pi}{3}$ or $\frac{2\pi}{52}w = \frac{4\pi}{3}$

$w = 17\frac{1}{3}$ $w = 34\frac{2}{3}$

The average temperature is 20°C at $17\frac{1}{3}$ weeks and $34\frac{2}{3}$ weeks.

15.
$$8 = -6 \sin\left(\frac{\pi}{10}(t+5)\right) + 6$$

$$-\frac{1}{3} = \sin\left(\frac{\pi}{10}(t+5)\right)$$

$$\sin^{-1}\left(-\frac{1}{3}\right) = \frac{\pi}{10}(t+5)$$

$$t = \frac{10 \sin^{-1}\left(-\frac{1}{3}\right)}{\pi} - 5$$

$$\sin^{-1}\left(-\frac{1}{3}\right) \doteq -0.34$$
$$\doteq 2\pi - 0.34 \text{ or } \doteq \pi + 0.34$$
$$\doteq 5.94 \qquad \doteq 3.48$$

$$t \doteq 6.08 \text{ or } t \doteq 13.92 \qquad \text{Period: } \frac{2\pi}{\frac{\pi}{10}} = 20$$

$$t \doteq 6.08 + 20 = 26.08$$
$$t \doteq 13.92 + 20 = 33.92 \text{ (over 30 minutes)}$$

The streetcar will be 8 km away from the station at 6.08 min, 13.92 min, and 26.08 min.

16.
$$1 = 4\cos^2\left(\frac{\pi}{12}t\right)$$

$$\frac{1}{4} = \cos^2\left(\frac{\pi}{12}t\right)$$

$$\cos\left(\frac{\pi}{12}t\right) = \pm\frac{1}{2}$$

$$\cos\frac{\pi}{3} = \frac{1}{2} \rightarrow \frac{\pi}{12}t = \frac{\pi}{3}, \ t = 4 \text{ (4 a.m.)}$$

$$\cos\frac{2\pi}{3} = -\frac{1}{2} \rightarrow \frac{\pi}{12}t = \frac{2\pi}{3}, \ t = 8 \text{ (8 a.m.)}$$

$$\cos\frac{4\pi}{3} = -\frac{1}{2} \rightarrow \frac{\pi}{12}t = \frac{4\pi}{3}, \ t = 16 \text{ (4 p.m.)}$$

$$\cos\frac{5\pi}{3} = \frac{1}{2} \rightarrow \frac{\pi}{12}t = \frac{5\pi}{3}, \ t = 20 \text{ (8 p.m.)}$$

The water level will be 1 m at 4 a.m., 8 a.m., 4 p.m., and 8 p.m.

17. The compound angle formulas are identical to the double angle formulas when the compound angles are the same.
e.g. $\sin(a+b) = \sin a \cos b + \cos a \sin b$ ← compound angle formula
if $a = b$, $\sin(a+a) = \sin a \cos a + \cos a \sin a$
$$\sin 2a = \sin a \cos a + \sin a \cos a$$
$$\sin 2a = 2\sin a \cos a \leftarrow \text{double angle formula}$$

18. In the unit circle, the radius is 1 while the triangle formed has a base of x and a height of y.
Express as trigonometric functions:
$$\sin\theta = \frac{y}{1} \text{ and } \cos\theta = \frac{x}{1}$$
Substitute the function into the Pythagorean theorem:
$$a^2 + b^2 = c^2$$
$$(\sin\theta)^2 + (\cos\theta)^2 = 1^2$$
$$\sin^2\theta + \cos^2\theta = 1$$

19. If $(\sin\theta - 2)(\cos\theta + 2) = 0$, then $\sin\theta - 2 = 0$ or $\cos\theta + 2 = 0$.
So we need solutions when $\sin\theta = 2$ or $\cos\theta = -2$. However, the range of both sine and cosine functions is $\{y \in \mathbb{R} \mid -1 \le y \le 1\}$, so there are no solutions.

20. Jason's reasoning is correct. However, $\tan^{-1}(-1) = -45°$ or $\tan^{-1}(-1) = -\frac{\pi}{4}$. The angles must be expressed in the same units, either in degrees or in radians.
So x is $180° - 45° = 135°$ or $360° - 45° = 315°$,
or x is $\pi - \frac{\pi}{4} = \frac{3\pi}{4}$ or $2\pi - \frac{\pi}{4} = \frac{7\pi}{4}$.

21a. $\sin^4 x - \cos^4 x$
$$= (\sin^2 x)^2 - (\cos^2 x)^2$$
$$= (\sin^2 x + \cos^2 x)(\sin^2 x - \cos^2 x)$$
$$= 1(\sin^2 x - (1 - \sin^2 x))$$
$$= 2\sin^2 x - 1$$

b. $\cos\left(\frac{3\pi}{4} - x\right) - \sin\left(\frac{3\pi}{4} + x\right)$
$$= \cos\frac{3\pi}{4}\cos x + \sin\frac{3\pi}{4}\sin x - \left(\sin\frac{3\pi}{4}\cos x + \cos\frac{3\pi}{4}\sin x\right)$$
$$= -\frac{\sqrt{2}}{2}\cos x + \frac{\sqrt{2}}{2}\sin x - \frac{\sqrt{2}}{2}\cos x - \left(-\frac{\sqrt{2}}{2}\right)\sin x$$
$$= -\sqrt{2}\cos x + \sqrt{2}\sin x$$
$$= -\sqrt{2}(\cos x - \sin x)$$

c. $\dfrac{\sin 2x}{1 - \cos 2x}$
$$= \frac{2\sin x \cos x}{1 - (1 - 2\sin^2 x)}$$
$$= \frac{2\sin x \cos x}{2\sin^2 x}$$
$$= \frac{\cos x}{\sin x}$$
$$= \cot x$$

d. $\dfrac{1}{\sin A(\tan A + \cot A)}$
$$= \frac{1}{\sin A\left(\frac{\sin A}{\cos A} + \frac{\cos A}{\sin A}\right)}$$
$$= \frac{1}{\sin A\left(\frac{\sin^2 A + \cos^2 A}{\sin A \cos A}\right)}$$
$$= \frac{1}{\sin A\left(\frac{1}{\sin A \cos A}\right)}$$
$$= \frac{1}{\frac{1}{\cos A}}$$
$$= \cos A$$

22a. $2\sin x \cos x = \cos x$
$$2\sin x \cos x - \cos x = 0$$
$$\cos x(2\sin x - 1) = 0$$
$\cos x = 0 \qquad$ or $\quad 2\sin x - 1 = 0$
$x = \frac{\pi}{2} \text{ or } \frac{3\pi}{2} \qquad 2\sin x = 1$
$$\sin x = \frac{1}{2}$$
$$\sin\frac{\pi}{6} = \frac{1}{2} \text{ or } \sin\frac{5\pi}{6} = \frac{1}{2}$$
$$x = \frac{\pi}{6} \text{ or } \frac{5\pi}{6}$$
$$\therefore x = \frac{\pi}{6}, \frac{\pi}{2}, \frac{5\pi}{6}, \text{ or } \frac{3\pi}{2}$$

b. $2\cos x - \sqrt{3} = 0$ or $\cot x = 0$
$$\cos x = \frac{\sqrt{3}}{2}$$
$$\cos\frac{\pi}{6} = \frac{\sqrt{3}}{2} \text{ and } \cos\frac{11\pi}{6} = \frac{\sqrt{3}}{2}$$
$$\cot\frac{\pi}{2} = 0 \text{ and } \cot\frac{3\pi}{2} = 0$$
$$\therefore x = \frac{\pi}{6} \text{ or } \frac{\pi}{2} \text{ or } \frac{3\pi}{2} \text{ or } \frac{11\pi}{6}$$

c. $\tan^2 x + 2\tan x - 3 = 0$
$(\tan x + 3)(\tan x - 1) = 0$
$\tan x + 3 = 0 \qquad$ or $\qquad \tan x - 1 = 0$
$\quad \tan x = -3 \qquad\qquad\qquad \tan x = 1$
$\tan^{-1}(-3) \doteq -1.25 \qquad \tan\frac{\pi}{4} = 1 \text{ or } \tan\frac{5\pi}{4} = 1$
$x \doteq \pi - 1.25 \text{ or } x \doteq 2\pi - 1.25 \qquad x = \frac{\pi}{4} \text{ or } x = \frac{5\pi}{4}$
$\quad \doteq 1.89 \qquad\quad \doteq 5.03$
$\therefore x = \frac{\pi}{4} \text{ or } \frac{5\pi}{4} \text{ or } 1.89 \text{ or } 5.03$

d. $4\sin^2 x - 5\sin x - 6 = 0$
$(4\sin x + 3)(\sin x - 2) = 0$
$4\sin x + 3 = 0 \qquad$ or $\qquad \sin x - 2 = 0$
$\sin x = -\frac{3}{4} \qquad\qquad\qquad \sin x = 2$
$\sin^{-1}\left(-\frac{3}{4}\right) \doteq -0.85 \qquad \text{no solutions}$
$x \doteq \pi + 0.85 \text{ or } x \doteq 2\pi - 0.85$
$\quad \doteq 3.99 \qquad\quad \doteq 5.43$
$\therefore x \doteq 3.99 \text{ or } 5.43$

6 Exponential and Logarithmic Functions

1. C	2. A	3. D
4. C	5. D	6. C
7. B	8. D	9. B

10a. $2^x = 64$
$2^x = 2^6$
$x = 6$

b. $25^{\log_{25}x} = 25^{0.5}$
$x = \sqrt{25}$
$x = 5$

c. $3\log_x 9 = 2$
$\log_x 9^3 = 2$
$x^2 = 9^3$
$x = \sqrt{729}$
$x = 27$

d. $5^{x+8} = 5^{-2}$
$x + 8 = -2$
$x = -10$

e. $(2^3)^{2x-1} = (2^4)^{x-1}$
$2^{6x-3} = 2^{4x-4}$
$6x - 3 = 4x - 4$
$x = -\dfrac{1}{2}$

f. $2^x = \dfrac{1}{\sqrt{8}}$
$2^x = 2^{-\frac{3}{2}}$
$x = -\dfrac{3}{2}$

g. $3^{3x+1} = \dfrac{1}{9}$
$3^{3x+1} = 3^{-2}$
$3x + 1 = -2$
$x = -1$

h. $3^{\log_3(5x-1)} = 3^2$
$5x - 1 = 9$
$x = 2$

i. $\log_x\left(\dfrac{5}{2}\right) = 1$
$x = \dfrac{5}{2}$

11.

	Exponential Form	Logarithmic Form
A	$x = 5^3$	$\log_5 x = 3$
B	$3x = \sqrt{6}$	$\log_6 3x = \dfrac{1}{2}$
C	$x^{-2} = \dfrac{1}{9}$	$\log_x\left(\dfrac{1}{9}\right) = -2$
D	$\dfrac{2}{x} = 2^{\frac{3}{2}}$	$\log_2\left(\dfrac{2}{x}\right) = \dfrac{3}{2}$
E	$2x^{-3} = \dfrac{27}{4}$	$\log_x\dfrac{27}{8} = -3$
F	$2^{\frac{x}{2}} = 8$	$\dfrac{1}{2}\log_2 8 = \dfrac{x}{4}$

A: $x = 5^3$
$x = 125$

B: $3x = \sqrt{6}$
$x = \dfrac{\sqrt{6}}{3}$

C: $x^{-2} = \dfrac{1}{9}$
$\dfrac{1}{x^2} = \dfrac{1}{9}$
$x^2 = 9$
$x = 3$

D: $\dfrac{2}{x} = 2^{\frac{3}{2}}$
$x = 2^{-\frac{1}{2}}$
$x = \dfrac{1}{\sqrt{2}}$

E: $\log_x\dfrac{27}{8} = -3$
$x^{-3} = \dfrac{27}{8}$
$\dfrac{1}{x^3} = \dfrac{27}{8}$
$x^3 = \dfrac{8}{27}$
$x = \dfrac{2}{3}$

F: $2^{\frac{x}{2}} = 8$
$2^{\frac{x}{2}} = 2^3$
$x = 6$

12a. $= \log 2^2 + \log 25$
$= \log (2^2 \times 25)$
$= \log 100$
$= 2$

b. $= \log_2 5^{\frac{1}{2}} - \log_2 10$
$= \log_2\left(\dfrac{\sqrt{5}}{10}\right)$

c. $= \log_3\left(\dfrac{7 \times 20}{9}\right)$
$= \log_3\left(\dfrac{140}{9}\right)$

d. $= \log_5 5 - \log_5(10 \times 3^2)$
$= \log_5\left(\dfrac{5}{90}\right)$
$= \log_5\left(\dfrac{1}{18}\right)$

13a. Domain: $\{x \in \mathbb{R} \mid x > -2\}$
Range: $\{y \in \mathbb{R}\}$
Asymptote: $x = -2$

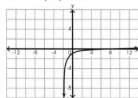

b. Domain: $\{x \in \mathbb{R} \mid x > 1\}$
Range: $\{y \in \mathbb{R}\}$
Asymptote: $x = 1$

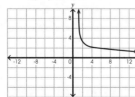

14. $\dfrac{10^{8.2}}{10^{7.1}} = 10^{8.2-7.1} = 10^{1.1} \doteq 12.59$
The initial earthquake was 12.59 times more intense than the aftershock.

15. $\text{pH} = -\log [H^+]$
$= -\log 0.000\,023$
$\doteq 4.64$
The pH of the water is 4.64.

16. $51\,200 = 400(2^{\frac{60x}{30}})$
$128 = 2^{2x}$
$2^7 = 2^{2x}$
$2x = 7$
$x = 3.5$
It will take 3.5 hours.

17. $2000 = 500(1 + i)^{18}$
$4 = (1 + i)^{18}$
$\log 4 = 18 \log (1 + i)$
$\dfrac{\log 4}{18} = \log (1 + i)$
$10^{\frac{\log 4}{18}} = 1 + i$
$i = 10^{\frac{\log 4}{18}} - 1$
$i \doteq 0.08$
The annual interest rate is 8%.

18. $11\,579 = 21\,000(1 - r)^3$
$0.551 = (1 - r)^3$
$\log 0.551 = 3 \log (1 - r)$
$(\log 0.551) \div 3 = \log (1 - r)$
$10^{(\log 0.551) \div 3} = 1 - r$
$r = 1 - 10^{(\log 0.551) \div 3}$
$r \doteq 0.18$
The annual depreciation rate is 18%.

19a. $375 = 3000\left(\dfrac{1}{2}\right)^{\frac{x}{5730}}$
$\dfrac{1}{8} = \left(\dfrac{1}{2}\right)^{\frac{x}{5730}}$
$\left(\dfrac{1}{2}\right)^3 = \left(\dfrac{1}{2}\right)^{\frac{x}{5730}}$
$\dfrac{x}{5730} = 3$
$x = 17\,190$
It takes 17 190 years.

b. $280 = A_o\left(\dfrac{1}{2}\right)^{\frac{8680}{5730}}$
$A_o = 280 \div \left(\dfrac{1}{2}\right)^{\frac{8680}{5730}}$
$A_o \doteq 800$
There was 800 mg of carbon-14 initially.

20. $1750 = 2100\left(\dfrac{1}{2}\right)^{\frac{1}{h}}$
$\dfrac{5}{6} = \left(\dfrac{1}{2}\right)^{\frac{1}{h}}$
$\dfrac{1}{h} = \log_{\frac{1}{2}}\dfrac{5}{6}$
$h = \dfrac{1}{\log_{\frac{1}{2}}\dfrac{5}{6}}$
$h \doteq 3.8$
The half-life of the isotope is 3.8 days.

21. $90 \times 20\% = 90(10^{-0.4d})$
$0.2 = 10^{-0.4d}$
$\log 0.2 = -0.4d$
$d = \log 0.2 \div (-0.4)$
$d \doteq 1.75$
It will be 1.75 km away.

22. It is an exponential function.
$f(x) = ab^x$
$f(0) = ab^0 = 5000$
$a = 5000$
$f(1) = 5000b^1 = 5200$
$b = 1.04$
$\therefore f(x) = 5000(1.04)^x$
$5000 \times 2 = 5000(1.04)^x$
$2 = 1.04^x$
$x = \log_{1.04} 2$
$x \doteq 17.67$
It will take 17.67 years.

ISBN: 978-1-77149-223-2

23. - reflect in the x-axis
    - vertical stretch by a factor of 2
    - horizontal compression by a factor of $\frac{1}{3}$
    - translate 2 units to the right
    - translate 5 units down

24. Consider its exponential form.
$$\log_a b = y$$
$$a^y = b$$
So b represents the power of a positive number, a, which must be positive.

25. $\log x^2$ is the logarithm of x squared while $(\log x)^2$ is the square of the logarithm of x.
    If $x = 10$,
    $\log 10^2 = \log 100 = 2$
    $(\log 10)^2 = 1^2 = 1$
    So $\log x^2 \neq (\log x)^2$.

26. Algebraically, swap the x and y in the equation and then rearrange the equation to isolate y using exponentials.
    Graphically, plot the logarithmic function and then reflect it in the line $y = x$.

27a. $= \log_{\frac{1}{3}} 27^{\frac{1}{2}}$

$= \frac{1}{2}\log_{\frac{1}{3}} 3^3$

$= \frac{3}{2}\log_{\frac{1}{3}}(\frac{1}{3})^{-1}$

$= -\frac{3}{2}\log_{\frac{1}{3}}(\frac{1}{3})$

$= -\frac{3}{2}$

b. $= \log_2(\frac{\sqrt{96}}{\sqrt{3}})$

$= \log_2\sqrt{32}$

$= \log_2 32^{\frac{1}{2}}$

$= \frac{1}{2}\log_2 2^5$

$= \frac{5}{2}\log_2 2$

$= \frac{5}{2}$

28a. $5^x(5^2 + 1) = 650$

$5^x(26) = 650$

$5^x = 25$

$x = 2$

b. $\frac{6}{5} = \frac{3^x}{2^x}$

$\frac{6}{5} = (\frac{3}{2})^x$

$x = \log_{\frac{3}{2}}\frac{6}{5}$

$x \doteq 0.45$

c. $3^{x^2}(9^x) = 27$
$3^{x^2}(3^{2x}) = 3^3$
$3^{x^2 + 2x} = 3^3$
$x^2 + 2x = 3$
$x^2 + 2x - 3 = 0$
$(x + 3)(x - 1) = 0$
$x = -3$ or $x = 1$

d. $\log_4 4^{2x} = \log_4 3^{x-1}$
$2x = (x - 1)\log_4 3$
$2x - (\log_4 3)x = -\log_4 3$
$x(2 - \log_4 3) = -\log_4 3$
$x = \frac{-\log_4 3}{(2 - \log_4 3)}$
$x \doteq -0.66$

e. $2^x - 1 = \pm 4$
$2^x = 1 \pm 4$
$2^x = 5$ or $2^x = -3$
$x = \log_2 5$ (not possible)
$x \doteq 2.32$

f. Let $z = 2^x$
$z^2 + 4z - 32 = 0$
$(z - 4)(z + 8) = 0$
$z = 4$ or $z = -8$
$2^x = 4$ or $2^x = -8$
$x = 2$ (not possible)

29.

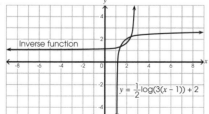

$y = -\frac{1}{2}\log(3(x - 1)) + 2$

Inverse function

a. Domain: $\{x \in \mathbb{R} \mid x > 1\}$
   Range: $\{y \in \mathbb{R}\}$
   Asymptote: $x = 1$

b. Domain: $\{x \in \mathbb{R}\}$
   Range: $\{y \in \mathbb{R} \mid y > 1\}$
   Asymptote: $y = 1$

30. $\log_a x = y$
$x = a^y$
$\log x = \log a^y$
$\log x = y \log a$
$y = \frac{\log x}{\log a}$
$\therefore \log_a x = \frac{\log x}{\log a}$

31. $\log_4 a = \frac{\log a}{\log 4} = \frac{\log a}{\log 2^2} = \frac{\log a}{2 \log 2} = \frac{\frac{1}{2}\log a}{\log 2} = \frac{\log a^{\frac{1}{2}}}{\log 2}$
$= \frac{\log\sqrt{a}}{\log 2} = \log_2 \sqrt{a}$
$\therefore \log_4 a = \log_2 \sqrt{a}$

7 Rates of Change

1. C 2. B 3. D
4. B 5a. A b. C
6. D 7. D

8a. $\frac{f(2) - f(-1)}{2 - (-1)}$

$= \frac{3(2)^2 - 3(-1)^2}{3}$

$= \frac{12 - 3}{3}$

$= 3$

b. $\frac{f(3) - f(-2)}{3 - (-2)}$

$= \frac{(3)^3 - 2(3) + 1 - ((-2)^3 - 2(-2) + 1)}{5}$

$= \frac{22 - (-3)}{5}$

$= 5$

c. $\frac{f(8) - f(4)}{8 - 4}$

$= \frac{(\frac{1}{8} + 4) - (\frac{1}{4} + 4)}{4}$

$= -\frac{1}{32}$

d. $\frac{f(1) - f(-1)}{1 - (-1)}$

$= \frac{(2\sin 1 - 1) - (2\sin(-1) - 1)}{2}$

$\doteq \frac{0.683 - (-2.683)}{2}$

$= 1.683$

e. $\frac{f(4) - f(2)}{4 - 2}$

$= \frac{(2^4 - 3) - (2^2 - 3)}{2}$

$= 6$

f. $\frac{f(5) - f(0.5)}{5 - 0.5}$

$= \frac{-\log 2(5) - (-\log 2(0.5))}{4.5}$

$\doteq \frac{(-1) - (0)}{4.5}$

$= -\frac{2}{9}$

9a. (Suggested answer)

$f(0) = -\frac{1}{2}$

$f(\pi) = -\frac{1}{2}$

$\frac{f(\pi) - f(0)}{\pi - 0} = 0$

$\therefore 0 \leq x \leq \pi$

b. $f(\frac{\pi}{2}) = 0.5$

$f(\frac{3\pi}{2}) = -1.5$

$\frac{f(\frac{3\pi}{2}) - f(\frac{\pi}{2})}{\frac{3\pi}{2} - \frac{\pi}{2}} = -\frac{2}{\pi}$

$\therefore \frac{\pi}{2} \leq x \leq \frac{3\pi}{2}$

10. $m = \frac{f(-2 + h) - f(-2)}{h}$

$= \frac{(-2 + h)^4 + 2(-2 + h)^3 - 3(-2 + h)^2 - 4(-2 + h) - (-4)}{h}$

$= \frac{(h^4 - 6h^3 + 9h^2 - 4) - (-4)}{h}$

$= \frac{h^4 - 6h^3 + 9h^2}{h}$

$= h^3 - 6h^2 + 9h$

When $h = 0.01$, $m \doteq 0.09$.
When $h = -0.01$, $m \doteq -0.09$.
Instantaneous rate of change:
$\frac{0.09 + (-0.09)}{2} \doteq 0$

$f(-1.99) \doteq -3.999$
$f(-2) = -4$
$f(-2.01) \doteq -3.999$
$(-2, -4)$ is a local minimum.

11a. $f(2.01) = -3(2.01)^2 + 5(2.01) = -2.0703$
$f(2) = -3(2)^2 + 5(2) = -2$
$m = \dfrac{-2.0703 - (-2)}{0.01} = -7.03$

b. $f(-1.99) = 2(-1.99)^3 - 3(-1.99)^2 - 3(-1.99) + 2 \doteq -19.6715$
$f(-2) = 2(-2)^3 - 3(-2)^2 - 3(-2) + 2 = -20$
$m = \dfrac{-19.6715 - (-20)}{0.01} = 32.85$

c. $f(-0.99) = \dfrac{2(-0.99)}{(-0.99) - 1} \doteq 0.995$
$f(-1) = \dfrac{2(-1)}{(-1) - 1} = 1$
$m = \dfrac{0.995 - 1}{0.01} = -0.5$

d. $f(\frac{3\pi}{4} + 0.01) = \frac{1}{2} \cos (2 (\frac{3\pi}{4} + 0.01)) \doteq 0.01$
$f(\frac{3\pi}{4}) = \frac{1}{2} \cos (2 (\frac{3\pi}{4})) = 0$
$m = \dfrac{0.01 - 0}{0.01} = 1$

e. $f(6.01) = 25(1.8)^{-6.01} \doteq 0.7307$
$f(6) = 25(1.8)^{-6} \doteq 0.7350$
$m = \dfrac{0.7307 - 0.7350}{0.01} = -0.43$

f. $f(16.01) = 49 \log 16.01 - 14 \doteq 45.0152$
$f(16) = 49 \log 16 - 14 \doteq 45.0019$
$m = \dfrac{45.0152 - 45.0019}{0.01} = 1.33$

12a. $\dfrac{V(2) - V(0)}{2 - 0}$
$= \dfrac{1.4(5 - 2)^3 - 1.4(5 - 0)^3}{2}$
$= \dfrac{37.8 - 175}{2}$
$= -68.6$
The average rate of change is -68.6 L/min.

b. $V(4.01) = 1.4(5 - 4.01)^3 \doteq 1.3584$
$V(4) = 1.4(5 - 4)^3 = 1.4$
$m = \dfrac{1.3584 - 1.4}{0.01} = -4.16$
The instantaneous rate of change at 4 minutes is -4.16 L/min. Since the rate is negative, the function is decreasing.

13a. $R(x) = xp(x) = \dfrac{3x}{x^2 + x + 2}$

b. $m = \dfrac{R(0.71) - R(0.7)}{0.01}$
$\doteq \dfrac{0.6627 - 0.6583}{0.01}$
$= 0.44$
When 700 doughnuts are sold, the marginal revenue is $0.44 per doughnut.

14. $m = \dfrac{d(3.51) - d(3.5)}{0.01}$
$\doteq \dfrac{5.1571 - 5}{0.01}$
$= 15.71$
The instantaneous speed is 15.71 cm/s at 3.5 s.

15. $f(t) = 1400(1.12)^{2t}$
$2 \times 1400 = 1400(1.12)^{2t}$
$2 = (1.12)^{2t}$
$\log 2 = 2t \log 1.12$
$t = \dfrac{\log 2}{2 \log 1.12}$
$t \doteq 3.058$
$m = \dfrac{f(3.059) - f(3.058)}{0.001}$
$\doteq \dfrac{2800.5537 - 2799.919}{0.001}$
$= 634.7$
The instantaneous rate of change is $634.70/year.

16. 20 minutes:
$m = \dfrac{m(20) - m(0)}{20 - 0}$
$\doteq \dfrac{55.4775 - 99.9832}{20}$
$\doteq -2.23$

8 hours:
$m = \dfrac{m(480) - m(0)}{480 - 0}$
$\doteq \dfrac{34.7811 - 99.9832}{480}$
$\doteq -0.14$

The average rates of change are -2.23%/min after 20 minutes and -0.14%/min after 8 hours.

17. The slope of the secant line is an approximation of the instantaneous rate of change at (x_1, y_1) provided that the secant line also passes through (x_2, y_2) and that $(x_2 - x_1)$ is nearly 0.

18. The average rate of change is the change of the dependent variable over an interval of values of the independent variable, while the instantaneous rate of change is the change of the dependent variable at a specific value of the independent variable. When the interval of values is extremely small, the average rate of change becomes a good estimate of the instantaneous rate of change.

19. The least instantaneous rate of change occurs in a sinusoidal function halfway from a local maximum to a local minimum. The greatest instantaneous rate of change occurs in a sinusoidal function halfway from a local minimum to a local maximum.

20. The instantaneous rate of change as x approaches a horizontal asymptote is nearly 0. The instantaneous rate of change as x approaches a vertical asymptote is a very large positive value or a very large negative value.

21a. $m = \dfrac{f(2.01) - f(2)}{0.01}$
$= \dfrac{24.1903 - 24}{0.01}$
$\doteq 19$
$f(2) = 24$
$24 = 19(2) + b$
$b = -14$
$\therefore y = 19x - 14$

b. $m = \dfrac{f(-2.99) - f(-3)}{0.01}$
$\doteq \dfrac{0.6645 - 0.6667}{0.01}$
$\doteq -0.22$ or $-\dfrac{2}{9}$
$f(-3) = \dfrac{2}{3}$
$\dfrac{2}{3} = (-\dfrac{2}{9})(-3) + b$
$b = 0$
$\therefore y = -\dfrac{2}{9}x$

22a. $m = \dfrac{f(x + h) - f(x)}{h}$
$= \dfrac{(x + h)^3 - x^3}{h}$
$= \dfrac{x^3 + 3x^2h + 3xh^2 + h^3 - x^3}{h}$
$= \dfrac{3x^2h + 3xh^2 + h^3}{h}$
$= 3x^2 + 3xh + h^2$
As $h \to 0$, $m = 3x^2$

b. $m = \dfrac{g(x + h) - g(x)}{h}$
$= \dfrac{(-\frac{3}{x + h}) - (-\frac{3}{x})}{h}$
$= \dfrac{\frac{3h}{x(x + h)}}{h}$
$= \dfrac{3}{x(x + h)}$
As $h \to 0$, $m = \dfrac{3}{x^2}$

23a. $3x^2 = 27$
$x^2 = 9$
$x = \pm 3$

b. $\dfrac{3}{x^2} = 27$
$x^2 = \dfrac{3}{27}$
$x = \pm \sqrt{\dfrac{1}{9}}$
$x = \pm \dfrac{1}{3}$

8 Combining Functions

1a. C   b. B   2. B   3. B
4a. B   b. C   c. B   d. C
5a. $= 1.2^x + 2 \sin x$ b. $= (-2x^2 + 1)(1.2^x)$
$= -2x^2(1.2^x) + 1.2^x$

c. $= 2 \sin x - 1.2^x$ d. $= \dfrac{-2x^2 + 1}{1.2^x}$

B ; A

D ; C

6a. $= \dfrac{1}{x^2} + 2^x$ b. $= \dfrac{1}{(2^x)^2}$

$\{x \in \mathbb{R} \mid x \neq 0\}$ $= \dfrac{1}{2^{2x}}$

$\{x \in \mathbb{R}\}$

c. $= \dfrac{\sin x}{\log x}$

$\{x \in \mathbb{R} \mid x > 0,\ x \neq 1\}$

d. $= \log (\sin x)$

$\{x \in \mathbb{R} \mid 2n\pi < x < (2n+1)\pi,\ n \in \mathbb{I}\}$

e. $= (x-1)(\sqrt{2x+3})$ f. $= \sqrt{2(x-1) + 3}$

$\{x \in \mathbb{R} \mid x \geq -\dfrac{3}{2}\}$ $= \sqrt{2x+1}$

$\{x \in \mathbb{R} \mid x \geq -\dfrac{1}{2}\}$

7a.

x	LS	RS
-2	$-3\frac{8}{9}$	8
-1	$-3\frac{2}{3}$	1
0	-3	0
1	-1	-1
2	5	-8

$\therefore x = 1$

b.

x	LS	RS
π	0.497	-1
$\frac{5\pi}{4}$	0.594	-0.707
$\frac{3\pi}{2}$	0.673	0
$\frac{7\pi}{4}$	0.740	0.707
2π	0.798	1

x	LS	RS
5.45	0.736	0.673
5.50	0.74	0.709
5.55	0.744	0.743

$\therefore x \doteq 5.55$

c.

x	LS	RS
2	1.828	1
1	1.646	4
0	1.449	N/A
-1	1.236	4
-2	1	1
-3	0.732	0.444
-4	0.414	0.25
-5	0	0.16
-6	-1	0.111

x	LS	RS
1.515	1.741	1.743
1.51	1.740	1.754
1.50	1.739	1.778

x	LS	RS
-4.50	0.225	0.198
-4.55	0.204	0.193
-4.58	0.192	0.191

$\therefore x \doteq 1.515, -2, \text{ or } -4.58$

d.

x	LS	RS
4	2	105
3	1	0
2	0	-15
1	-1	0
0	-2	9
-1	-1	0
-2	0	-15
-3	1	0
-4	2	105

x	LS	RS
3.021	1.021	1.028
1.058	-0.942	-0.941
-1.058	-0.942	-0.941
-3.021	1.021	1.028

$\therefore x \doteq 3.021, 1.058, -1.058, \text{ or } -3.021$

8a. $P(x) = R(x) - C(x)$

$= 12x - 0.5x^2 - (2x + 4)$

$= -0.5x^2 + 10x - 4$

b. $P(15) = -0.5(15)^2 + 10(15) - 4 = 33.5$

The profit is \$33.50.

c. $P(10) = -0.5(10)^2 + 10(10) - 4 = 46$

$P(10.01) = 45.99995$

$m_1 = \dfrac{P(10.01) - P(10)}{10.01 - 10} = -0.005$

$P(9.99) = 45.99995$

$m_2 = \dfrac{P(10) - P(9.99)}{10 - 9.99} = 0.005$

$\dfrac{m_1 + m_2}{2} = 0$

(10,46) is a local maximum.

Yes, washing 10 cars will make the maximum profit.

9a. $P(t) = \dfrac{c}{1 + ab^t}$

$c = 100$

When $t = 0$, $P(t) = 27$.

When $t = 3$, $P(t) = 65$.

$27 = \dfrac{100}{1 + ab^0}$ $65 = \dfrac{100}{1 + 2.7b^3}$

$1 + a = \dfrac{100}{27}$ $1 + 2.7b^3 = \dfrac{100}{65}$

$a \doteq 2.70$ $b^3 \doteq 0.199$

$b \doteq 0.584$

$\therefore P(t) = \dfrac{100}{1 + 2.7(0.584)^t}$

b. $80 = \dfrac{100}{1 + 2.7(0.584)^t}$

$1 + 2.7(0.584^t) = 1.25$

$0.584^t = 0.0926$

$t = \dfrac{\log 0.0926}{\log 0.584}$

$t \doteq 4.42$

The students need to study approximately 4.42 hours to get an average of 80 marks.

c. $\dfrac{P(5) - P(0)}{5 - 0}$

$= \dfrac{84.5 - 27}{5}$

$= 11.5$

The average rate of change is 11.5 marks/hour.

10a. The function is an exponential function in the form of $f(t) = c - ab^t$, where c is the carrying capacity.

The maximum radius of an orange is 4 cm.

b. $V(r) = \dfrac{4}{3}\pi r^3$

$\therefore V(t) = \dfrac{4}{3}\pi(4 - 4(0.65^t))^3$

c. $V(10) = \dfrac{4}{3}\pi(4 - 4(0.65^{10}))^3 \doteq 257.27$

The volume is 257.27 cm³.

11. (Suggested answers)

a.

Plants over Time

$n(t) = \dfrac{940}{1 + 10(0.6^{t - 2005})}$

b. $n(2020) = \dfrac{940}{1 + 10(0.6^{2020 - 2005})}$

$= \dfrac{940}{1 + 10(0.6^{15})}$

$\doteq 936$

There should be about 936 plants in 2020.

c. $10 = \dfrac{940}{1 + 10(0.6^{t - 2005})}$

$1 + 10(0.6^{t - 2005}) = 94$

$0.6^{t - 2005} = 9.3$

$t - 2005 = \dfrac{\log 9.3}{\log 0.6}$

$t \doteq 2001$

They were introduced in 2001.

12. $(f + g)(x) = 0$
$f(x) + g(x) = 0$
$f(x) = -g(x)$
$f(x)$ and $g(x)$ are reflections of each other in the x-axis.

13. When $f(x)$ and $g(x)$ are combined with an operation, the domain is the intersection of the domains of $f(x)$ and $g(x)$. In a division, there is an additional restriction such that $g(x) \neq 0$ when $g(x)$ is the denominator.
In a composition of $f(x)$ and $g(x)$, the domain of $(f \circ g)(x)$ is the subset of the domain of $g(x)$ while $g(x)$ is in the domain of $f(x)$.

14. While it is usually true that $(f \circ g)(x) \neq (g \circ f)(x)$, there are functions where it is true.
e.g. $f(x) = x^2$, $g(x) = \dfrac{1}{x}$
$(f \circ g)(x) = (\dfrac{1}{x})^2 = \dfrac{1}{x^2}$ $(g \circ f)(x) = \dfrac{1}{x^2}$
$\therefore (f \circ g)(x) = (g \circ f)(x)$

15. When making an inverse function, all the operations in the functions are reversed in the opposite order. So when $f(x)$ and $f^{-1}(x)$ are composed together, all the operations "cancel out" and x remains.
e.g. $f(x) = 2x^2 + 3$ $f^{-1}(x) = \sqrt{\dfrac{x - 3}{2}}$
$(f \circ f^{-1})(x) = 2(\sqrt{\dfrac{x - 3}{2}})^2 + 3 = x$

16. Exponential model: Logistic model:
$f(x) = c - ab^x$ $f(x) = \dfrac{c}{1 + ab^x}$
Both functions have c as a carrying capacity. The exponential model approaches 1 limit at 1 horizontal asymptote, while it is unbounded in the opposite direction. The logistic model approaches 2 limits at 2 horizontal asymptotes, creating a boundary for the possible y-values.

17. $f(x) + g(x) = -2x^2 - 2x + 5$
$+\ \ f(x) - g(x) = 2x^2 - 8x + 1$
———————————————
$2f(x) = -10x + 6$
$f(x) = -5x + 3$
$g(x) = -2x^2 - 2x + 5 - f(x)$
$= -2x^2 - 2x + 5 - (-5x + 3)$
$= -2x^2 + 3x + 2$
$\therefore f(x) = -5x + 3$ and $g(x) = -2x^2 + 3x + 2$

18a. $(f + g)(0) = -6$ $(f - g)(0) = 2$
$(0^2 + n) + (0p + q) = -6$ $(0^2 + n) - (0p + q) = 2$
$n + q = -6$ $n - q = 2$

$n + q = -6$
$+\ \ n - q = 2$
————————
$2n = -4$
$n = -2$
$q = -6 - (-2) = -4$
$(f \times g)(-2) = 4$
$((-2)^2 - 2) \times (-2p - 4) = 4$
$-4p - 8 = 4$
$p = -3$
Check: $(\dfrac{f}{g})(-1) = \dfrac{(-1)^2 + (-2)}{-3(-1) + (-4)} = \dfrac{-1}{-1} = 1$
$\therefore f(x) = x^2 - 2$ and $g(x) = -3x - 4$

b. $(f \circ g)(x) = (g \circ f)(x)$
$(-3x - 4)^2 - 2 = -3(x^2 - 2) - 4$
$9x^2 + 24x + 16 - 2 = -3x^2 + 6 - 4$
$12x^2 + 24x + 12 = 0$
$12(x^2 + 2x + 1) = 0$
$12(x + 1)^2 = 0$
$x = -1$
$\therefore x = -1$

19a. $r(x) = x^3$ (Domain: $\{x \in \mathbb{R}\}$)
$q(x) = x + 2$ (Domain: $\{x \in \mathbb{R}\}$)
$p(x) = \sqrt{x}$ (Domain: $\{x \in \mathbb{R} \mid x \geq 0\}$) $\rightarrow x^3 + 2 \geq 0$
$x^3 \geq -2$
$x \geq -1.26$
The domain of $f(x)$ is $\{x \in \mathbb{R} \mid x \geq -1.26\}$.

b. $r(q(p(x))) = (\sqrt{x} + 2)^3$
Domain: $\{x \in \mathbb{R} \mid x \geq 0\}$

c. $p(q(r^{-1}(r(x)))) = p(q(x)) = \sqrt{x + 2} \rightarrow x + 2 \geq 0$
$x \geq -2$
Domain: $\{x \in \mathbb{R} \mid x \geq -2\}$

20a.
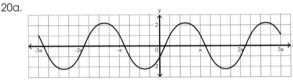

b.
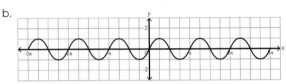

Cumulative Review

1. A   2. C   3. C   4. B
5. D   6. D   7. B   8. A
9. C   10. A   11. C

12a. $x = -2, \dfrac{1}{3}, 1$, or 3
b. $x = 3$
c. $x = \dfrac{\pi}{4}$ or $\dfrac{3\pi}{4}$ d. $x = -3$
e. $x = 8$ f. $x = \dfrac{\pi}{12}$ or $\dfrac{5\pi}{12}$

13a. 4 ; negative   b. 5 ; positive
c. 3 ; negative

14a. $= \dfrac{(2x + 1)(x - 2)}{2(x - 2)}$ b. $= \dfrac{(2x + 1)(x - 4)}{(2x + 1)(x + 3)}$
$= x + \dfrac{1}{2}$ $= \dfrac{(x - 4)}{(x + 3)}$

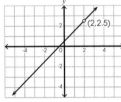

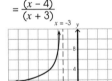

$\{x \in \mathbb{R} \mid x \neq 2\}$ $\{x \in \mathbb{R} \mid x \neq -3, -0.5\}$
$\{y \in \mathbb{R} \mid y \neq 2.5\}$ $\{y \in \mathbb{R} \mid y \neq -1.8, 1\}$
Positive: $x > -0.5$, $x \neq 2$ Positive: $x < -3$, $x > 4$
Negative: $x < -0.5$ Negative: $-3 < x < 4$

15a. 16 ; $-\dfrac{1}{24}$; $\dfrac{2}{7}$; 2.3625   b. 10 ; -7.2

16a. π ; 2 ; 4 ; 0 ; $\{x \in \mathbb{R} \mid -2\pi \leq x \leq 2\pi\}$; $\{y \in \mathbb{R} \mid 0 \leq y \leq 4\}$
b. (Suggested answers)   c. Greatest: 4
$f(x) = 2 \sin (2(x - \dfrac{\pi}{2})) + 2$ Least: -4
$g(x) = 2 \cos (2(x + \dfrac{\pi}{4})) + 2$

17a. $-2 \leq x \leq 1$ or $x \geq 3$ b. $-6 < x < -3$ or $-2 < x < 2$

18a. The population will be 21 900 in the year 2020.
b. The population will fall below 14 400 after 2045.
c. The average rate of change from 2018 to 2028 is 390 people/year.
d. The instantaneous rate of change in 2037 is about -569 people/year.

19a. Gunter will gain about $81.53 after 5 years.
b. The instantaneous rate of change in 10 years is about $63.15/year.
20a. The value of the machinery will decrease by 39% after 26 months.
b. The minimum value is more than $4000.
c. The total payment will exceed the value of the machinery after 40 months.
21a. Her speed is 9 m/s.
b. No, Camilla is not running at the maximum speed at 50 minutes.
c. The average rate of change from 20 min to 25 min is 0.35 m/s.
22a. The total width of the hill is 180 m.
b. The instantaneous rate of change is about -1 m per metre.
c. Yes, the maximum height of the hill is at $x = 90$.
23a. $S(x) = \dfrac{200}{200(0.95^x) + 1}$
b. The predicted maximum number of students infected is 200.
c. It will take about 130 days for 80% of the students to be infected.
24. A 5th degree polynomial with a positive leading coefficient has end behaviours:
As $x \to \infty$, $y \to \infty$ and as $x \to -\infty$, $y \to -\infty$.
The possible numbers of x-intercepts are 1, 2, 3, 4, and 5.
e.g. 1 x-intercept: $f(x) = x^5$
2 x-intercepts: $f(x) = x^4(x - 1)$
3 x-intercepts: $f(x) = x^3(x - 1)(x - 2)$
4 x-intercepts: $f(x) = x^2(x - 1)(x - 2)(x - 3)$
5 x-intercepts: $f(x) = x(x - 1)(x - 2)(x - 3)(x - 4)$
25. $\dfrac{1}{f(x)} = \dfrac{(x + 1)}{(x + 3)(x - 2)}$
$f(x)$ has 1 vertical asymptote at $x = -1$ and an oblique asymptote because the degree of the numerator is greater than the degree of the denominator by exactly 1.
$\dfrac{1}{f(x)}$ has 2 vertical asymptotes at $x = 2$ and $x = -3$ and a horizontal asymptote at $y = 0$.
26. (Suggested answer)
- horizontal reflection
- vertical compression by a factor of $\dfrac{1}{4}$
- horizontal stretch by a factor of $\dfrac{12}{\pi}$
- vertical translation of 7 units up
27. $(f \circ g)(x) = \log(10^x) = x$
$(g \circ f)(x) = 10^{\log x} = x$
However, consider the domain and range of each function.
$f(x)$: Domain: $\{x \in \mathbb{R} \mid x > 0\}$ Range: $\{y \in \mathbb{R}\}$
$g(x)$: Domain: $\{x \in \mathbb{R}\}$ Range: $\{y \in \mathbb{R} \mid y > 0\}$
$(f \circ g)(x)$: Domain: $\{x \in \mathbb{R}\}$ Range: $\{y \in \mathbb{R}\}$
$(g \circ f)(x)$: Domain: $\{x \in \mathbb{R} \mid x > 0\}$ Range: $\{y \in \mathbb{R} \mid y > 0\}$
$(f \circ g)(x)$ and $(g \circ f)(x)$ are not equal.
28a. $x = 3$
b. $x = 0, \dfrac{3\pi}{2}$, or 2π
c. $x = 2$
d. $x = -\dfrac{\pi}{4}$
29a. $0 < x < 1, \dfrac{\pi}{2} < x < \pi$
b. $-2 < x < 0$
c. $0 \le x \le \pi, x = 2\pi$
d. $-\dfrac{\pi}{3} \le x \le \dfrac{\pi}{3}, x = -\pi, x = \pi$

30a.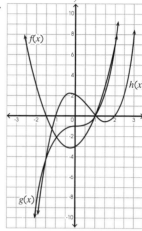
b. 6
c. (Suggested answer)
$-1 < x < 1$

31a. $\dfrac{\cos \theta - \sin 2\theta}{\cos 2\theta + \sin \theta - 1}$
$= \dfrac{\cos \theta - 2\cos \theta \sin \theta}{1 - 2\sin^2 \theta + \sin \theta - 1}$
$= \dfrac{\cos \theta (1 - 2\sin \theta)}{\sin \theta (1 - 2\sin \theta)}$
$= \dfrac{\cos \theta}{\sin \theta}$
$= \cot \theta$
b. $\sin 2x \tan^2 x$
$= 2\sin x \cos x (\dfrac{\sin x}{\cos x}) \tan x$
$= 2\sin^2 x \tan x$
$= 2(1 - \cos^2 x)\dfrac{1}{\cot x}$
$= \dfrac{2 - 2\cos^2 x}{\cot x}$

Calculus and Vectors

1 Limits

1. B
2. D
3. C
4. B
5. C
6. C
7. A
8. B

9a. $= \dfrac{\sqrt{7} + \sqrt{2}}{\sqrt{3}} \times \dfrac{\sqrt{3}}{\sqrt{3}}$
$= \dfrac{\sqrt{3}\sqrt{7} + \sqrt{3}\sqrt{2}}{3}$
$= \dfrac{\sqrt{21} + \sqrt{6}}{3}$

b. $= \dfrac{4\sqrt{5} - 2\sqrt{3}}{3\sqrt{2}} \times \dfrac{\sqrt{2}}{\sqrt{2}}$
$= \dfrac{4\sqrt{2}\sqrt{5} - 2\sqrt{2}\sqrt{3}}{3(2)}$
$= \dfrac{4\sqrt{10} - 2\sqrt{6}}{6}$
$= \dfrac{2\sqrt{10} - \sqrt{6}}{3}$

c. $= \dfrac{\sqrt{7} + \sqrt{2}}{\sqrt{3}} \times \dfrac{\sqrt{7} - \sqrt{2}}{\sqrt{7} - \sqrt{2}}$
$= \dfrac{7 - 2}{\sqrt{3}\sqrt{7} - \sqrt{3}\sqrt{2}}$
$= \dfrac{5}{\sqrt{21} - \sqrt{6}}$

d. $= \dfrac{4\sqrt{5} - 2\sqrt{3}}{3\sqrt{2}} \times \dfrac{4\sqrt{5} + 2\sqrt{3}}{4\sqrt{5} + 2\sqrt{3}}$
$= \dfrac{16(5) - 4(3)}{12\sqrt{2}\sqrt{5} + 6\sqrt{3}\sqrt{2}}$
$= \dfrac{68}{12\sqrt{10} + 6\sqrt{6}}$
$= \dfrac{34}{6\sqrt{10} + 3\sqrt{6}}$

10a. $= 3$
b. $= \lim_{x \to -2} x + \lim_{x \to -2} -2$
$= -2 + (-2)$
$= -4$

c. $= 3(\lim_{x \to 2} x)$
$= 3(2)$
$= 6$

d. $= (\lim_{x \to -1} x)^2$
$= (-1)^2$
$= 1$

e. $= (\lim_{x \to 1} x - 1)(\lim_{x \to 1} x + 2)$
$= (0)(3)$
$= 0$

f. $= \dfrac{\lim_{x \to 4}(x + 3)}{\lim_{x \to 4}(x - 2)}$
$= \dfrac{7}{2}$

ANSWERS

11a.

- $\lim_{x\to -1} -\frac{1}{2}x^2$

$= -\frac{1}{2}(\lim_{x\to -1} x^2)$

$= -\frac{1}{2}(\lim_{x\to -1} x)^2$

$= -\frac{1}{2}(-1)^2$

$= -\frac{1}{2}$

- $m = \lim_{h\to 0}\frac{f(a+h)-f(a)}{h}$

$= \lim_{h\to 0}\frac{-\frac{1}{2}(-1+h)^2-(-\frac{1}{2}(-1)^2)}{h}$

$= \lim_{h\to 0}\frac{h-\frac{1}{2}h^2}{h}$

$= \lim_{h\to 0} 1-\frac{1}{2}h$

$= 1$

$y = mx+b$

$-\frac{1}{2} = 1(-1)+b$

$b = \frac{1}{2}$

$\therefore y = x+\frac{1}{2}$

b.

- $\lim_{x\to 5}\sqrt{x-1}$

$= \sqrt{(\lim_{x\to 5} x-1)}$

$= \sqrt{4}$

$= 2$

- $m = \lim_{h\to 0}\frac{f(a+h)-f(a)}{h}$

$= \lim_{h\to 0}\frac{\sqrt{h+4}-2}{h}$

$= \lim_{h\to 0}\frac{\sqrt{h+4}-2}{h}\times\frac{\sqrt{h+4}+2}{\sqrt{h+4}+2}$

$= \lim_{h\to 0}\frac{1}{\sqrt{h+4}+2}$

$= \frac{1}{4}$

$y = mx+b$

$2 = \frac{1}{4}(5)+b$

$b = \frac{3}{4}$

$\therefore y = \frac{1}{4}x+\frac{3}{4}$

12a. $\frac{1}{x^2}-1 \leftarrow$ asymptote

$x^2 \neq 0$

$x \neq 0$

infinite discontinuity at $x=0$

$\lim_{x\to 1^-} f(x) = 0$

$\lim_{x\to 1^+} f(x) = 1$

jump discontinuity at $x=1$

$\frac{x^2-2x}{x-2} = \frac{x(x-2)}{x-2} = x$

$x-2 \neq 0$

$x \neq 2$

point discontinuity at $x=2$

b. $\lim_{x\to -1} f(x)$

$= \lim_{x\to -1}(\frac{1}{x^2}-1)$

$= \frac{1}{(\lim_{x\to -1} x)^2}-1$

$= 0$

c. $\lim_{x\to 3} f(x)$

$= \lim_{x\to 3}\frac{x^2-2x}{x-2}$

$= \lim_{x\to 3} x$

$= 3$

13a. $\frac{S(5)-S(0)}{5-0} = \frac{350-0}{5} = 70$

The average velocity of the truck is 70 km/h.

b. $\lim_{h\to 0}\frac{S(3+h)-S(3)}{h}$

$= \lim_{h\to 0}\frac{10(3+h)(5+h)-150}{h}$

$= \lim_{h\to 0}\frac{10h^2+80h}{h}$

$= \lim_{h\to 0} 10h+80$

$= 80$

The instantaneous velocity at $t=3$ is approximately 80 km/h.

c. $\lim_{h\to 0}\frac{S(5+h)-S(5)}{h}$

$= \lim_{h\to 0}\frac{10(5+h)(7+h)-350}{h}$

$= \lim_{h\to 0}\frac{10h^2+120h}{h}$

$= \lim_{h\to 0} 10h+120$

$= 120$

The velocity at $t=5$ is 120 km/h.

14a. $\frac{S(20)-S(0)}{20-0} = \frac{0-80}{20} = -4$

The average velocity of the balloon is -4 m/s.

b. $\frac{S(1.5)-S(1)}{1.5-1} = \frac{79.55-79.8}{0.5} = -0.5$

The average velocity of the balloon between 1 s and 1.5 s is -0.5 m/s.

c. $\lim_{h\to 0}\frac{S(2+h)-S(2)}{h}$

$= \lim_{h\to 0}\frac{80-0.2(2+h)^2-79.2}{h}$

$= \lim_{h\to 0}\frac{-0.2h^2-0.8h}{h}$

$= \lim_{h\to 0} -0.2h-0.8$

$= -0.8$

The velocity at 2 s is -0.8 m/s.

15. To evaluate $\lim_{x\to 4} f(x)$, you can simply substitute 4 into the function. However, you cannot do the same for $\lim_{x\to 1} f(x)$ because it results in an indeterminate form ($\frac{0}{0}$). So you will need to rationalize the denominator to evaluate the limit.

16. $\lim_{x\to a} f(x)$ exists when $\lim_{x\to a^-} f(x) = \lim_{x\to a^+} f(x)$, even if $f(a)$ is not defined.

17. $\lim_{x\to 2^-}\frac{x}{x-2}$ is a very large negative number.

$\lim_{x\to 2^+}\frac{x}{x-2}$ is a very large positive number.

Since $\lim_{x\to 2^-}\frac{x}{x-2} \neq \lim_{x\to 2^+}\frac{x}{x-2}$, $\lim_{x\to 2}\frac{x}{x-2}$ does not exist.

18. (Suggested answers)
- direct substitution: substitute the value of x directly into the function and evaluate
- rationalization: rationalize the function before substitution
- change of variable: change the variable so that the denominator is not zero

19a. $= 5(3)^2+2(3)-3$

$= 48$

b. $= \frac{(-2)^2-3(-2)+4}{3(-2)^3+2(-2)+1}$

$= -\frac{14}{27}$

c. $= \sqrt{25-(-4)^2}$

$= \sqrt{9}$

$= 3$

d. $= \sqrt{\frac{4(12)^2}{12-2}}$

$= \sqrt{\frac{576}{10}}$

$= \frac{24}{\sqrt{10}}$

e. $= \lim_{x\to 4}\frac{(x-4)(x-2)}{x-4}$

$= \lim_{x\to 4}(x-2)$

$= 4-2$

$= 2$

f. $= \lim_{x\to 0}\frac{\sqrt{x+4}-2}{x}\times\frac{\sqrt{x+4}+2}{\sqrt{x+4}+2}$

$= \lim_{x\to 0}\frac{x+4-4}{x(\sqrt{x+4}+2)}$

$= \lim_{x\to 0}\frac{1}{\sqrt{x+4}+2}$

$= \frac{1}{\sqrt{0+4}+2}$

$= \frac{1}{4}$

g. let $u = (x+81)^{\frac{1}{4}}$

$x = u^4-81$

when $x=0$, $u=3$

$= \lim_{u\to 3}\frac{u-3}{u^4-81}$

$= \lim_{u\to 3}\frac{u-3}{(u-3)(u+3)(u^2+9)}$

$= \lim_{u\to 3}\frac{1}{(u+3)(u^2+9)}$

$= \frac{1}{(3+3)(3^2+9)}$

$= \frac{1}{108}$

h. $= \lim\limits_{x \to 5}\begin{cases} \dfrac{x-5}{x-5}, & \text{if } x > 5 \\ \dfrac{-(x-5)}{x-5}, & \text{if } x \le 5 \end{cases}$

$= \lim\limits_{x \to 5}\begin{cases} 1, & \text{if } x > 5 \\ -1, & \text{if } x \le 5 \end{cases}$

$\lim\limits_{x \to 5^+}\dfrac{|x-5|}{x-5} = 1, \; \lim\limits_{x \to 5^-}\dfrac{|x-5|}{x-5} = -1$

$\therefore \lim\limits_{x \to 5}\dfrac{|x-5|}{x-5}$ does not exist.

2   Derivatives and Their Applications

1. D   2. D   3. C
4. D   5. B   6. B
7. B   8. A   9. C

10a. $f'(x) = 10x + 2$ b. $f'(x) = 9x^2 - \dfrac{1}{2}$

c. $f'(x) = 6x^5 + 14x - 5$ d. $f'(x) = \dfrac{3}{\sqrt{x}}$

e. $f'(x) = -\dfrac{2}{x^2} + \dfrac{10}{x^3}$ f. $f'(x) = \dfrac{1}{\sqrt{x}} - 6 + 21x^2$

g. $f'(x) = 1(x^2 + 1) + x(2x)$ h. $f'(x) = 1(4x^4 - 2) + (x+3)(16x^3)$
$= 3x^2 + 1$ $= 20x^4 + 48x^3 - 2$

i. $f'(x) = -\dfrac{1}{(x+2)^2}$

j. $f'(x) = \dfrac{(2)(x^2 - 1) - (2x + 1)(2x)}{(x^2 - 1)^2}$
$= \dfrac{-2(x^2 + x + 1)}{(x^2 - 1)^2}$

k. $f'(x) = \dfrac{3x^2(4 - x^2) - x^3(-2x)}{(4 - x^2)^2}$
$= \dfrac{x^2(12 - x^2)}{(4 - x^2)^2}$

l. $f'(x) = 2(x - 5)(x + 2)^3 + 3(x - 5)^2(x + 2)^2$
$= (x - 5)(x + 2)^2(5x - 11)$

m. $f'(x) = \dfrac{2x + 3}{2\sqrt{x^2 + 3x}}$

n. $f'(x) = 6(\sqrt{x} - 5)(\dfrac{1}{2\sqrt{x}})$
$= \dfrac{3(\sqrt{x} - 5)}{\sqrt{x}}$

11a. $f'(x) = \dfrac{3x^2(5 - 3x^2) - x^3(-6x)}{(5 - 3x^2)^2}$
$= \dfrac{15x^2 - 3x^4}{(5 - 3x^2)^2}$
$f'(1) = \dfrac{15(1)^2 - 3(1)^4}{(5 - 3(1)^2)^2} = 3$
The slope of the tangent at (1,0.5) is 3.

b. $f'(x) = 2(x - 2)(x + 1)^3 + 3(x - 2)^2(x + 1)^2$
$= (x - 2)(x + 1)^2(5x - 4)$
$f'(-2) = (-2 - 2)(-2 + 1)^2(5(-2) - 4) = 56$
The slope of the tangent at (-2,-16) is 56.

12.

$y' = 2x\sqrt{x-3} + x^2\dfrac{1}{2\sqrt{x-3}}$ $= \dfrac{4x(x-3) + x^2}{2\sqrt{x-3}}$ $= \dfrac{5x^2 - 12x}{2\sqrt{x-3}}$	$y' = \dfrac{2(x^2) - (2x+1)(2x)}{(x^2)^2}$ $= \dfrac{-2x^2 - 2x}{x^4}$ $= \dfrac{-2(x+1)}{x^3}$	$y' = \dfrac{1}{2\sqrt{(2x+1)-3}}(2)$ $= \dfrac{1}{\sqrt{2x-2}}$
$y'' = \dfrac{(10x-12)(2\sqrt{x-3}) - \dfrac{(5x^2-12x)}{\sqrt{x-3}}}{(2\sqrt{x-3})^2}$ $= \dfrac{(10x-12)(2x-6) - (5x^2-12x)}{4(x-3)\sqrt{x-3}}$ $= \dfrac{15x^2 - 72x + 72}{4(x-3)^{\frac{3}{2}}}$	$y'' = \dfrac{-2(x^3) - (-2(x+1))(3x^2)}{(x^3)^2}$ $= \dfrac{4x^3 + 6x^2}{x^6}$ $= \dfrac{4x + 6}{x^4}$	$y'' = -\dfrac{1}{2}(2x-2)^{-\frac{3}{2}}(2)$ $= -\dfrac{1}{(2x-2)^{\frac{3}{2}}}$

13a. $f'(x) = -6x + 108$
$0 = -6x + 108$
$x = 18$
$f(18) = -3(18)^2 + 108(18) - 722 = 250$
$\therefore (18,250)$

b. $f'(x) = (2x + 1)(x - 1) + (x^2 + x + 1)(1)$
$= 3x^2$
$0 = 3x^2$
$x = 0$
$f(0) = (0^2 + 0 + 1)(0 - 1) = -1$
$\therefore (0,-1)$

14a. $f'(x) = (2x)(x + 3) + (x^2 + 3)(1)$
$= 3x^2 + 6x + 3$
$0 = 3x^2 + 6x + 3$
$x = -1$
$f(0) = (0^2 + 3)(0 + 3) = 9$
$f(-1) = ((-1)^2 + 3)((-1) + 3) = 8$
$f(-3) = ((-3)^2 + 3)((-3) + 3) = 0$
absolute maximum: (0,9)
absolute minimum: (-3,0)

b. $g'(x) = \dfrac{2x(x) - (x^2 + 4)(1)}{x^2}$
$= \dfrac{x^2 - 4}{x^2}$
$0 = \dfrac{x^2 - 4}{x^2}$
$x = \pm 2$
$g'(1) = \dfrac{1^2 + 4}{1} = 5$
$g'(2) = \dfrac{2^2 + 4}{2} = 4$
$g'(5) = \dfrac{5^2 + 4}{5} = 5.8$
absolute maximum: (5,5.8)
absolute minimum: (2,4)

15. $h'(t) = -9.8t$
$h'(4) = -9.8(4) = -39.2$
The ball is falling at 39.2 m/s.

16. $V'(t) = 13\,000(1 - \dfrac{t}{20})(-\dfrac{1}{20})$
$= -650(1 - \dfrac{t}{20})$
$V'(5) = -650(1 - \dfrac{5}{20}) = -487.5$
The water is flowing at 487.5 L/min.

17. $v(t) = 2(4 + 3t)(3)\sqrt{t + 3} + \dfrac{(4 + 3t)^2}{2\sqrt{t + 3}}$
$= \dfrac{5(3t + 4)(3t + 8)}{2\sqrt{t + 3}}$
$v(6) = \dfrac{5(3(6) + 4)(3(6) + 8)}{2\sqrt{6 + 3}} \doteq 476.67$
The velocity of the car is 476.67 m/min.

18. $V(t) = \dfrac{4}{3}\pi(0.5t^2)^3 = \dfrac{1}{6}\pi t^6$
$V'(t) = \pi t^5$
$V'(4) = \pi(4)^5 \doteq 3215.36$
The rate will be 3215.36 cm³/s.

19a. $v(t) = 8t - 6t^2$ $a(t) = 8 - 12t$
$v(1) = 8(1) - 6(1)^2 = 2$ $a(1) = 8 - 12(1) = -4$
The velocity is 2 km/min and the acceleration is -4 km/min².

b. $0 = 8t - 6t^2$
$0 = t(8 - 6t)$
$t = 0$ or $t \doteq 1.33$
The train stops at 0 minutes and 1.33 minutes.

c. $0 = 4t^2 - 2t^3$
$0 = 2t^2(2 - t)$
$t = 0$ or $t = 2$
The train will return to the station at 2 minutes.

ISBN: 978-1-77149-223-2

d. $v(3) = 8(3) - 6(3)^2 = -30$
   $s(3) = 4(3)^2 - 2(3)^3 = -18$
   The train is moving away from the station at 3 minutes.

20. $A = w(300 - 2w)$
   $A' = 1(300 - 2w) + w(-2)$
   $= 300 - 4w$
   $0 = 300 - 4w$
   $w = 75$
   $l = 300 - 2(75) = 150$
   Dimensions of 150 m by 75 m will enclose the largest possible area.

21.
   $A = lw$
   $= w(\dfrac{3600 - 3w}{2})$
   $= 1800w - \dfrac{3}{2}w^2$
   $A' = 1800 - 3w$
   $0 = 1800 - 3w$
   $w = 600$
   $l = \dfrac{3600 - 3(600)}{2} = 900$
   Dimensions of 900 m by 600 m will maximize the area.

22. $R(x) = (8000 - 125x)(50 + x)$
   $R'(x) = (-125)(50 + x) + (8000 - 125x)(1)$
   $= -6250 - 125x + 8000 - 125x$
   $= 1750 - 250x$
   $0 = 1750 - 250x$
   $x = 7$
   Passagers: $6000 \le 8000 - 125x$ Fare: $0 \le 50 + x$
   $16 \ge x$ $-50 \le x$
   $\therefore 16 \ge x \ge -50$
   $R(16) = (8000 - 125(16))(50 + 16) = 396\ 000$
   $R(7) = (8000 - 125(7))(50 + 7) = 406\ 125 \leftarrow$ maximum
   $R(-50) = (8000 - 125(-50))(50 + (-50)) = 0$
   Fare: $50 + 7 = 57$
   Passengers: $8000 - 125(7) = 7125$
   The fare is $57 with 7125 passengers when the revenue is maximized.

23. $d = \sqrt{(28 - 6t)^2 + (8t)^2}, 2 \ge t \ge 0$
   $= 2\sqrt{25t^2 - 84t + 196}$
   $d' = \dfrac{50t - 84}{\sqrt{25t^2 - 84t + 196}}$
   $0 = \dfrac{50t - 84}{\sqrt{25t^2 - 84t + 196}}$
   $0 = 50t - 84$
   $t = 1.68$
   $d(2) = \sqrt{(28 - 6(2))^2 + (8(2))^2} \doteq 22.63$
   $d(1.68) = \sqrt{(28 - 6(1.68))^2 + (8(1.68))^2} = 22.4 \leftarrow$ minimum
   $d(0) = \sqrt{(28 - 6(0))^2 + (8(0))^2} = 28$
   Anastasia and Rubin will be closest in distance after 1.68 h.

24. $\dfrac{7}{7 - x} = \dfrac{24}{y}$
   $y = \dfrac{24}{7}(7 - x)$
   $A = \dfrac{24}{7}x(7 - x), 7 \ge x \ge 0$
   $A' = \dfrac{24}{7}(7 - x) + \dfrac{24}{7}x(-1)$
   $= 24 - \dfrac{48}{7}x$
   $0 = 24 - \dfrac{48}{7}x$
   $x = 3.5$
   $A(3.5) = \dfrac{24}{7}(3.5)(7 - 3.5) = 42 \leftarrow$ maximum
   $A(0) = \dfrac{24}{7}(0)(7 - 0) = 0$
   $A(7) = \dfrac{24}{7}(7)(7 - 7) = 0$
   The area of the largest rectangle is 42 cm².

25. Volume: $s^2h = 8000$
   $h = \dfrac{8000}{s^2}$
   Surface area: $y = 2s^2 + 4sh$
   $= 2s^2 + 4s(\dfrac{8000}{s^2})$
   $= 2s^2 + \dfrac{32\ 000}{s}, s > 0$
   $y' = 4s - \dfrac{32\ 000}{s^2}$
   $0 = 4s - \dfrac{32\ 000}{s^2}$
   $4s = \dfrac{32\ 000}{s^2}$
   $s^3 = 8000$
   $s = 20$
   $h = \dfrac{8000}{20^2} = 20$
   Dimensions of 20 cm by 20 cm by 20 cm will use the least amount of cardboard.

26. - when there is a point discontinuity or an asymptote
   - when there is a cusp (the slopes on either side of a point are not equal)
   - when the tangent to the graph is vertical

27. $f(x) = |x - 1|$ is not differentiable at $x = 1$ because the limits on either side are not equal.
   $|x - 1| = \begin{cases} x - 1, \text{ if } x > 1 \\ -(x - 1), \text{ if } x \le 1 \end{cases}$
   $\lim\limits_{x \to 1^+} \dfrac{f(x + h) - f(x)}{h} = \lim\limits_{x \to 1^+} \dfrac{((1 + h) - 1) - (1 - 1)}{h} = \dfrac{h}{h} = 1$
   $\lim\limits_{x \to 1^-} \dfrac{f(x + h) - f(x)}{h} = \lim\limits_{x \to 1^-} \dfrac{-((1 + h) - 1) - (-(1 - 1))}{h} = -\dfrac{h}{h} = -1$
   So $\lim\limits_{x \to 1^+} \ne \lim\limits_{x \to 1^-}$, and the function is not differentiable at $x = 1$.

28. They are both correct.
   $f(x) = \dfrac{p(x)}{q(x)}$
   quotient rule: $f'(x) = \dfrac{p'(x)q(x) - p(x)q'(x)}{(q(x))^2}$
   product rule: rewrite function as a product
   $f(x) = p(x)q(x)^{-1}$
   $f'(x) = p'(x)q(x)^{-1} + p(x)(-1)q(x)^{-2}q'(x)$
   $= \dfrac{p'(x)}{q(x)} - \dfrac{p(x)q'(x)}{q(x)^2}$
   $= \dfrac{p'(x)q(x) - p(x)q'(x)}{(q(x))^2}$
   Either method will give the same answer.

29. 1. Write a function to model the problem.
   2. Sketch a graph.
   3. Determine the domain to be optimized.
   4. Find the derivative.
   5. Solve for any local max./min. and the extreme values.
   6. Identify the absolute maximum or minimum value.

30a. $y' = 2(1 - 5x^2)(-10x)$ b. $y' = 3(4x - 1)^2(4)$
   $= -20x + 100x^3$ $= 12(4x - 1)^2$
   $y'' = -20 + 300x^2$ $y'' = 24(4x - 1)(4)$
   $y''' = 600x$ $= 96(4x - 1)$
   $y'''' = 600$ $y''' = 384$
                                            $y'''' = 0$

31a. $f'(x) = 9x^2 + 10x^{-3}$
   $f'(-1) = 9(-1)^2 + 10(-1)^{-3} = -1$
   $f(-1) = 3(-1)^3 - 5(-1)^{-2} = -8$
   $y = mx + b$
   $-8 = -1(-1) + b$
   $b = -9$
   $\therefore y = -x - 9$

b. $g'(x) = \dfrac{2(2x+5)(2)\sqrt{x-1} - \dfrac{(2x+5)^2}{2\sqrt{x-1}}}{(\sqrt{x-1})^2}$

$= \dfrac{8(2x+5)(x-1) - (2x+5)^2}{2\sqrt{x-1}(x-1)}$

$= \dfrac{(2x+5)(6x-13)}{2(x-1)^{\frac{3}{2}}}$

$g(2) = \dfrac{(2(2)+5)^2}{\sqrt{2-1}}$

$= 81$

$g'(2) = \dfrac{(2(2)+5)(6(2)-13)}{2(2-1)^{\frac{3}{2}}}$

$= -4.5$

$y = mx + b$

$81 = -4.5(2) + b$

$b = 90$

$\therefore y = -4.5x + 90$

32a. $f(-2) = 3(-2)^3 - 5(-2)^{-2} = -25.25$

$f'(-2) = 9(-2)^2 + 10(-2)^{-3} = 34.75$

$m = -\dfrac{1}{34.75} = -\dfrac{4}{139}$

$-25.25 = -\dfrac{4}{139}(-2) + b$

$b = -25\dfrac{171}{556}$

$\therefore y = -\dfrac{4}{139}x - 25\dfrac{171}{556}$

b. $g(5) = \dfrac{(2(5)+5)^2}{\sqrt{5-1}} = 112.5$

$g'(5) = \dfrac{(2(5)+5)(6(5)-13)}{2(5-1)^{\frac{3}{2}}} = \dfrac{255}{16}$

$m = -\dfrac{1}{\dfrac{255}{16}} = -\dfrac{16}{255}$

$112.5 = -\dfrac{16}{255}(5) + b$

$b = 112\dfrac{83}{102}$

$\therefore y = -\dfrac{16}{255}x + 112\dfrac{83}{102}$

33. $f'(x) = 4x \qquad g'(x) = -2x$

$f'(a) = 4a \qquad g'(b) = -2b$

$4a = -2b$

$b = -2a$

$\dfrac{f(a) - g(b)}{a - b} = 4a$

$\dfrac{2a^2 + 6 - (-b^2)}{a - b} = 4a$

$2a^2 + b^2 + 6 = 4a(a - b)$

$2a^2 + (-2a)^2 + 6 = 4a(a - (-2a))$

$6a^2 + 6 = 12a^2$

$a = \pm 1$

$a = 1$	$a = -1$
$f(1) = 2(1)^2 + 6 = 8$	$f(-1) = 2(-1)^2 + 6 = 8$
$f'(1) = 4(1) = 4$	$f'(-1) = 4(-1) = -4$
$8 = 4(1) + b$	$8 = -4(-1) + b$
$b = 4$	$b = 4$
$\therefore y = 4x + 4$	$\therefore y = -4x + 4$

3 Curve Sketching

1. B	2. D	3. D	4. B
5. A	6. B	7. D	8. B
9. A	10. C		

11a. $f'(x) = -4x + 3$

$0 = -4x + 3$

$x = \dfrac{3}{4}$

	$x < \frac{3}{4}$	$x > \frac{3}{4}$
$f'(x)$	+	−

$f(\dfrac{3}{4}) = -2(\dfrac{3}{4})^2 + 3(\dfrac{3}{4}) + 2 = 3\dfrac{1}{8}$

$\therefore (\dfrac{3}{4}, 3\dfrac{1}{8})$ is a local maximum.

b. $g'(x) = \dfrac{8x+2}{2\sqrt{4x^2+2x+1}} = \dfrac{4x+1}{\sqrt{4x^2+2x+1}}$

$0 = \dfrac{4x+1}{\sqrt{4x^2+2x+1}}$

$x = -\dfrac{1}{4}$

	$x < -\frac{1}{4}$	$x > -\frac{1}{4}$
$g'(x)$	−	+

$g(-\dfrac{1}{4}) = \sqrt{4(-\dfrac{1}{4})^2 + 2(-\dfrac{1}{4}) + 1} = \dfrac{\sqrt{3}}{2}$

$\therefore (-\dfrac{1}{4}, \dfrac{\sqrt{3}}{2})$ is a local minimum.

12a. $x + 4 \neq 0$

$x \neq -4$

$\lim_{x \to +\infty} h(x) = 1 \quad \lim_{x \to -\infty} h(x) = 1$

$\therefore$ vertical asymptote at $x = -4$ and horizontal asymptote at $y = 1$

b. $x^2 + 4x + 4 \neq 0$

$(x + 2)^2 \neq 0$

$x \neq -2$

$\lim_{x \to +\infty} k(x) = 0 \quad \lim_{x \to -\infty} k(x) = 0$

$\therefore$ vertical asymptote at $x = -2$ and horizontal asymptote at $y = 0$

13a. $p'(x) = 3x^2 - 6x$

$3x^2 - 6x = 0$

$3x(x - 2) = 0$

$x = 0$ or $x = 2$

$p(0) = 0^3 - 3(0)^2 = 0$

$p(2) = 2^3 - 3(2)^2 = -4$

	$x < 0$	$0 < x < 2$	$x > 2$
$p'(x)$	+	−	+

$\therefore$ local maximum at $(0,0)$ and local minimum at $(2,-4)$, no asymptotes

A

b. $q'(x) = \dfrac{4x}{(x^2+2)^2}$

$0 = \dfrac{4x}{(x^2+2)^2}$

$x = 0$

$q(0) = \dfrac{0^2}{0^2 + 2} = 0$

$x^2 + 2 \neq 0$

$x^2 \neq -2 \leftarrow$ no real values

$\lim_{x \to +\infty} q(x) = 1 \quad \lim_{x \to -\infty} q(x) = 1$

$\therefore$ local minimum at $(0,0)$, horizontal asymptote at $y = 1$

A

	$x < 0$	$x > 0$
$q'(x)$	−	+

14a. • $f'(x) = -2x + 5$

$-2x + 5 = 0$

$x = 2.5$

	$x < 2.5$	$x > 2.5$
$f'(x)$	+	−
interval	increase	decrease

• $g'(x) = -3x^2 + 12x$

$-3x^2 + 12x = 0$

$-3x(x - 4) = 0$

$x = 0$ or $x = 4$

	$x < 0$	$0 < x < 4$	$x > 4$
$g'(x)$	−	+	−
interval	decrease	increase	decrease

• $p'(x) = \dfrac{-7}{(x-1)^2}, (x-1)^2 \neq 0$

$x \neq 1$

$\dfrac{-7}{(x-1)^2} = 0$

$\therefore$ no local max./min.

	$x < 1$	$x > 1$
$p'(x)$	−	−
interval	decrease	decrease

• $q'(x) = \dfrac{4x-9}{3(x-3)^{\frac{2}{3}}}, (x-3)^{\frac{2}{3}} \neq 0$

$x \neq 3$

$\dfrac{4x-9}{3(x-3)^{\frac{2}{3}}} = 0$

$4x - 9 = 0$

$x = 2.25$

	$x < 2.25$	$2.25 < x < 3$	$x > 3$
$q'(x)$	−	+	+
interval	decrease	increase	increase

b. • $f''(x) = -2$

	x
$f''(x)$	–
concave	down

• $g''(x) = -6x + 12$
$-6x + 12 = 0$
$x = 2$

	$x < 2$	$x > 2$
$g''(x)$	+	–
concave	up	down

• $p''(x) = \dfrac{14}{(x-1)^3}$, $(x-1)^3 \neq 0$
$\quad x \neq 1$
$\dfrac{14}{(x-1)^3} = 0$
∴ no points of inflection

	$x < 1$	$x > 1$
$p''(x)$	–	+
concave	down	up

• $q''(x) = \dfrac{4x - 18}{9(x-3)^{\frac{5}{3}}}$, $(x-3)^{\frac{5}{3}} \neq 0$
$\quad x \neq 3$
$\dfrac{4x - 18}{9(x-3)^{\frac{5}{3}}} = 0$
$4x - 18 = 0$
$x = 4.5$

	$x < 3$	$3 < x < 4.5$	$x > 4.5$
$q''(x)$	+	–	+
concave	up	down	up

15a. A ; B ; E ; F
• x-intercept:
$3(x^3 - 3x^2) = 0$
$x^2(x - 3) = 0$
$x = 0$ or $x = 3$
∴ (0,0) and (3,0)

• y-intercept:
$f(0) = 3(0^3 - 3(0)^2) = 0$
∴ (0,0)

• local max./min.:
$f'(x) = 9x^2 - 18x$
$9x^2 - 18x = 0$
$9x(x - 2) = 0$
$x = 0$ or $x = 2$

	$x < 0$	$0 < x < 2$	$x > 2$
$f'(x)$	+	–	+
interval	increase	decrease	increase

$f(0) = 0$ local max. at (0,0)
$f(2) = -12$ local min. at (2,-12)

• concavity:
$f''(x) = 18x - 18$
$18x - 18 = 0$
$x = 1$

	$x < 1$	$x > 1$
$f''(x)$	–	+
concave	down	up

• point of inflection:
$f(1) = -6$
∴ (1,-6)

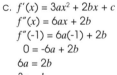

b. A ; B ; C ; E ; F
• x-intercept:
$-\dfrac{2x^3 - 3x^2}{x^3} = 0$ $\quad x \neq 0$
$-x^2(2x - 3) = 0$
$x = 0$ or $x = \dfrac{3}{2}$
(undefined)
∴ $\left(\dfrac{3}{2},0\right)$

• y-intercept:
$f(0) = -\dfrac{2(0)^3 - 3(0)^2}{0^3}$ (undefined)
∴ no y-intercept

• vertical/horizontal asymptotes:
$x^3 \neq 0$
$x \neq 0$ $\quad \lim_{x \to +\infty} f(x) = -2$ $\quad \lim_{x \to -\infty} f(x) = -2$
∴ vertical asymptote at $x = 0$
horizontal asymptote at $y = -2$

• concavity:
$f''(x) = \dfrac{6}{x^3}$
$x \neq 0$

	$x < 0$	$x > 0$
$f''(x)$	–	+
concave	down	up

• local max./min.:
$f'(x) = -\dfrac{3}{x^2}$
$x \neq 0$

	$x < 0$	$x > 0$
$f'(x)$	–	–
interval	decrease	decrease

∴ no local max./min.

• point of inflection:
$f(0) =$ undefined
∴ no point of inflection

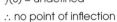

16. $f'(x) = -0.2(3x^2 - 22x + 40)$
$-0.2(3x^2 - 22x + 40) = 0$
$-0.2(3x - 10)(x - 4) = 0$
$3x - 10 = 0$ or $x - 4 = 0$
$x = \dfrac{10}{3}$ $\qquad x = 4$

	$x < \frac{10}{3}$	$\frac{10}{3} < x < 4$	$x > 4$
$f'(x)$	–	+	–
interval	decrease	increase	decrease

No, the path is not always decreasing. The interval of increase is $\dfrac{10}{3} < x < 4$.

17. $C'(t) = \dfrac{(t - 7)(t + 8)}{(2t + 1)^2}$, where $t \neq -\dfrac{1}{2}$
$\dfrac{(t - 7)(t + 8)}{(2t + 1)^2} = 0$
$t - 7 = 0$ or $t + 8 = 0$
$t = 7$ $\qquad t = -8$

	$0 < t < 7$	$t > 7$	← time cannot be negative
$C'(t)$	–	+	
interval	decrease	increase	

The algae concentration will increase after 7 months.

18. 1. Use the function to find the x- and y-intercepts, and any asymptotes and discontinuities.
2. Use the first derivative to find the critical numbers, any local maxima or minima, and the intervals of increase and decrease.
3. Use the second derivative to find any points of inflection and the intervals of concavity.
4. Calculate the values of the critical points and points of inflection and graph the function.

19. The number of possible x-intercepts is equal to the number of solutions to $f(x)$, which is n.
The number of possible critical numbers is equal to the number of solutions to $f'(x) = np^{n-1}$, which is $n - 1$.
The number of possible points of inflection is equal to the number of solutions to $f''(x) = n \cdot (n - 1)p^{n-2}$, which is $n - 2$.

20a.
$$\begin{array}{r} x + 2 \\ x - 1 \overline{)\, x^2 + x - 3} \\ \underline{x^2 - x} \\ 2x - 3 \\ \underline{2x - 2} \\ -1 \end{array}$$
∴ $y = x + 2$

b.
$$\begin{array}{r} -x - 3 \\ x^2 - 3x \overline{)\, -x^3 \quad\quad - x + 9} \\ \underline{-x^3 + 3x^2} \\ -3x^2 - x + 9 \\ \underline{-3x^2 + 9x} \\ -10x + 9 \end{array}$$
∴ $y = -x - 3$

21a. $f'(x) = 2x + b$
$f'(1) = 0$
$2(1) + b = 0$
$b = -2$
$(1)^2 - 2(1) + c = 6$
$c = 7$
∴ $f(x) = x^2 - 2x + 7$

c. $f'(x) = 3ax^2 + 2bx + c$
$f''(x) = 6ax + 2b$
$f''(-1) = 6a(-1) + 2b$
$0 = -6a + 2b$
$6a = 2b$
$3a = b$
$f'(2) = 3a(2)^2 + 2b(2) + c$
$0 = 12a + 4b + c$
$0 = 12a + 4(3a) + c$
$-24a = c$
$f(x) = ax^3 + 3ax^2 - 24ax + d$
$8 = a(2)^3 + 3a(2)^2 - 24a(2) + d$
$8 = -28a + d$ ①
$-10 = a(-1)^3 + 3a(-1)^2 - 24a(-1) + d$
$-10 = 26a + d$ ②
$-18 = 54a$ ② – ①
$a = -\dfrac{1}{3}$ $\qquad c = 8$
$b = -1$ $\qquad d = -\dfrac{4}{3}$
∴ $f(x) = -\dfrac{1}{3}x^3 - x^2 + 8x - \dfrac{4}{3}$

b. $f(0) = a(0)^3 + b(0)^2 + c$
$c = 12$
$f'(x) = 3ax^2 + 2bx$
$f''(x) = 6ax + 2b$
$f''(-2) = 6a(-2) + 2b$
$0 = -12a + 2b$
$6a = b$
$f(x) = ax^3 + 6ax^2 + 12$
$f(-2) = a(-2)^3 + 6a(-2)^2 + 12$
$4 = -8a + 24a + 12$
$-8 = 16a$
$a = -\dfrac{1}{2}$
$b = -3$
∴ $y = -\dfrac{1}{2}x^3 - 3x^2 + 12$

ISBN: 978-1-77149-223-2

4 Derivatives of Exponential and Trigonometric Functions

1. B 　　　2. C 　　　3. C 　　　4. A
5. D 　　　6. A 　　　7. B 　　　8. D
9. C 　　　10. D 　　　11. A

12a. $f'(x) = -4e^{x^3} \cdot 3x^2$
　　$= -12x^2 e^{x^3}$

b. $f'(x) = 4xe^{3x} + 2x^2 e^{3x} \cdot 3$
　　$= 2xe^{3x}(2 + 3x)$

c. $f'(x) = -\sin x^4 \cdot 4x^3$
　　$= -4x^3 \sin x^4$

d. $f'(x) = 6 \sin x \cos x$

13a. $f'(x) = (6x - 2)e^{3x^2 - 2x - 5}$
　　$f'(-1) = (6(-1) - 2)e^{3(-1)^2 - 2(-1) - 5}$
　　　$= -8e^0$
　　　$= -8$
　　$\therefore$ The slope is -8.

b. $f'(x) = 2x \tan x + x^2 \sec^2 x$
　　$f'(\pi) = 2\pi \tan \pi + \pi^2 \sec^2 \pi$
　　　$= \pi^2$
　　$\therefore$ The slope is π^2.

14a. $f'(x) = 5e^x$
　　$f'(\ln 5) = 5e^{\ln 5}$
　　　$= 25$
　　$f(\ln 5) = 5e^{\ln 5} = 25$
　　　$25 = 25 \ln 5 + b$
　　　$b = 25(1 - \ln 5)$
　　$\therefore y = 25x + 25(1 - \ln 5)$

b. $f'(x) = \dfrac{e^x(x - 3)}{2x^4}$
　　$f'(3) = \dfrac{e^3(3 - 3)}{2(3)^4} = 0$
　　$f(3) = \dfrac{e^3}{2(3)^3} = \dfrac{e^3}{54}$
　　$\dfrac{e^3}{54} = 0(3) + b$
　　$b = \dfrac{e^3}{54}$
　　$\therefore y = \dfrac{e^3}{54}$

c. $f'(x) = 2x \cos 3x - 3x^2 \sin 3x$
　　$f'(\frac{\pi}{6}) = 2(\frac{\pi}{6}) \cos (\frac{3\pi}{6}) - 3(\frac{\pi}{6})^2 \sin (\frac{3\pi}{6})$
　　　$= -\dfrac{\pi^2}{12}$
　　$f(\frac{\pi}{6}) = (\frac{\pi}{6})^2 \cos (\frac{3\pi}{6}) = 0$
　　$0 = -\dfrac{\pi^2}{12}(\frac{\pi}{6}) + b$
　　$b = \dfrac{\pi^3}{72}$
　　$\therefore y = -\dfrac{\pi^2}{12}x + \dfrac{\pi^3}{72}$

d. $f'(x) = 3 \sec^2 (3x - 1)$
　　$f'(\pi) = 3 \sec^2 (3\pi - 1) \doteq 10.28$
　　$f(\pi) = \tan (3\pi - 1) \doteq -1.56$
　　$-1.56 = 10.28\pi + b$
　　$b \doteq -33.84$
　　$\therefore y = 10.28x - 33.84$

15. $\lim\limits_{t \to \infty} P(t) = \lim\limits_{t \to \infty} \dfrac{500}{1 + 9e^{-0.01t}} = \dfrac{500}{1 + 9 \lim\limits_{t \to \infty} e^{-0.01t}} = \dfrac{500}{1 + 9(0)} = 500$
The largest possible population is 500.

16. $S'(t) = 90e^{-\frac{t}{9}} + 90te^{-\frac{t}{9}} \cdot (-\frac{1}{9})$
　　$= 10(9 - t)e^{-\frac{t}{9}}$
　　$10(9 - t)e^{-\frac{t}{9}} = 0$ 　　$0 \le t \le 21$
　　$9 - t = 0$ or $e^{-\frac{t}{9}} = 0$
　　　$t = 9$ 　　no solution
　　$S(9) = 90 \cdot 9 \cdot e^{-\frac{9}{9}} \doteq 298 \leftarrow$ local max.
　　$S(0) = 90(0) \cdot e^{-\frac{0}{9}} = 0$
　　$S(21) = 90(21) \cdot e^{-\frac{21}{9}} \doteq 183$
The most pieces, that is 298 pieces, were sold after 9 days.

17. $S'(x) = -2(x - 4)3^{-0.1x} + (-(x - 4)^2)3^{-0.1x}(-0.1\ln 3)$
　　$= (x - 4)3^{-0.1x}(-2 + 0.1\ln 3(x - 4))$
　　$(x - 4)3^{-0.1x}(-2 + 0.1\ln 3(x - 4)) = 0$
　　$x - 4 = 0$ or $3^{-0.1x} = 0$ or $-2 + 0.1\ln 3(x - 4) = 0$
　　　$x = 4$ 　　no solutions 　　　$x = \dfrac{2}{0.1\ln 3} + 4 \doteq 22$
　　$0 \le x \le 30$
　　$S(0) = -(0 - 4)^2 \cdot 3^{-0.1(0)} + 38 = 22$
　　$S(4) = -(4 - 4)^2 \cdot 3^{-0.1(4)} + 38 = 38 \leftarrow$ local max.
　　$S(22) = -(22 - 4)^2 \cdot 3^{-0.1(22)} + 38 \doteq 9 \leftarrow$ local min.
　　$S(30) = -(30 - 4)^2 \cdot 3^{-0.1(30)} + 38 \doteq 13$
The stock will have the highest price 4 days into April and the lowest price 22 days into April.

18. 　　$0 = 1.5^{\frac{t + 22}{5}} - 3^{\frac{t + 5}{10}}$
　　$1.5^{\frac{t + 22}{5}} = 3^{\frac{t + 5}{10}}$
　　$\dfrac{t + 22}{5} \ln 1.5 = \dfrac{t + 5}{10} \ln 3$
　　$(2 \ln 1.5 - \ln 3)t = 5 \ln 3 - 44 \ln 1.5$
　　　$t = \dfrac{5 \ln 3 - 44 \ln 1.5}{2 \ln 1.5 - \ln 3}$
　　　$t \doteq 43$
　　$0 \le t \le 43$
　　$N'(t) = \dfrac{1}{5} \ln 1.5 \cdot 1.5^{\frac{t + 22}{5}} - \dfrac{1}{10} \ln 3 \cdot 3^{\frac{t + 5}{10}}$
　　$0 = \dfrac{1}{5} \ln 1.5 \cdot 1.5^{\frac{t + 22}{5}} - \dfrac{1}{10} \ln 3 \cdot 3^{\frac{t + 5}{10}}$
　　$\ln (\frac{\ln 1.5}{5}) + \dfrac{t + 22}{5} \ln 1.5 = \ln (\frac{\ln 3}{10}) + \dfrac{t + 5}{10} \ln 3$
　　$t(\frac{\ln 1.5}{5} - \frac{\ln 3}{10}) = \ln (\frac{\ln 3}{10}) + \dfrac{5 \ln 3}{10} - \ln (\frac{\ln 1.5}{5}) - \dfrac{22 \ln 1.5}{5}$
　　　$t \doteq 32$
　　$N(0) \doteq 4.22$
　　$N(32) \doteq 21.5 \leftarrow$ local max.
　　$N(43) \doteq 0$
The park is empty at 43°C. There is a maximum number of visitors at 32°C.

19. $A = \dfrac{(4)(4) \sin \theta}{2} = 8 \sin \theta$
　　$A' = 8 \cos \theta$
　　$8 \cos \theta = 0$
　　　$\cos \theta = 0$
　　　　$\theta = 90°$ or $270°$ (not applicable)
An angle of 90° will maximize the area of the triangle.

20. $H'(t) = -10 \sin (\frac{\pi}{15}t - \pi)(\frac{\pi}{15})$
　　$0 = -\dfrac{10\pi}{15} \sin (\frac{\pi}{15}t - \pi)$
　　$\sin (\frac{\pi}{15}t - \pi) = 0$
　　$\dfrac{\pi}{15}t - \pi = -\pi$ or $\dfrac{\pi}{15}t - \pi = 0$ or $\dfrac{\pi}{15}t - \pi = \pi$
　　　$t = 0$ 　　　　　$t = 15$ 　　　　$t = 30$
　　$0 \le t \le 30$
　　$H(0) = 10 \cos (\frac{\pi}{15}(0) - \pi) + 13 = 3 \leftarrow$ local min.
　　$H(15) = 10 \cos (\frac{\pi}{15}(15) - \pi) + 13 = 23 \leftarrow$ local max.
　　$H(30) = 10 \cos (\frac{\pi}{15}(30) - \pi) + 13 = 3 \leftarrow$ local min.
The maximum height is 23 m and the minimum height is 3 m.

21. e is an irrational number that is approximately 2.718. The exponential function, $f(x) = e^x$, is equal to its derivative. That is, $f'(x) = e^x$.

22. He is incorrect. Even when there are no critical values from 2 to 6, the maximum value can be found using the extreme values in the domain.
　　$f(2) = \tan \dfrac{2}{5} \doteq 0.42$
　　$f(6) = \tan \dfrac{6}{5} \doteq 2.57 \leftarrow$ maximum value
The maximum value for $f(x) = \tan \dfrac{x}{5}$ when $2 \le x \le 6$ is 2.57.

23a. $f'(x) = \frac{1}{2}(x+1)^{-\frac{1}{2}} \cdot e^x + \sqrt{x+1} \cdot e^x$

$= \frac{e^x(2x+3)}{2\sqrt{x+1}}$

b. $g'(x) = e^{x^3} \cdot 3x^2 + 4e^{-2x} \cdot (-2)$

$= 3x^2 e^{x^3} - 8e^{-2x}$

c. $y' = 15 \sin^4 x \cos x + 6 \cos^2 x \sin x$

$= 3 \sin x \cos x (5 \sin^3 x + 2 \cos x)$

d. $y' = 3(\cos x + \tan x)^2(-\sin x + \sec^2 x)$

$= 3(\cos x + \tan x)^2(\sec^2 x - \sin x)$

e. $g'(x) = -\sin x \cdot 3 \sin x + \cos x \cdot 3 \cos x$

$= 3(\cos^2 x - \sin^2 x)$

$= 3 \cos 2x$

f. $y' = \cos(e^{\tan x}) \cdot e^{\tan x} \cdot \sec^2 x$

24a. $f'(x) = 2 \sin x \cos x$

$0 = 2 \sin x \cos x$

$\sin x = 0$ or $\cos x = 0$

$x = 0$ or π or 2π $x = \frac{\pi}{2}$ or $\frac{3\pi}{2}$

$f(0) = \sin^2(0) = 0$

$f(\frac{\pi}{2}) = \sin^2(\frac{\pi}{2}) = 1$

$f(\pi) = \sin^2(\pi) = 0$

$f(\frac{3\pi}{2}) = \sin^2(\frac{3\pi}{2}) = 1$

$f(2\pi) = \sin^2(2\pi) = 0$

The max. is 1 and the min. is 0.

b. $f'(x) = -\sin(\sin x) \cdot \cos x$

$0 = -\sin(\sin x) \cos x$

$\sin(\sin x) = 0$ or $\cos x = 0$

$\sin x = 0$ or $\sin x = \pi$ or $\sin x = 2\pi$ $x = \frac{\pi}{2}$ or $\frac{3\pi}{2}$

$x = 0$ or π or 2π

$f(0) = \cos(\sin(0)) = 1$

$f(\frac{\pi}{2}) = \cos(\sin(\frac{\pi}{2})) \doteq 0.54$

$f(\pi) = \cos(\sin(\pi)) = 1$

$f(\frac{3\pi}{2}) = \cos(\sin(\frac{3\pi}{2})) \doteq 0.54$

$f(2\pi) = \cos(\sin(2\pi)) = 1$

The max. is 1 and the min. is 0.54.

25.

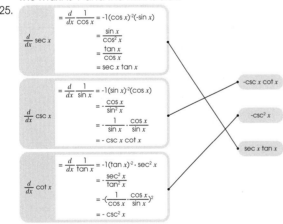

$\frac{d}{dx} \sec x$

$= \frac{d}{dx} \frac{1}{\cos x} = -1(\cos x)^{-2}(-\sin x)$

$= \frac{\sin x}{\cos^2 x}$

$= \frac{\tan x}{\cos x}$

$= \sec x \tan x$

$\frac{d}{dx} \csc x$

$= \frac{d}{dx} \frac{1}{\sin x} = -1(\sin x)^{-2}(\cos x)$

$= -\frac{\cos x}{\sin^2 x}$

$= -\frac{1}{\sin x} \cdot \frac{\cos x}{\sin x}$

$= -\csc x \cot x$

$\frac{d}{dx} \cot x$

$= \frac{d}{dx} \frac{1}{\tan x} = -1(\tan x)^{-2} \cdot \sec^2 x$

$= -\frac{\sec^2 x}{\tan^2 x}$

$= -(\frac{1}{\cos x} \cdot \frac{\cos x}{\sin x})^2$

$= -\csc^2 x$

$-\csc x \cot x$

$-\csc^2 x$

$\sec x \tan x$

26a. $f'(x) = e^x + xe^x$

$f''(x) = e^x + e^x + xe^x$

$= e^x(x+2)$

b. $f'(x) = \frac{xe^x - e^x}{x^2}$

$f''(x) = \frac{(e^x + xe^x - e^x)x^2 - (xe^x - e^x) \cdot 2x}{x^4}$

$= \frac{e^x(x^2 - 2x + 2)}{x^3}$

c. $y' = -\csc^2 x$

$y'' = -2(\csc x)(-\csc x \cot x)$

$= 2(\csc^2 x)(\cot x)$

d. $y' = 4 \sin^3 x \cdot \cos x$

$y'' = 12 \sin^2 x \cos x \cdot \cos x + 4 \sin^3 x (-\sin x)$

$= 4 \sin^2 x (3 \cos^2 x - \sin^2 x)$

e. $f'(x) = e^{\sin x} \cdot \cos x$

$f''(x) = e^{\sin x} \cdot \cos x \cdot \cos x + e^{\sin x}(-\sin x)$

$= e^{\sin x}(\cos^2 x - \sin x)$

f. $y' = e^x \cos x - e^x \sin x$

$y'' = e^x \cos x - e^x \sin x - (e^x \sin x + e^x \cos x)$

$= -2e^x \sin x$

5 Vectors

1. C   2a. D   b. B   c. D

3. C   4. C

5a. B   b. A   c. D   d. C

6.

(-3,5,2)	(2,-5,-3)	(5,-10,-5)
$-3\vec{i} + 5\vec{j} + 2\vec{k}$	$2\vec{i} - 5\vec{j} - 3\vec{k}$	$5\vec{i} - 10\vec{j} - 5\vec{k}$
$\sqrt{38}$	$\sqrt{38}$	$5\sqrt{6}$
$\frac{1}{\sqrt{38}}(-3,5,2)$	$\frac{1}{\sqrt{38}}(2,-5,-3)$	$\frac{1}{5\sqrt{6}}(5,-10,-5)$

7a. $|\vec{x} + \vec{y}|^2 = |\vec{x}|^2 + |\vec{y}|^2 - 2|\vec{x}||\vec{y}| \cos \theta$

$|\vec{x} + \vec{y}|^2 = 7^2 + 5^2 - 2(7)(5) \cos 60°$

$|\vec{x} + \vec{y}|^2 = 39$

$|\vec{x} + \vec{y}| = \sqrt{39}$

b. $\frac{\sin \theta}{|\vec{y}|} = \frac{\sin 60°}{|\vec{x} + \vec{y}|}$

$\frac{\sin \theta}{5} = \frac{\sin 60°}{\sqrt{39}}$

$\theta \doteq 44°$

The direction of $\vec{x} + \vec{y}$ is 44° from $\vec{x}$.

c. $|2\vec{x} - \vec{y}|^2 = |2\vec{x}|^2 + |-\vec{y}|^2 - 2|2\vec{x}||-\vec{y}| \cos \theta$

$|2\vec{x} - \vec{y}|^2 = 14^2 + 5^2 - 2(14)(5) \cos 120°$

$|2\vec{x} - \vec{y}|^2 = 291$

$|2\vec{x} - \vec{y}|^2 = \sqrt{291}$

8a. $|\vec{a} - \vec{b}|^2 = |\vec{a}|^2 + |\vec{b}|^2 - 2|\vec{a}||\vec{b}| \cos \theta$

$|\vec{a} - \vec{b}|^2 = 2^2 + 3^2 - 2(2)(3) \cos 45°$

$|\vec{a} - \vec{b}|^2 \doteq 4.51$

$|\vec{a} - \vec{b}| \doteq 2.12$

b. $\frac{\sin \alpha}{|\vec{a}|} = \frac{\sin 45°}{|\vec{a} - \vec{b}|}$

$\frac{\sin \alpha}{2} = \frac{\sin 45°}{2.12}$

$\alpha \doteq 42°$

$\theta = 180° - 42° = 138°$

The direction of $\vec{a} - \vec{b}$ is 138° from $\vec{b}$.

c. $|3\vec{a} + 2\vec{b}|^2 = |3\vec{a}|^2 + |2\vec{b}|^2 - 2|3\vec{a}||2\vec{b}| \cos \theta$

$|3\vec{a} + 2\vec{b}|^2 = 6^2 + 6^2 - 2(6)(6) \cos 135°$

$|3\vec{a} + 2\vec{b}|^2 \doteq 122.91$

$|3\vec{a} + 2\vec{b}| \doteq 11.09$

9a. $|\vec{a}| = \sqrt{(-25)^2 + 17^2} = \sqrt{914}$

b. $|\vec{b}| = \sqrt{(-25)^2 + (-8)^2} = \sqrt{689}$

c. $\vec{a} + \vec{b} = (-25,17) + (-25,-8) = (-50,9)$

$|\vec{a} + \vec{b}| = \sqrt{(-50)^2 + 9^2} = \sqrt{2581}$

d. $\vec{a} - \vec{b} = (-25,17) - (-25,-8) = (0,25)$

$|\vec{a} - \vec{b}| = \sqrt{0^2 + 25^2} = 25$

10a. $\vec{AB} = \vec{OB} - \vec{OA} = (5,8,2) - (-4,2,-3)$

$= (9,6,5)$

b. $|\vec{AB}| = \sqrt{9^2 + 6^2 + 5^2} = \sqrt{142}$

c. $\frac{1}{\sqrt{142}}(9,6,5)$ d. $-\frac{1}{\sqrt{142}}(9,6,5)$

 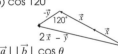

11a. $\vec{a} + 2\vec{b} = (2\vec{i} - \vec{j} - \vec{k}) + 2(3\vec{i} - 2\vec{j} + 4\vec{k})$
$= 2\vec{i} - \vec{j} - \vec{k} + 6\vec{i} - 4\vec{j} + 8\vec{k}$
$= 8\vec{i} - 5\vec{j} + 7\vec{k}$

  b. $3\vec{b} - 2\vec{c} = 3(3\vec{i} - 2\vec{j} + 4\vec{k}) - 2(\vec{i} + 5\vec{k})$
$= 9\vec{i} - 6\vec{j} + 12\vec{k} - 2\vec{i} - 10\vec{k}$
$= 7\vec{i} - 6\vec{j} + 2\vec{k}$

  c. $\vec{a} - \vec{b} + 2\vec{c} = (2\vec{i} - \vec{j} - \vec{k}) - (3\vec{i} - 2\vec{j} + 4\vec{k}) + 2(\vec{i} + 5\vec{k})$
$= 2\vec{i} - \vec{j} - \vec{k} - 3\vec{i} + 2\vec{j} - 4\vec{k} + 2\vec{i} + 10\vec{k}$
$= \vec{i} + \vec{j} + 5\vec{k}$

  d. $2(\vec{a} + \vec{b} - \vec{c}) = 2((2\vec{i} - \vec{j} - \vec{k}) + (3\vec{i} - 2\vec{j} + 4\vec{k}) - (\vec{i} + 5\vec{k}))$
$= 2(4\vec{i} - 3\vec{j} - 2\vec{k})$
$= 8\vec{i} - 6\vec{j} - 4\vec{k}$

12a. $2a - 3(1) = 7$
$a = 5$
$2(2) - 3b = -2$
$b = 2$

  b. $a + 4(-1) = 6$
$a = 10$
$3 + 4b = -1$
$b = -1$
$c + 4(-2) = 2c$
$c = -8$

13a. R^2 ; $\vec{a}$ and $\vec{b}$ are noncollinear.

  b. R^3 ; $\vec{c}$ and $\vec{a}$ are noncollinear.

  c. ✗ ; $\vec{e} = (1,-2,-1)$
$\vec{f} = (-6,12,6) = -6(1,-2,-1)$
$\vec{e}$ and $\vec{f}$ are collinear.

  d. ✗ ; $\vec{g} = (12,9) = 3(4,3)$
$\vec{h} = (-20,-15) = -5(4,3)$
$\vec{g}$ and $\vec{h}$ are collinear.

14a. $a(2,3) + b(-1,4) = (8,1)$
$2a - b = 8$ ① $11a = 33$ ① × 4 + ②
$3a + 4b = 1$ ② $a = 3$
                 $b = -2$
$\therefore \vec{a} = 3(2,3) - 2(-1,4)$

  b. $a(2,-1) + b(-3,2) = (1,0)$
$2a - 3b = 1$ ① $b = 1$ ① + ② × 2
$-a + 2b = 0$ ② $a = 2$
$\therefore \vec{b} = 2(2,-1) + (-3,2)$

  c. $a(2,1,-1) + b(-1,-2,1) + c(1,2,-2) = (8,10,-9)$
$2a - b + c = 8$ ①
$a - 2b + 2c = 10$ ② $-b = 1$ ② + ③
$-a + b - 2c = -9$ ③ $b = -1$
                            $3b - 3c = -12$ ① − ② × 2
                            $3(-1) - 3c = -12$
                            $c = 3$
                            $a = 2$
$\therefore \vec{c} = 2(2,1,-1) - (-1,-2,1) + 3(1,2,-2)$

  d. $a(-1,2,1) + b(0,-1,2) + c(2,-1,-5) = (0,-7,8)$
$-a + 2c = 0$ ①
$2a - b - c = -7$ ②
$a + 2b - 5c = 8$ ③
$4a - 2b - 2c = -14$ ② × 2
$+) \quad a + 2b - 5c = 8$ ③ $-a + 2c = 0$
$\overline{\quad 5a \quad\quad - 7c = -6}$ ④ $-a + 2(-2) = 0$
$-5a + 10c = 0$ ① × 5 $a = -4$
$+) \; 5a - 7c = -6$ ④ $2a - b - c = -7$
$\overline{\quad\quad 3c = -6}$ $2(-4) - b - (-2) = -7$
$c = -2$ $b = 1$
$\therefore \vec{d} = -4(-1,2,1) + (0,-1,2) - 2(2,-1,-5)$

15. $|\vec{v} + \vec{w}|^2 = |\vec{v}|^2 + |\vec{w}|^2 - 2|\vec{v}||\vec{w}| \cos \theta$
$|\vec{v} + \vec{w}|^2 = 350^2 + 120^2 - 2(350)(120) \cos 110°$
$|\vec{v} + \vec{w}|^2 \doteq 165\,629.69$
$|\vec{v} + \vec{w}| \doteq 406.98$
$\dfrac{\sin \alpha}{120} = \dfrac{\sin 110°}{406.98}$
$\sin \alpha \doteq 0.28$
$\alpha \doteq 16°$
bearing: $20° + 16° = 36°$
The resultant velocity is 406.98 km/h, N36°E.

16. $|\vec{s} + \vec{r}|^2 + |\vec{r}|^2 = |\vec{s}|^2$
$|\vec{s} + \vec{r}| = \sqrt{|\vec{s}|^2 - |\vec{r}|^2}$
$|\vec{s} + \vec{r}| = \sqrt{7^2 - 4^2}$
$|\vec{s} + \vec{r}| = \sqrt{33}$
$|\vec{s} + \vec{r}| \doteq 5.74$
$\sin \theta = \dfrac{|\vec{r}|}{|\vec{s}|}$
$\sin \theta = \dfrac{4}{7}$
$\theta \doteq 35°$

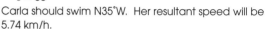

Carla should swim N35°W. Her resultant speed will be 5.74 km/h.

17. • vector addition:
commutative property: $\vec{a} + \vec{b} = \vec{b} + \vec{a}$
associative property: $(\vec{a} + \vec{b}) + \vec{c} = \vec{a} + (\vec{b} + \vec{c})$
distributive property: $k(\vec{a} + \vec{b}) = k\vec{a} + k\vec{b}, \; k \in \mathbb{R}$
• scalar multiplication:
associative law: $m(n\vec{a}) = (mn)\vec{a} = mn\vec{a}$
distributive law: $(m + n)\vec{a} = m\vec{a} + n\vec{a}$

18. Collinear vectors are vectors that are parallel or lie on the same line. They cannot form a spanning set. Coplanar vectors are vectors that are noncollinear and have different directions. They can form a spanning set.

19a. $m(-5,8,13) + n(-4,2,3) = (2,-1,4)$
$-5m - 4n = 2$ ①
$8m + 2n = -1$ ②
$13m + 3n = 4$ ③
$11m = 0$ ① + ② × 2
$m = 0$
$8(0) + 2n = -1$
$n = -\dfrac{1}{2}$
Check in ③:
$13(0) + 3(-\dfrac{1}{2}) = -\dfrac{3}{2} \neq 4$ ← inconsistent result
The vectors do not lie on the same plane.

  b. $m(3,15,3) + n(3,4,-2) = (-2,1,3)$
$3m + 3n = -2$ ①
$15m + 4n = 1$ ②
$3m - 2n = 3$ ③
$5n = -5$ ① − ③
$n = -1$
$3m + 3(-1) = -2$
$m = \dfrac{1}{3}$
Check in ②:
$15(\dfrac{1}{3}) + 4(-1) = 1$ ← consistent result
The vectors lie on the same plane.

  c. $m(-2,3,4) + n(3,1,-5) = (-2,-8,15)$
$-2m + 3n = -2$ ①
$3m + n = -8$ ②
$4m - 5n = 15$ ③
$n = 11$ ① × 2 + ③
$-2m + 3(11) = -2$
$m = \dfrac{35}{2}$
Check in ②:
$3(\dfrac{35}{2}) + 11 = 63\dfrac{1}{2} \neq 8$ ← inconsistent result
The vectors do not lie on the same plane.

d. $m(8,9,31) + n(-1,2,3) = (2,1,5)$

$8m - n = 2$ ①

$9m + 2n = 1$ ②

$31m + 3n = 5$ ③

$55m = 11$ ① × 3 + ③

$m = \dfrac{1}{5}$

$8(\dfrac{1}{5}) - n = 2$

$n = -\dfrac{2}{5}$

Check in ②:

$9(\dfrac{1}{5}) + 2(-\dfrac{2}{5}) = 1$ ← consistent result

The vectors lie on the same plane.

20a. $m\vec{a}$ and $n\vec{b}$ must be equal but opposite vectors.

Since they are collinear, $\vec{a} = k\vec{b}$, $k \in \mathbb{R}$

$mk\vec{b} + n\vec{b} = \vec{0}$

$mk\vec{b} = -n\vec{b}$

$mk = -n \leftarrow k = \dfrac{|\vec{a}|}{|\vec{b}|}$

$m\dfrac{|\vec{a}|}{|\vec{b}|} = -n$

$\therefore m = -n\dfrac{|\vec{b}|}{|\vec{a}|}$, $n = -m\dfrac{|\vec{a}|}{|\vec{b}|}$

b. $\vec{0}$ is directionless and has a magnitude of 0.
Since $\vec{a}$ and $\vec{b}$ are coplanar, they are noncollinear.
The only possible linear combination of two noncollinear vectors to result in $\vec{0}$ is if m and n are both 0.

$\therefore m = 0$, $n = 0$

6 Applications of Vectors

1. D   2. B   3. A   4. C

5a. C   b. C   c. B   d. D

e. B   f. C

6. $|\vec{R}|^2 = 55^2 + 43^2 - 2(55)(43) \cos 100°$

$|\vec{R}| \doteq 75.47$

$\dfrac{\sin \alpha}{55} = \dfrac{\sin 100°}{75.47}$

$\alpha \doteq 46°$

$\beta \doteq 180° - 46° = 134°$

$|\vec{E}| = |\vec{R}| = 75.47$

The resultant is 75.47 N and makes an angle of 46° with the 43 N force and the equilibrant is 75.47 N and makes an angle of 134° with the 43 N force.

7. $|\vec{R}| = 45 \times 9.8 = 441$ N

$\dfrac{\sin 45°}{|\vec{T_1}|} = \dfrac{\sin 80°}{441}$

$|\vec{T_1}| \doteq 316.64$

$\dfrac{\sin 55°}{|\vec{T_2}|} = \dfrac{\sin 80°}{441}$

$|\vec{T_2}| \doteq 366.82$

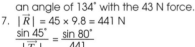

The tensions are 316.64 N and 366.82 N.

8. $|\vec{R}| = 7t \cos 47° + 5t \cos 30°$

$= t(7 \cos 47° + 5 \cos 30°)$

$\doteq 9.1t$

$9.1t = 0.5$

$t \doteq 0.055$ h $\doteq 3.3$ min

It will take approximately 3.3 min.

9. $|\vec{h}| = 90 \cos 50° \doteq 57.85$

$W = (57.85)(150) = 8677.5$

8677.55 J of work was done.

10. $|\vec{r} \times \vec{f}| = |\vec{r}||\vec{f}| \sin \theta = (\dfrac{0.2}{2})(30) \sin 75° \doteq 2.9$

The magnitude of the torque is approximately 2.9 J.

11. The dot product is the scalar projection of one vector onto another. It is a scalar result.
The cross product is the vector product of two vectors. It is perpendicular to both vectors. It is a vector result.

12. - for $0 \le \theta < 90°$, $\cos \theta > 0$, so $\vec{a} \cdot \vec{b} > 0$
- for $\theta = 90°$, $\cos \theta = 0$, so $\vec{a} \cdot \vec{b} = 0$
- for $90° \le \theta < 180°$, $\cos \theta < 0$, so $\vec{a} \cdot \vec{b} < 0$

13. $(\vec{a} \times \vec{b}) \cdot \vec{c}$ is possible because $(\vec{a} \times \vec{b})$ results in a vector, which can then be used to find the dot product with $\vec{c}$. However, in $(\vec{a} \cdot \vec{b}) \times \vec{c}$, $(\vec{a} \cdot \vec{b})$ results in a scalar, which cannot be used to find a cross product with $\vec{c}$. It is therefore meaningless.

14. The cross product $(\vec{a} \times \vec{b})$ is perpendicular to both $\vec{a}$ and $\vec{b}$. Since the dot product of two perpendicular vectors is zero, $\vec{a} \cdot (\vec{a} \times \vec{b}) = 0$ and $\vec{b} \cdot (\vec{a} \times \vec{b}) = 0$.

15. torque $= |\vec{r}||\vec{f}| \sin \theta$

The torque is maximized when the angle θ between the force and the object is 90° ($\sin \theta = 1$), and when the force is applied as far away from the turning point as possible.

16a. $\vec{AB} = (-3 - 2, 2 - 5, 1 - 3) = (-5,-3,-2)$

$\vec{AC} = (2 - 2, 0 - 5, -5 - 3) = (0,-5,-8)$

$\vec{AB} \cdot \vec{AC} = |\vec{AB}||\vec{AC}| \cos \theta$

$\cos \theta = \dfrac{\vec{AB} \cdot \vec{AC}}{|\vec{AB}||\vec{AC}|}$

$= \dfrac{(-5,-3,-2) \cdot (0,-5,-8)}{\sqrt{38}\sqrt{89}}$

$= \dfrac{31}{\sqrt{38}\sqrt{89}}$

$\doteq 0.53$

$\theta \doteq 58°$

The angle at A is 58°.

b. $\vec{AB} \times \vec{AC} = ((-3)(-8) - (-2)(-5), (-2)(0) - (-5)(-8), (-5)(-5) - (-3)(0))$

$= (14,-40,25)$

$|\vec{AB} \times \vec{AC}| = \sqrt{14^2 + (-40)^2 + 25^2} = \sqrt{2421} \doteq 49.20$

The area of the parallelogram is 49.2 units².

17. $\cos \alpha = \dfrac{2}{\sqrt{2^2 + (-3)^2 + 3^2}}$ $\cos \beta = \dfrac{-3}{\sqrt{2^2 + (-3)^2 + 3^2}}$

$\alpha \doteq 65°$ $\beta \doteq 130°$

$\cos \gamma = \dfrac{3}{\sqrt{2^2 + (-3)^2 + 3^2}}$

$\gamma \doteq 50°$

The angles are 65°, 130°, and 50° respectively.

18. $\vec{a} \times \vec{b} = ((-2)(5) - (1)(-1), (1)(2) - (3)(5), (3)(-1) - (-2)(2))$

$= (-9,-13,1)$

$|\vec{a} \times \vec{b}| = \sqrt{(-9)^2 + (-13)^2 + (1)^2} = \sqrt{251}$

unit vector: $\dfrac{1}{\sqrt{251}}(-9,-13,1) = (-\dfrac{9}{\sqrt{251}}, -\dfrac{13}{\sqrt{251}}, \dfrac{1}{\sqrt{251}})$

19. $|\vec{a}| = 1$

$|\vec{b}| = 1$

$|\vec{a} + \vec{b}| = \sqrt{3}$

$|\vec{a} \times \vec{b}|^2 = |\vec{a}|^2 + |\vec{b}|^2 - 2|\vec{a}||\vec{b}| \cos \alpha$

$(\sqrt{3})^2 = 1^2 + 1^2 - 2(1)(1) \cos \alpha$

$3 = 2 - 2 \cos \alpha$

$\cos \alpha = -\dfrac{3 - 2}{2}$

$\alpha = 120°$ $\theta = 180° - 120° = 60°$

$(\vec{a} - 2\vec{b}) \cdot (2\vec{a} + 3\vec{b})$

$= 2\vec{a} \cdot \vec{a} + 3\vec{a} \cdot \vec{b} - 4\vec{a} \cdot \vec{b} - 6\vec{b} \cdot \vec{b}$

$= 2|\vec{a}|^2 - \vec{a} \cdot \vec{b} - 6|\vec{b}|^2$

$= -\vec{a} \cdot \vec{b} - 4$

$= -|\vec{a}||\vec{b}| \cos \theta - 4$

$= -(1)(1) \cos 60° - 4$

$= -\dfrac{1}{2} - 4$

$= -4\dfrac{1}{2}$

ISBN: 978-1-77149-223-2

7 Equations of Lines and Planes

1. B   2. B   3. C   4. C
5. B   6. A   7. C   8. B
9. C

10.

$\vec{r} = (1,2) + s(2,-3),$ $s \in \mathbb{R}$	$\vec{r} = (0,3) + s(1,-2),$ $s \in \mathbb{R}$	$\vec{r} = (0,3) + s(2,-1),$ $s \in \mathbb{R}$
$x = 1 + 2s,$ $y = 2 - 3s,$ $s \in \mathbb{R}$	$x = s,$ $y = 3 - 2s,$ $s \in \mathbb{R}$	$x = 2s,$ $y = 3 - s,$ $s \in \mathbb{R}$
$\dfrac{x-1}{2} = \dfrac{y-2}{-3}$	$x = \dfrac{y-3}{-2}$	$\dfrac{x}{2} = -y + 3$
$3x + 2y - 7 = 0$	$4x + 2y - 6 = 0$	$x + 2y - 6 = 0$
$y = -\dfrac{3}{2}x + \dfrac{7}{2}$	$y = -2x + 3$	$y = -\dfrac{1}{2}x + 3$

11a. • vector form: $\vec{r} = (2,3,5) + s(-1,2,1) + t(4,2,3)$
          $s, t \in \mathbb{R}$
     • Cartesian form: $(-1,2,1) \times (4,2,3) = (4,7,-10)$
          $4(2) + 7(3) - 10(5) + D = 0$
          $D = 21$
     $\therefore 4x + 7y - 10z + 21 = 0$

  b. • parametric form: $x = -\dfrac{5}{4}s + \dfrac{3}{4}t - \dfrac{1}{2},$
          $y = s,$
          $z = t,$
          $s, t \in \mathbb{R}$
     • vector form: $\vec{r} = (-\dfrac{1}{2},0,0) + s(-5,4,0) + t(3,0,4),$
          $s, t \in \mathbb{R}$

12. (9,-16):
     $3s = 9$ $8 - 8s = -16$
     $s = 3$ $s = 3$
     (9,-16) exists on the line.

    (5,7):
     $3s = 5$ $8 - 8s = 7$
     $s = \dfrac{5}{3}$ $s = \dfrac{1}{8}$
     (5,7) does not exist on the line.

13. (Suggested answers)
     $s = 0, t = 0$ $\therefore (2,3,5)$
     $s = 1, t = 0$ $\therefore (1,5,6)$
     $s = 0, t = 1$ $\therefore (6,5,8)$

14. (Suggested answers)
     $(a,b) \cdot (1,-2) = 0$ $\therefore \vec{r} = (-3,2) + s(2,1), s \in \mathbb{R}$
     $a - 2b = 0$ $\therefore x = -3 + 2s, y = 2 + s, s \in \mathbb{R}$
     $(a,b) = (2,1)$ $\therefore x - 2y + 7 = 0$

15. $\theta = \cos^{-1}(\dfrac{(1,5,-1) \cdot (2,3,-5)}{\sqrt{1^2 + 5^2 + (-1)^2}\sqrt{2^2 + 3^2 + (-5)^2}})$
     $\theta = \cos^{-1}(\dfrac{22}{\sqrt{27}\sqrt{38}})$
     $\theta \doteq 47°$

16. (Suggested answers)
     $\overrightarrow{AB} = (-1,-3,-2) = -1(1,3,2)$
     $\overrightarrow{BC} = (0,1,-1)$
     $\therefore \vec{r} = (1,1,1) + s(1,3,2) + t(0,1,-1), s, t \in \mathbb{R}$
     $\therefore x = 1 + s, y = 1 + 3s + t, z = 1 + 2s - t, s, t \in \mathbb{R}$
     $(1,3,2) \times (0,1,-1) = (-5,1,1)$
     $(-5)(1) + 1(1) + 1(1) + D = 0$
          $D = 3$
     $\therefore -5x + y + z + 3 = 0$

17. $\vec{v_1} = (6,-2,0) = 2(3,-1,0)$
     $\vec{v_2} = (6,0,3) = 3(2,0,1)$
     $(3,-1,0) \times (2,0,1) = (-1,-3,2)$
     The normal is $(-1,-3,2)$.

18. $\vec{r} = (2,-4,3) + s(2,4,-2) + t(3,0,-5), s, t \in \mathbb{R}$
     $(2,4,-2) \times (3,0,-5) = (-20,4,-12)$
          $= -4(5,-1,3)$
     $5(2) - 1(-4) + 3(3) + D = 0$
          $D = -23$
     $\therefore 5x - y + 3z - 23 = 0$

19. For π_1: $\vec{n_1} = (1,-1,-1)$
          $|\vec{n_1}| = \sqrt{1^2 + (-1)^2 + (-1)^2} = \sqrt{3}$
     For π_2: $\vec{n_2} = (1,-1,1)$
          $|\vec{n_2}| = \sqrt{1^2 + (-1)^2 + 1^2} = \sqrt{3}$
     $\theta = \cos^{-1}(\dfrac{(1,-1,-1) \cdot (1,-1,1)}{\sqrt{3}\sqrt{3}})$
     $\theta = \cos^{-1}(\dfrac{1}{3})$
     $\theta \doteq 71°$

20. (Suggested answers)
  a. $0x + 3y - 2z = -1$
     y-intercept: $(0,-\dfrac{1}{3},0)$
     z-intercept: $(0,0,\dfrac{1}{2})$
     parallel to x-axis

  b. $x - 2y + 4z = 2$
     x-intercept: $(2,0,0)$
     y-intercept: $(0,-1,0)$
     z-intercept: $(0,0,\dfrac{1}{2})$

21. A: $5 + s = 0$ $16 - 4s = a$
          $s = -5$ $a = 36$
     B: $16 - 4s = 0$ $5 + s = b$
          $s = 4$ $b = 9$
     $\triangle AOB$: $36 \times 9 \div 2 = 162$
     The area of $\triangle AOB$ is 162 units^2.

22. $(3,-2,0) \times (1,1,5) = (-10,-15,5)$
          $= -5(2,3,-1)$
     $2(-2) + 3(1) - 1(5) + D = 0$
          $D = 6$
     $\therefore 2x + 3y - z + 6 = 0$
     x-intercept: $(-3,0,0)$
     y-intercept: $(0,-2,0)$
     z-intercept: $(0,0,6)$
     Volume: $\dfrac{1}{3}((3)(2) \div 2)6 = 6$
     The volume of the pyramid is 6 units^3.

23. Symmetric equations cannot represent a plane in R^3. Cartesian equations cannot represent a line in R^3.

24. - Check whether their direction vectors are parallel by determining if they are scalar multiples of each other.
    - Substitute one point on one line into the other line to check if it is consistent.
    - If one point on one line lies on the other line, then the two lines are parallel and coincident.
    - If one point on one line does not lie on the other line, then the two lines are parallel and non-coincident.

25. The dot product can be used to find the angle between two planes and to determine if they are perpendicular. The cross product can be used to find the normal of two planes and to determine if they are parallel.

26. Case 1: The planes are either the coordinates planes (xy-plane, yz-plane, and xz-plane) or are parallel to them.
    Case 2: The planes are parallel to one of the x-, y-, or z-axes.
    Case 3: The planes either pass through (0,0,0), or cross the x-, y-, and z- axes.

27. Parametric equation: yz-plane: $x = 0$
     $x = 2 + 4s$ $0 = 2 + 4s$
     $y = 4 - 2s$ $s = -\dfrac{1}{2}$
     $z = s$ $y = 4 - 2(-\dfrac{1}{2}) = 5$
                                 $z = -\dfrac{1}{2}$
     The coordinates of the point are $(0,5,-\dfrac{1}{2})$.

28a. For π_1: $\vec{n}_1 = (4,-2,k)$ For π_2: $\vec{n}_2 = (k,-1,1)$

$(4,-2,k) = s(k,-1,1)$

$4 = sk$

$-2 = -s$ $k = s$

$s = 2$ $k = 2$

$\therefore k = 2$

b. $(4,-2,k) \cdot (k,-1,1) = 0$

$4k + 2 + k = 0$

$5k = -2$

$k = -\dfrac{2}{5}$

$\therefore k = -\dfrac{2}{5}$

29. π_1: $x = -4s - 5t$ $a = -4s - 5t$

$y = s + 2t$ $0 = s + 2t$

$z = 2s + 3t$ $1 = 2s + 3t$

$s = 2, t = -1, a = -3$

$\vec{n}_1 = (-4,1,2) \times (-5,2,3) = (-1,2,-3)$

$(1,b,1) \cdot (-1,2,-3) = 0$ $(2,1,c) \cdot (-1,2,-3) = 0$

$-1 + 2b - 3 = 0$ $-2 + 2 - 3c = 0$

$b = 2$ $c = 0$

$\therefore a = -3, b = 2, c = 0$

30. L_1: $x = 2 + 3s$

$y = 1 - 2s$

$z = 2s$

$\overrightarrow{AB} = (2 + 3s - 2, 1 - 2s - 2, 2s - (-16))$

$= (3s, -1 - 2s, 16 + 2s)$

$(3s, -1 - 2s, 16 + 2s) \cdot (3,-2,2) = 0$

$3(3s) - 2(-1 - 2s) + 2(16 + 2s) = 0$

$9s + 2 + 4s + 32 + 4s = 0$

$17s + 34 = 0$

$s = -2$

B: $(2,1,0) + (-2)(3,-2,2) = (-4,5,-4)$

B is $(-4,5,-4)$.

8   Points, Lines, and Planes

1. D   2. D   3. A   4. D

5. A   6. D   7. D   8. D

9A: L: $x = 1 + 4s, y = -2 - 5s, z = 1 - s$

$2(1 + 4s) + (-2 - 5s) + 3(1 - s) - 3 = 0$

$2 + 8s - 2 - 5s + 3 - 3s - 3 = 0$

$0s = 0$

$\therefore$ infinite points of intersection

B: L: $x = 1 + 2s, y = 2 - 3s, z = 5 - 5s$

$3(1 + 2s) + 2(2 - 3s) - (5 - 5s) - 7 = 0$

$3 + 6s + 4 - 6s - 5 + 5s - 7 = 0$

$s = 1$

$(3,-1,0)$

$\therefore$ one point of intersection

C: L: $x = 2 + 7s, y = -2 - 3s, z = -1 - 2s$

$(2 + 7s) + (-2 - 3s) + 2(-1 - 2s) - 3 = 0$

$2 + 7s - 2 - 3s - 2 - 4s - 3 = 0$

$0s = 5$

$\therefore$ no points of intersection

B ; C ; A

10a. $(2,-4,-8) = -2(-1,2,4)$

$\vec{a}$: $x = -2 - s, y = 1 + 2s, z = 3 + 4s$

$-1 = -2 - s$ $\rightarrow s = -1$

$5 = 1 + 2s$ $\rightarrow s = 2$

$11 = 3 + 4s$ $\rightarrow s = 2$

The lines are parallel and there are no intersections.

b. $(2,2,-6) = -2(-1,-1,3)$

$\vec{b}$: $x = 1 - t, y = 4 - t, z = 4 + 3t$

$3 = 1 - t$ $\rightarrow t = -2$

$6 = 4 - t$ $\rightarrow t = -2$

$-2 = 4 + 3t$ $\rightarrow t = -2$

The lines are parallel and coincident.

c. $(-1,-1,3) \neq k(2,-4,-8)$

$\vec{b}$: $x = 1 - t, y = 4 - t, z = 4 + 3t$

$\vec{c}$: $x = -1 + 2u, y = 5 - 4u, z = 11 - 8u$

$\left.\begin{array}{l} 1 - t = -1 + 2u \\ 4 - t = 5 - 4u \\ 4 + 3t = 11 - 8u \end{array}\right\} \begin{array}{l} u = \dfrac{1}{2} \\ t = 1 \end{array}$

$\vec{b}$: $x = 0, y = 3, z = 7$

$\vec{c}$: $x = 0, y = 3, z = 7$

The lines intersect at $(0,3,7)$.

d. $(-1,2,4) \neq k(2,2,-6)$

$\vec{a}$: $x = -2 - s, y = 1 + 2s, z = 3 + 4s$

$\vec{d}$: $x = 3 + 2v, y = 6 + 2v, z = -2 - 6v$

$-2 - s = 3 + 2v$

$\left.\begin{array}{l} 1 + 2s = 6 + 2v \\ 3 + 4s = -2 - 6v \end{array}\right\} \begin{array}{l} s = 1 \\ v = -\dfrac{3}{2} \end{array}$

$\vec{a}$: $x = -3, y = 3, z = 7$

$\vec{d}$: $x = 0, y = 3, z = 7$

The lines are skew.

11.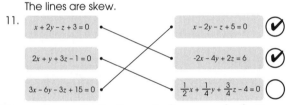

12a. $x + 3y - z + 2 = 0$ ①

$x - 3y + z - 4 = 0$ ②

$6y - 2z + 6 = 0$ ① − ②

$6y - 2z + 6 = 0$ $z = s$

$y = \dfrac{1}{3}s - 1$

$x + 3(\dfrac{1}{3}s - 1) - s + 2 = 0$

$x = 1$

$\therefore$ line of intersection:

$x = 1, y = \dfrac{1}{3}s - 1, z = s$

b. $2x - y + z - 3 = 0$ ①

$x - 3z + 7 = 0$ ②

$-y + 7z - 17 = 0$ ① − ② × 2

$-y + 7s - 17 = 0$ $z = s$

$y = 7s - 17$

$2x - (7s - 17) + s - 3 = 0$

$x = 3s - 7$

$\therefore$ line of intersection:

$x = 3s - 7, y = 7s - 17, z = s$

c. $x + 2y - 4z + 11 = 0$ ①

$-2x + 5y - z + 5 = 0$ ②

$3x - 6z + 15 = 0$ ③

④ $0x - 6y + 6z - 18 = 0$ ③ − ① × 3

⑤ $0x + 9y - 9z + 27 = 0$ ② + ① × 2

⑥ $0x - y + z - 3 = 0$ ④ ÷ 6

⑦ $0x + y - z + 3 = 0$ ⑤ ÷ 9

$0x + 0y + 0z = 0$ ⑥ + ⑦

$-y + t - 3 = 0$ ⑥: $z = t$

$y = t - 3$

$3x - 6t + 15 = 0$

$x = 2t - 5$

$\therefore$ line of intersection: $x = 2t - 5, y = t - 3, z = t$

d. $3x + y - 2z - 7 = 0$ ①

$x - y + z + 2 = 0$ ②

$x + y + 3z = 0$ ③

④ $0x + 4y - 5z - 13 = 0$ ① − ② × 3

⑤ $0x - 2y - 2z + 2 = 0$ ② − ③

$0x + 0y - 9z - 9 = 0$ ④ + ⑤ × 2

$z = -1$

$-2y - 2(-1) + 2 = 0$

$y = 2$

$x + 2 + 3(-1) = 0$

$x = 1$

$\therefore$ point of intersection $(1,2,-1)$

13. Cartesian form: $2x - 3y + 19 = 0$

$d = \dfrac{|2(1) + (-3)(4) + 19|}{\sqrt{2^2 + (-3)^2}}$

$d = \dfrac{9}{\sqrt{13}}$

$d \doteq 2.50$

14. $d = \dfrac{|3(1) + 2(4) + (-5)6 + 8|}{\sqrt{3^2 + 2^2 + (-5)^2}}$

$d = \dfrac{11}{\sqrt{38}}$

$d \doteq 1.78$

15. $\overrightarrow{QP} = (3 - 2, 1 - 4, 6 - 3) = (1,-3,3)$

$d = \dfrac{|(-1,5,-2) \times (1,-3,3)|}{|(-1,5,-2)|}$

$d = \dfrac{|(9,1,-2)|}{|(-1,5,-2)|}$

$d = \dfrac{\sqrt{86}}{\sqrt{30}}$

$d \doteq 1.69$

The least amount of cable required is 1.69 km.

16. $\vec{n} = (2,1,2) \times (3,-5,2) = (12,2,-13)$

π_1: $12(1) + 2(5) - 13(8) + D = 0$

$D = 82$

$\therefore 12x + 2y - 13z + 82 = 0$

$d = \dfrac{|12(3) + 2(-2) - 13(0) + 82|}{\sqrt{12^2 + 2^2 + (-13)^2}}$

$d = \dfrac{114}{\sqrt{317}}$

$d \doteq 6.40$

The least distance between the ski lifts is 6.4 m.

17a. • The line intersects the plane at exactly one point.
  • The line does not intersect the plane because it is parallel to the plane.
  • The line lies on the plane.

b. • The lines intersect at a point.
  • The lines are coincident.
  • The lines are parallel.
  • The lines are skew.

c. • The two planes intersect along a line.
  • The two planes are parallel.
  • The two planes are coincident.

d. • The three planes intersect at a point.
  • The three planes intersect along a line.
  • The three planes are coincident.
  • A triangle prism is formed by the three planes.
  • Two parallel planes intersect a third plane.
  • Two coincident planes intersect a third plane along a line.
  • Two coincident planes are parallel to a third plane.
  • Three planes are parallel.

18. A consistent system has either one solution or an infinite number of solutions.
An inconsistent system has no solutions.

19. Any lines can extend to infinity on both ends. Therefore, it is impossible for non-parallel lines to not intersect in R^2.

20. No, it is not. Any plane can extend to infinity. Therefore, two non-parallel planes in R^3 must intersect.

21a. $x - 3y + z = 2$ ①
  $2x + y - z = -2$ ②
  $3x - 2y + pz = q$ ③
  ④ $0x + 7y - 3z = -6$ ② – ① × 2
  ⑤ $0x + 7y + (p - 3)z = q - 6$ ③ – ① × 3
  $0x + 0y + (-3 - (p - 3))z = -6 - (q - 6)$ ④ – ⑤
  $pz = q$
  $z = \dfrac{q}{p}$

1 solution when $z = \dfrac{q}{p}$

$\therefore p \neq 0, q \in \mathbb{R}$

b. no solutions when $0z = n$ ← non-zero
  $\therefore p = 0, q \neq 0$

c. infinitely many solutions when $0z = 0$
  $\therefore p = 0, q = 0$

22. Line of intersection:
  $3x + y - 2z = 3$ ①
  $2y + z = 1$ ②
  $3x + 5y = 5$ ① + ② × 2
  $3x + 5s = 5$ $y = s$
  $x = -\dfrac{5}{3}s + \dfrac{5}{3}$
  $z = -2s + 1$

Direction vector:
$(-\dfrac{5}{3}, 1, -2) \to (-5,3,-6)$

Equation of the line:
$\vec{r} = (2,-1,3) + s(-5,3,-6)$
$\therefore \vec{r} = (2,-1,3) + s(-5,3,-6)$

23a. P_1: $x = 0, y = 0$
  $0 + 2(0) - z + 9 = 0$
  $z = 9$
  $\therefore (0,0,9)$
  $d = \dfrac{|1(0) + 2(0) - 1(9) + 5|}{\sqrt{1^2 + 2^2 + (-1)^2}}$
  $d = \dfrac{4}{\sqrt{6}}$
  $d \doteq 1.63$

b. P_1: $x = 0, y = 0$
  $2(0) - (0) + z - 6 = 0$
  $z = 6$
  $\therefore (0,0,6)$
  $d = \dfrac{|4(0) - 2(0) + 2(6) - 3|}{\sqrt{4^2 + (-2)^2 + 2^2}}$
  $d = \dfrac{9}{\sqrt{24}}$
  $d \doteq 1.84$

Cumulative Test

1. C   2. B   3. B   4. D
5. C   6. A   7. C   8. B
9. C   10. A   11. B
12a. 7   b. -6
13a. $6x^2 - 2x + 1$ b. $6x^2 - 2x$
  c. $\dfrac{1}{\sqrt{x}}$ d. $\dfrac{-2x}{(x^2 - 1)^2}$
  e. $\dfrac{2x - 1}{2\sqrt{x^2 - x + 1}}$ f. $5e^{5x}$
  g. $3^x(x \ln 3 + 1)$ h. $-3 \sec^2 3x$
14a. $6(x - 1)^{-3}$ b. 4
  c. $2 \cos (x^2 - x) - (2x - 1)^2 \sin (x^2 - x)$
  d. $-4 (\cos^2 x - \sin^2 x)$
15a. -3   b. $\ln 2$
16a. $(\dfrac{1}{5}, -\dfrac{1}{5})$ b. $(2, \dfrac{1}{4})$
17a. $x = 0$ is a local maximum.
  b. There is no local maximum or minimum.
18. local max. at $(-\dfrac{5}{3}, 9\dfrac{13}{27})$
  local min. at $(1,0)$
  point of inflection at $(-\dfrac{1}{3}, 4\dfrac{20}{27})$

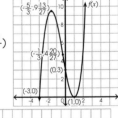

19.

20. $5(1,-2,5) + 7(-3,1,2)$ 21. $42°$
22. Parametric equations:
  $x = 7 - 9s$
  $y = 4s$
  $z = 5 - 2s$

Symmetric equations:
$\dfrac{x - 7}{-9} = \dfrac{y}{4} = \dfrac{z - 5}{-2}$

23. Vector equation:
  $\vec{r} = (4,-2,3) + s(1,1,1) + t(2,3,2)$
  Cartesian equation:
  $-x + z + 1 = 0$

24. Vector equation:
$\vec{r} = (4,7,-1) + s(4,8,-4) + t(1,-2,-3)$
Parametric equations:
$x = 4 + 4s + t$
$y = 7 + 8s - 2t$
$z = -1 - 4s - 3t$
Cartesian equation:
$-4x + y - 2z + 7 = 0$

25. 1.64

26. $x = 5, y = s, z = 1 - s$
Two planes are coincident and intersect the third plane along the line $\vec{r} = (5,0,1) + s(0,1,-1)$.

27a. The lines are skew.
b. The planes intersect along $\vec{r} = (1,-3,0) + s(2,11,3)$.

28a. The average rate of change is 1000 cats/year.
b. The instantaneous rate of change is 800 cats/year.

29. The price should be $15 to maximize their revenue.

30a. The average rate of change is -9890 bugs/week.
b. The instantaneous rate of change is -1624 bugs/week.

31. The player should practise for 1.41 hours. The maximum percent of successful baskets is 12.87%.

32. The radius and height should be 3.91 cm and 7.81 cm respectively.

33. The tensions in the ropes are 505.87 N and 644.67 N.

34. Irene should pull 207.73 N at S60°W.

35. The nth derivative will be $n(n-1)(n-2)...(1)a$.
Since $n > 0$ and $a > 0$, the leading coefficient of each derivative will be positive.

36. $f'(x) = \cos x$
$f''(x) = -\sin x$
$f'''(x) = -\cos x$
$f''''(x) = \sin x \leftarrow$ same as $f(x)$
The derivatives repeat every 4 derivatives.
∴ When n is a multiple of 4 (i.e. 4, 8, 12...etc.), then the nth derivative is equivalent to $f(x)$.

37. 1. three lines intersecting at a point
2. two parallel lines intersecting a third line at two points
3. three lines intersecting at three points
4. three parallel lines, so no points of intersection
5. three coincident lines, so infinitely many solutions
6. two coincident lines and a third parallel line
7. two coincident lines intersecting a third line at a point

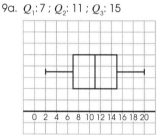

38. 1. all three planes intersecting along a line
2. two planes are coincident and intersecting a third plane along a line
3. three coincident planes

39a. $4(3x^2 - 5x + 1)^3(6x - 5)$ b. $(2\sin x + \cos x)e^{2x-1}$
c. $x^2(3^x)(3 + x \ln 3)$
d. $-2(4x - 5) \sin (2x^2 - 5x + 3) \cos (2x^2 - 5x + 3)$

40. $a = -1, b = -4$

41a. The max. value is 4 and the min. value is 3.
b. The max. value is $\sqrt{2}$ or 1.41, and the min. value is -1.

42. $a = 2, b = -6, c = 8$

43. (Suggested answers)

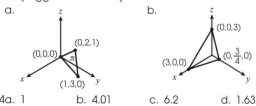

44a. 1   b. 4.01   c. 6.2   d. 1.63
45. The area of the triangle is 38.12 units^2.

Mathematics of Data Management

1 One-variable Statistics

1a. C   b. B   c. D
d. C   e. B   2. D
3. B   4. B   5. A
6. A   7. C

8a. Set A: mean = 19.8, median = 20, mode = 18, 20, 21, 22
Set B: mean = 21, median = 21.5, mode = 24
b. Set A: $\sigma \doteq 1.66$ Set B: $\sigma \doteq 2.72$
Set A is more consistent because the standard deviation is smaller.
c. Set A: $z = \dfrac{17 - 19.8}{1.66} \doteq -1.69$ Set B: $z = \dfrac{17 - 21}{2.72} \doteq -1.47$
$z = \dfrac{24 - 19.8}{1.66} \doteq 2.53$ $z = \dfrac{24 - 21}{2.72} \doteq 1.10$

9a. Q_1: 7 ; Q_2: 11 ; Q_3: 15

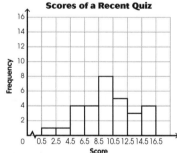

b. 5: first quartile ; 10: second quartile ; 16: fourth quartile ; 20: fourth quartile
c. 6.5 ; 15 ; 18
d. 4: 10th ; 14: 70th ; 16: 80th ; 18: 90th

10a. bin width = $\dfrac{15 - 1}{8} = 1.75 \doteq 2$

Score	Tally	Frequency
0.5 – 2.5	I	1
2.5 – 4.5	I	1
4.5 – 6.5	IIII	4
6.5 – 8.5	IIII	4
8.5 – 10.5	HH III	8
10.5 – 12.5	HH	5
12.5 – 14.5	III	3
14.5 – 16.5	IIII	4

Scores of a Recent Quiz

b. $\mu \doteq 9.67$
$\sigma^2 = \dfrac{\Sigma(x - \mu)^2}{N} \doteq 12.62$
The variance is 12.62.

11. $\mu = \dfrac{16(27) + 14(32) + 12(37) + 13(42) + 11(47) + 13(52) + 6(57) + 4(62) + 2(67)}{91}$
$= \dfrac{3787}{91}$
$\doteq 41.62$
The median is the 46th datum. It belongs in the 40-44 age range. The approximate value of the median is 42.
The mean age is 41.62. The median age is 42.

12. $Q_1 = 61$ $Q_3 = (90 + 92) \div 2 = 91$
$IQR = 91 - 61 = 30$
$Q_1 - 1.5 \, IQR = 61 - 1.5 \times 30 = 16$
$Q_3 + 1.5 \, IQR = 91 + 1.5 \times 30 = 136$
x is an outlier when $x < 16$ or $x > 136$.
Yes, there is. 145 decibels is an outlier.

13a. - convenient overview of the distribution of the scores
- reveals trends in the data
b. - shows the running total of the frequencies from lowest score up
c. - shows the frequency of a score as a fraction of all scores

14. An index relates the value of a variable to a base level, allowing for comparisons and understanding the change in value.
(Suggested answer)
An example of an index is the consumer price index.

15. Sample standard deviation has $n - 1$ as the denominator instead of N, for n and N representing the number of data. This is because a sample tends to underestimate the deviation, so the denominator is one less to compensate.

16. A z-score represents the number of standard deviations a value is from the mean.

17. The standard deviation accounts for all the data in a set but can be easily skewed by outliers. The semi-interquartile range does not account for all the data in a set but is not affected by outliers.

18. (Suggested answers)
   a. Sample all the students in the cafeteria.
   b. Sample all the students whose student numbers end in 1.
   c. Sample 10 students from each grade.
   d. Sample all the students in a class.
   e. Pick 4 random classes and survey 5 students in each class.
   f. Sent out surveys to all the students and collect the responses.

19a. There is a sampling bias. People in Ontario are more likely to support their local team. To avoid bias, survey Canadians from different provinces as well.

   b. There is a measurement bias. There is a leading question; it suggests that the only choices for the best Canadian province are Nova Scotia and New Brunswick. To avoid bias, remove the mention of any specific provinces in the question.

   c. There is a response bias. Customers are more likely to give positive reviews due to the discount incentive. To avoid bias, remove the discount offer.

20a. $3.2 = \dfrac{120 - \mu}{4.5}$
   $\mu = 105.6$

   b. $-1.95 = \dfrac{65.25 - 75}{s}$
   $s = 5$

21. Since the mode is 52, x is less than 10.
For the median to be 53, there must be an equal number of values above and below 53. There are 15 values less than 53 and 8 values greater than 53. So x is greater than 7.
$\therefore 7 < x < 10$
The possible values are 8 or 9.

22. $IQR = 15 \times 2 = 30$
   $14 < Q_1 - 1.5 \times 30$ \qquad $138 > Q_3 + 1.5 \times 30$
   $14 < Q_1 - 45$ \qquad $138 > Q_3 + 45$
   $59 < Q_1$ \qquad $93 > Q_3$
   $Q_3 - Q_1 = 30$
   $\therefore Q_1 = 60, Q_3 = 90$ or $Q_1 = 61, Q_3 = 91$ or $Q_1 = 62, Q_3 = 92$

23. median $= 165$ cm ; $Q_1 = 162.5$ cm ; $Q_3 = 167.5$ cm
interquartile range $= 167.5 - 162.5 = 5$

2 Two-variable Statistics

1. B	2. C	3. A	4. D
5. D	6. D	7. D	8. C

9a. linear ; -1 \qquad b. linear ; $r = 0$
   c. linear ; $r = -0.5$ \qquad d. exponential ; $r^2 = 0.2$
   e. cubic ; $r^2 = 1$ \qquad f. quadratic ; $r^2 = 0.8$

10a. B ; $r = \dfrac{3(477) - (24)(72)}{\sqrt{(3(210) - (24)^2)(3(2274) - (72)^2)}}$
   $\doteq -0.9986$
   $r = -0.9986$

   b. A ; $a = \dfrac{3(477) - (24)(72)}{3(210) - (24)^2}$
   $= -5.5$
   A ; $b = 24 - (-5.5)(8)$
   $= 68$
   $a = -5.5$; $b = 68$; $y = -5.5x + 68$

11a. The slope of the line is 0.12. This suggests that for every 1% increase in the smoking rate, the heart disease rate increases by 0.12%.

   b. The r value suggests that there is a weak positive linear correlation between the smoking rate and the heart disease rate.

12a.

Time x	Calories y	x^2	y^2	xy
14	71	196	5041	994
19	107	361	11 449	2033
25	142	625	20 164	3550
23	113	529	12 769	2599
10	67	100	4489	670
18	91	324	8281	1638
29	159	841	25 281	4611
34	176	1156	30 976	5984
Sum: 172	926	4132	118 450	22 079

$r = \dfrac{8(22\ 079) - (172)(926)}{\sqrt{(8(4132) - (172)^2)(8(118\ 450) - (926)^2)}}$
$\doteq 0.9814$

   b. The two variables have a very strong positive linear relationship.

   c.

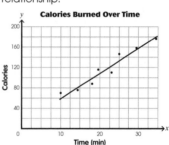

   d. $a = \dfrac{8(22\ 079) - (172)(926)}{8(4132) - (172)^2} = 5$
   $b = \dfrac{926}{8} - 5(\dfrac{172}{8}) = 8.25$
   $\therefore y = 5x + 8.25$

   e. $x = 20$, $y = 5(20) + 8.25 = 108.25$
   $x = 45$, $y = 5(45) + 8.25 = 233.25$
   It is estimated that 108.25 calories are burned at 20 minutes and 233.25 calories are burned at 45 minutes.
   (Suggested answer)
   The results are reasonable. The line of best fit is suitable for both interpolation and extrapolation.

13a. This is an accidental relationship. There is no direct way for the sales of yoga mats to affect the number of traffic tickets. This correlation is likely accidental.

   b. This is a cause-and-effect relationship. The increase in toxic dumping directly causes the decrease in fish population.

   c. This is a reverse cause-and-effect relationship. It is the temperature increase that causes the increased sales of ice cream, not the reverse.

   d. This is a common-cause relationship. The increase in both cyclists and pedestrians is likely due to a common cause, such as an increase in temperature.

e. This is a presumed relationship. While it is likely that as the basketball viewership increases, fewer people will visit the beach, this relationship cannot be directly observed.

14. (Suggested answer)
The statement is not necessarily true. This is because the correlation is only made with 3 data points, which is insufficient to draw a conclusion.

15. A control group accounts for extraneous variables by comparing the experimental group and the control group. The control group is kept as similar as possible to the experimental group. As the independent variable changes in the experimental group, any difference can be attributed to the changes in the independent variable and not to the extraneous variables.

16. The correlation coefficient applies to linear regressions while the correlation of determination applies to non-linear regressions. The correlation coefficient ranges from -1 to 1, while the correlation of determination ranges from 0 to 1.

17. While a regression might be a good fit over a set of data, extrapolation outside of data may not always be accurate. For example, an exponential regression might generate very large values and a quadratic regression might generate negative values that are not applicable.

18a. The sample size is too small to generate a valid statistical claim.

b. There is an intentional bias of sampling only bestselling books.

c. A hidden variable is possible. The experiment does not account for other aspects of the players, such as their gaming skills and enjoyment of video games.

19. A hidden variable is an extraneous variable that is difficult to detect. To detect hidden variables, look for unusual patterns or analyze additional data.

20a. linear: $y = -0.8835x + 76.575$; 0.9334
quadratic: $y = 0.0169x^2 - 1.7334x + 83.293$; 0.9963
cubic: $y = -0.0002x^3 + 0.0338x^2 - 2.0581x + 84.467$; 0.9985
exponential: $y = 78.643e^{-0.016x}$; 0.9758

b. The cubic regression has the highest r^2 value, so it is the best fit for the set of data.

c. Initial values:
linear: 76.575 ; quadratic: 83.293 ; cubic: 84.467 ;
exponential: 78.643
The cubic model gives the closest initial value of 84°C. The cubic regression models the initial value the best.

d. $x = 100$:
linear: -11.775 ; quadratic: 78.953 ; cubic: 16.657 ;
exponential: 15.878
The cubic and exponential models give the most reasonable values. The quadratic model gives a value that is too high and the linear model gives a value that is too low. The cubic and exponential models are the best for extrapolation.

e. (Suggested answer)
The cubic model is the best. This is because its r^2 value is the highest and the initial value is the closest to 84. Also, it extrapolates the data better than the other models.

3 Permutations and Counting

1a. C
b. B
c. B
2. D
3. B
4. A
5. C
6. B
7. D
8. C
9. D
10. B

11a.
```
                1
              1   1
            1   2   1
          1   3   3   1
        1   4   6   4   1
      1   5  10  10   5   1
    1   6  15  20  15   6   1
  1   7  21  35  35  21   7   1
1   8  28  56  70  56  28   8   1
```

b. 3 ; 4 ; 1

c. $t_{5,2}$; $t_{8,4} + t_{8,5}$; $t_{14,9} + t_{14,10}$

12. 6 ; 25 ; 2 ; 34 ; 80 ; 167

13a. $= \dfrac{5!}{(5 - 0)!}$

$= \dfrac{5!}{5!}$

$= 1$

b. $= \dfrac{8!}{(8 - 2)!}$

$= \dfrac{8!}{6!}$

$= \dfrac{8 \times 7 \times 6!}{6!}$

$= 8 \times 7$

$= 56$

c. $= \dfrac{(7 \times 6 \times 5 \times 4!)(5 \times 4 \times 3!)}{4!3!}$

$= 7 \times 6 \times 5 \times 5 \times 4$

$= 4200$

d. $= \dfrac{3!}{(3 - 3)!}$

$= \dfrac{3!}{0!}$

$= \dfrac{3 \times 2 \times 1}{1}$

$= 6$

14a. $\dfrac{8!}{4!}$

b. $\dfrac{8!}{5!3!}$

c. $\dfrac{10!}{5!7!}$

d. $\dfrac{9!3!}{7!}$

e. $\dfrac{10!4!}{7!5!}$

15a. $n + 1 = 12$
$n = 11$

b.
$\dfrac{(n + 1)!}{(n + 1 - 3)!} = \dfrac{12(n - 1)!}{(n - 1 - 2)!}$

$\dfrac{(n + 1)!}{(n - 2)!} = \dfrac{12(n - 1)!}{(n - 3)!}$

$(n + 1)(n)(n - 1) = 12(n - 1)(n - 2)$

$n^2 + n = 12n - 24$

$n^2 - 11n + 24 = 0$

$(n - 3)(n - 8) = 0$

$n = 3$ or $n = 8$

16.
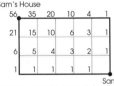

Sam's House

56	35	20	10	4	1
21	15	10	6	3	1
6	5	4	3	2	1
1	1	1	1	1	

Sam

There are 56 possible routes.

17. $\dfrac{6!}{4!2!} = 15$
They can occur in 15 orders.

18a. Indirect method:
(All possible) – (5 and 6 together)
$5! - 4! \times 2$
$= 120 - 48$
$= 72$
72 numbers can be made.

b. The first digit must be 8 or 9.
$2 \times 4 \times 3 \times 2 \times 1$
$= 48$
48 numbers can be made.

c. The last digit must be 6 or 8.
$4 \times 3 \times 2 \times 1 \times 2$
$= 48$
48 numbers can be made.

d. The first digit must be 5, 6, or 7 and the last digit must be 5, 7, or 9.
First digit 5: $1 \times 3 \times 2 \times 1 \times 2 = 12$
First digit 6: $1 \times 3 \times 2 \times 1 \times 3 = 18$
First digit 7: $1 \times 3 \times 2 \times 1 \times 2 = 12$
Total: $12 + 18 + 12 = 42$
42 numbers can be made.

19a. $\frac{10!}{3!2!2!} = 151\ 200$
151 200 arrangements can be made.

b. Consonants: S, C, F, L
$\frac{9!}{2!2!2!} + \frac{9!}{3!2!} + \frac{9!}{3!2!2!} + \frac{9!}{3!2!2!}$
$= 45\ 360 + 30\ 240 + 15\ 120 + 15\ 120$
$= 105\ 840$
105 840 arrangements can be made.

c. Consider "LESS" as a single letter.
Remaining letters: S, U, C, C, F, U
$\frac{7!}{2!2!} = 1260$
1260 arrangements can be made.

d. U _ _ _ _ _ _ _ _ U
$\frac{1 \times 8! \times 1}{3!2!} = 3360$
3360 arrangements can be made.

20.
There are 70 paths.

21.
$4 + 13 + 9 + 1 = 27$
There are 27 paths.

22. 5^{40}; The test can be answered in 5^{40} ways.

23a. $6! = 720$
There are 720 different formations.

b. $5!2! = 240$
There are 240 different formations.

c. Indirect method:
(All formations) – (Hannah with Jen) – (Hannah with Anna) + (Hannah between Anna and Jen)
$6! - 5!2! - 5!2! + 4!2!$
$= 720 - 240 - 240 + 48$
$= 288$
There are 288 different formations.

24. General formula for moving m blocks south and n blocks west: $\frac{(m + n)!}{m!n!}$
$\frac{(3 + 8)!}{3!8!} \times \frac{(3 + 2)!}{3!2!} \times \frac{(2 + 6)!}{2!6!}$
$= \frac{11!}{3!8!} \times \frac{5!}{3!2!} \times \frac{8!}{2!6!}$
$= 46\ 200$
There are 46 200 possible pathways.

25. $_nP_r = \frac{n!}{(n - r)!} = \frac{(n)(n - 1)(n - 2)...(1)}{(n - r)(n - r - 1)...(1)} = (n)(n - 1)(n - 2)...(n - r + 1)$
Since $n > r$, $_nP_r$ will be a product of whole numbers.
Yes, all permutations $_nP_r$ are whole numbers.

26. $_nP_n = n!$
$\frac{n!}{(n - n)!} = n!$
$\frac{n!}{0!} = n!$
$\therefore 0! = 1$

27. • powers of 2:
The sum of the terms in row n of Pascal's triangle in 2^n.
• triangular numbers:
The nth triangular number is equal to the term $t_{n + 1, 2}$ in Pascal's triangle.
• perfect squares:
Each perfect square greater than 1 is equal to $t_{n, 2} + t_{n + 1, 2}$ for $n > 1$.

28. It may be more efficient and require fewer steps to use an indirect method.
(Suggested answer)
For example, there are 4 balls that can be arranged such that 2 of the balls cannot be next to each other.
Direct method:
$(1 \times 2 \times 2 \times 1) + (2 \times 1 \times 1 \times 1) + (1 \times 2 \times 1 \times 1) + (1 \times 2 \times 2 \times 1) = 12$
Indirect method:
$4! - 3!2! = 12$
So the indirect method is faster.

29a.
There are 1450 possible routes.

b.
There are 250 possible routes.

30. Last digit 5: $6 \times 6 \times 5 \times 1 = 180$
Last digit 0: $7 \times 6 \times 5 \times 1 = 210$
Total: $180 + 210 = 390$
390 four-digit numbers can be formed.

31. (food cargo cars) × (furniture cargo cars) × (remaining cars)
$(5 \times 4) \times (4 \times 3) \times (6!)$
$= 172\ 800$
The cargo cars can be arranged in 172 800 ways.

32a. $\frac{8!}{8} = 7! = 5040$
They can be seated in 5040 ways.

b. $\frac{4!}{4} \times 2!2!2!2! = 3!2!2!2!2! = 96$
They can be seated in 96 ways.

4 Combinations and Binomial Theorem

1. C   2. B   3. A   4. C
5. D   6. C   7. C
8a. B   b. B   9. B
10a.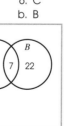
78 ; 56 ; 100

b.
11 ; 3 ; 150

11a. $\frac{10!}{3!(10 - 3)!} = \frac{10!}{3!7!} = 120$ b. $\frac{9!}{7!(9 - 7)!} = \frac{9!}{7!2!} = 36$

c. $\frac{12!}{4!(12 - 4)!} = \frac{12!}{4!8!} = 495$ d. $\frac{8!}{8!(8 - 8)!} = \frac{8!}{8!0!} = 1$

e. $\frac{6!}{0!(6 - 0)!} = \frac{6!}{0!6!} = 1$ f. $\frac{10!}{7!(10 - 7)!} = \frac{10!}{7!3!} = 120$

ANSWERS

12.

Single Term	$_{16}C_4$	$_{22}C_{14}$	$_{17}C_3$
Addition	$_{15}C_3 + _{15}C_4$	$_{21}C_{13} + _{21}C_{14}$	$_{16}C_2 + _{16}C_3$
Subtraction	$_{17}C_4 - _{16}C_3$ or $_{17}C_5 - _{16}C_5$	$_{23}C_{14} - _{22}C_{13}$ or $_{23}C_{15} - _{22}C_{15}$	$_{18}C_3 - _{17}C_2$

13a. $C(13,6)x^7y^6$ b. $\binom{17}{8}x^9y^8$ c. $\binom{8}{2}x^6y^2$

$a = 6$ $a = 17$ $a = \binom{8}{2} = 28$

14.

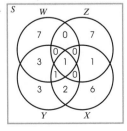

a. $15 + 24 + 20 = 59$
  59 students have exactly one of the three classes.
b. $203 - 7 = 196$
  196 students have at least one of the three classes.
c. $7 + 15 + 24 + 20 = 66$
  66 students have fewer than two classes.

15a. $_{30}C_3 \times _{21}C_4 = 4060 \times 5985 = 24\ 299\ 100$
  There are 24 299 100 ways.
  b. $_{51}C_7 - _{21}C_7 - _{30}C_7 = 115\ 775\ 100 - 116\ 280 - 2\ 035\ 800 = 113\ 623\ 020$
  There are 113 623 020 ways.

16. 0 clubs: $_8C_0 = 1$ 2 clubs: $_8C_2 = 28$
  1 club: $_8C_1 = 8$ 3 clubs: $_8C_3 = 56$
  Total: $1 + 8 + 28 + 56 = 93$
  A student can choose in 93 ways.

17. $(3 + 1)(3 + 1)(4 + 1) - 1$
  $= (4)(4)(5) - 1$
  $= 79$
  She can get them in 79 ways.

18. The order is important in permutations while it is not important in combinations. The formula for $_nP_r$ is $\frac{n!}{(n-r)!}$ and that for $_nC_r$ is $\frac{n!}{(n-r)!r!}$.
  (Suggested answer)
  Example of permutation: How many ways are there to line up 8 people in a row?
  Example of combination: How many ways are there to choose 3 people from a group of 8?

19. $(p + 1)(q + 1)(r + 1)\dots - 1$ is used to find the total number of selections that can be made with at least one item from p items of one kind, q of a second kind, r of a third kind, and so on.
  e.g. Build a sundae with up to 3 scoops of vanilla ice cream and 2 scoops of chocolate ice cream.
  $2^n - 1$ is used to find the total number of selections of at least one item from n items.
  e.g. Add toppings from a choice of 5 toppings.

20. (Suggested answer)
  How many combinations can be made using 4 letters from the letters in "BOOKKEEPER"?
  - Break the situation into 4 cases: 4 different letters, 1 pair of same letter and 2 other different letters, 2 pairs of same letter, 3 same letters and 1 other.
  - Find the combinations of each case and add them up.

21. The coefficients of the terms in the expansion of $(a + b)^n$ correspond to the terms in row n of Pascal's triangle.

22a.

b. • $6 + 2 + 1 + 1 + 1 + 3 + 7 = 21$
  • 1
  • $6 + 1 + 7 + 2 + 1 + 1 + 3 + 3 + 7 = 31$

23. Jessie and Mitch on Friday: $(_2C_2\ _{11}C_1)(_{10}C_5)(_5C_5) = 2772$
  Jessie and Mitch on Saturday: $(_{11}C_3)(_2C_2\ _8C_3)(_5C_5) = 9240$
  Jessie and Mitch on Sunday: $(_{11}C_3)(_8C_5)(_2C_2\ _3C_3) = 9240$
  Total: $2772 + 9240 + 9240 = 21\ 252$
  The students can be scheduled in 21 252 ways.

24a. $_{13}C_5 \times 4 = 5148$ b. $_4C_4 \times 13 \times 48 = 624$
  There are 5148 ways.   There are 624 ways.

25a. $= \binom{4}{0}(2x)^4\left(-\frac{2}{x^2}\right)^0 + \binom{4}{1}(2x)^3\left(-\frac{2}{x^2}\right)^1 + \binom{4}{2}(2x)^2\left(-\frac{2}{x^2}\right)^2 +$
  $\binom{4}{3}(2x)^1\left(-\frac{2}{x^2}\right)^3 + \binom{4}{4}(2x)^0\left(-\frac{2}{x^2}\right)^4$
  $= 16x^4 - 64x + \frac{96}{x^2} - \frac{64}{x^5} + \frac{16}{x^8}$

  b. $= \binom{6}{0}(4y)^6\left(\frac{3}{\sqrt{y}}\right)^0 + \binom{6}{1}(4y)^5\left(\frac{3}{\sqrt{y}}\right)^1 + \binom{6}{2}(4y)^4\left(\frac{3}{\sqrt{y}}\right)^2 +$
  $\binom{6}{3}(4y)^3\left(\frac{3}{\sqrt{y}}\right)^3 + \binom{6}{4}(4y)^2\left(\frac{3}{\sqrt{y}}\right)^4 + \binom{6}{5}(4y)^1\left(\frac{3}{\sqrt{y}}\right)^5 +$
  $\binom{6}{6}(4y)^0\left(\frac{3}{\sqrt{y}}\right)^6$
  $= 4096y^6 + 18\ 432y^{4.5} + 34\ 560y^3 + 34\ 560y^{1.5} + 19\ 440 + 5832y^{-1.5} + 729y^{-3}$

26a. $\binom{20}{10}(6x)^{10}\left(-\frac{1}{3x}\right)^{10}$ b. $\binom{20}{18}(6x)^2\left(-\frac{1}{3x}\right)^{18}$
  $= 189\ 190\ 144$ $= \frac{760}{43\ 046\ 721x^{16}}$

27a. $= (x^2 - y^2)^{20}$
  $\binom{20}{0}(x^2)^{20}(-y^2)^0, \binom{20}{1}(x^2)^{19}(-y^2)^1, \binom{20}{2}(x^2)^{18}(-y^2)^2, \binom{20}{3}(x^2)^{17}(-y^2)^3,$
  $\binom{20}{4}(x^2)^{16}(-y^2)^4$
  $\therefore x^{40}, -20x^{38}y^2, 190x^{36}y^4, -1140x^{34}y^6, 4845x^{32}y^8$
  b. $= [(2x + y)(2x - y)]^{10}$
  $= (4x^2 - y^2)^{10}$
  $\binom{10}{0}(4x^2)^{10}(-y^2)^0, \binom{10}{1}(4x^2)^9(-y^2)^1, \binom{10}{2}(4x^2)^8(-y^2)^2,$
  $\binom{10}{3}(4x^2)^7(-y^2)^3, \binom{10}{4}(4x^2)^6(-y^2)^4$
  $\therefore 1\ 048\ 576x^{20}, -2\ 621\ 440x^{18}y^2, 2\ 949\ 120x^{16}y^4, -1\ 996\ 080x^{14}y^6, 860\ 160x^{12}y^8$

28. $_{199}C_{102} + _{199}C_{103} - _{200}C_{97}$
  $= _{200}C_{103} - _{200}C_{97}$
  $= \frac{200!}{103!(200 - 103)!} - \frac{200!}{97!(200 - 97)!}$
  $= \frac{200!}{103!97!} - \frac{200!}{97!103!}$
  $= 0$

5 Probability

1. D   2. C   3. B   4. A
5. A   6. C   7. D   8. A
9a. $P(A) + P(A') = 1$
  The sum of their probabilities must be 1 because A and A' together contain all possible outcomes.
b.

$P(A)$	0.3	75%	$\frac{3}{8}$	0.8	$\frac{3}{10}$
$P(A')$	0.7	25%	$\frac{5}{8}$	0.2	$\frac{7}{10}$
odds in favour of A	$\frac{3}{7}$	3:1	$\frac{3}{5}$	4:1	3:7
odds against A	$\frac{7}{3}$	1:3	$\frac{5}{3}$	1:4	7:3

    ISBN: 978-1-77149-223-2

10a.

+	1	2	3	4	5	6
1	2	3	4	5	6	7
2	3	4	5	6	7	8
3	4	5	6	7	8	9
4	5	6	7	8	9	10
5	6	7	8	9	10	11
6	7	8	9	10	11	12

b. $\dfrac{6}{36} = \dfrac{1}{6}$

c. $\dfrac{15}{36} = \dfrac{5}{12}$

d. $1 - \dfrac{5}{12} = \dfrac{7}{12}$

11a. $\dfrac{{}_4C_2}{{}_{52}C_2} = \dfrac{6}{1326} = \dfrac{1}{221}$ b. $\dfrac{{}_2C_1 \cdot {}_4C_1}{{}_{52}C_2} = \dfrac{8}{1326} = \dfrac{4}{663}$

12a. $1 - 30\% - 45\% = 25\%$ b. $1 - 30\% - 45\% + 10\% = 35\%$

13.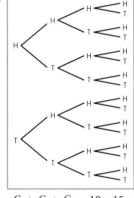

a. The odds in favour are 5:11.

b. The probability is $\dfrac{1}{2}$.

c. The probability is $\dfrac{3}{4}$.

14. $\dfrac{{}_5C_2 + {}_6C_2 + {}_4C_2}{{}_{15}C_2} = \dfrac{10 + 15 + 6}{105} = \dfrac{31}{105}$

The probability is $\dfrac{31}{105}$.

15. $\dfrac{1 \times 39 \times 39}{40 \times 40 \times 40} + \dfrac{39 \times 1 \times 39}{40 \times 40 \times 40} + \dfrac{39 \times 39 \times 1}{40 \times 40 \times 40}$

$= \dfrac{4563}{64\,000}$

$= 7.13\%$

The probability is 7.13%.

16. $\dfrac{{}_2C_2 \cdot {}_5C_3 \cdot 2!4!}{{}_7P_5} = \dfrac{480}{2520} = \dfrac{4}{21}$

The probability is $\dfrac{4}{21}$.

17a. $\dfrac{{}_6C_2 \cdot {}_3C_1}{{}_9C_3} = \dfrac{45}{84} = \dfrac{15}{28}$ b. $\left(\dfrac{6}{9}\right)\left(\dfrac{6}{9}\right)\left(\dfrac{3}{9}\right)\left(\dfrac{3!}{2!}\right) = \dfrac{4}{9}$

The probability is $\dfrac{15}{28}$.   The probability is $\dfrac{4}{9}$.

18a. $\dfrac{1}{7} \times 45\% = \dfrac{9}{140} \doteq 6.43\%$ b. $\dfrac{6}{7} \times 15\% + \dfrac{1}{7} \times 45\%$

The probability is 6.43%. $= \dfrac{27}{140}$

$\doteq 19.29\%$

The probability is 19.29%.

19. $(60\%)(5\%) + (40\%)(80\%) = 35\%$

The chance of rain tomorrow is 35%.

20. Theoretical probability is determined from the analysis of the possible outcomes. It is found by $P(A) = \dfrac{n(A)}{n(S)}$, where $n(A)$ is the number of outcomes in A and $n(S)$ is the total number of outcomes, and all outcomes are equally likely.

Empirical probability is determined from measured results. It is the number of times an event occurs divided by the number of trials.

Subjective probability is an estimation based on intuition and experience.

21. Probability is the ratio between the number of outcomes of an event and the total number of outcomes.

Odds is the ratio between the number of outcomes of an event and the number of outcomes that the event will not occur.

22. Independent events are events that have no effect on another while in dependent events, one event affects the probability of another.

Independent events: $P(A \text{ and } B) = P(A) \times P(B)$

Dependent events: $P(A \text{ and } B) = P(A) \times P(B|A)$

23. Yes, they are. The complement of an event is given by $P(A') = 1 - P(A)$. There is no overlap between an event and its complement, so they are mutually exclusive.

24. $\dfrac{7}{7 + 11} + \dfrac{5}{5 + 13} + \dfrac{1}{1 + 2}$

$= \dfrac{7}{18} + \dfrac{5}{18} + \dfrac{1}{3}$

$= 1$

Since all the probabilities add up to 1, Shanna's predictions are possible.

25. I _ _ _ _ _ _ _ _ _ _ _ O

Remaining letters: 2R, 1I, 1G, 1O, 1N, 1M, 1E, 1T, 1Y

$\dfrac{1 \times \dfrac{10!}{2!} \times 1}{12!} = \dfrac{1}{264}$

The probability is $\dfrac{1}{264}$.

26. $P(\text{even}) = \left(\dfrac{1}{5}\right)\left(\dfrac{2}{5}\right) + \left(\dfrac{4}{5}\right)\left(\dfrac{5}{10}\right) = \dfrac{12}{25}$

$P(\text{orange and even}) = \left(\dfrac{1}{5}\right)\left(\dfrac{2}{5}\right) = \dfrac{2}{25}$

$P(\text{orange and even}) = P(\text{even}) \times P(\text{orange} \mid \text{even})$

$P(\text{orange} \mid \text{even}) = \dfrac{P(\text{orange and even})}{P(\text{even})}$

$= \dfrac{2}{25} \div \dfrac{12}{25}$

$= \dfrac{1}{6}$

The probability is $\dfrac{1}{6}$.

27. Monday: $P(\text{regular}) = 60\%$, $P(\text{chocolate}) = 40\%$

Tuesday: $P(\text{regular}) = (60\%)(40\%) + (40\%)(20\%) = 32\%$
$P(\text{chocolate}) = 1 - 32\% = 68\%$

Wednesday: $P(\text{regular}) = (32\%)(40\%) + (68\%)(20\%) = 26.4\%$
$P(\text{chocolate}) = 1 - 26.4\% = 73.6\%$

Thursday: $P(\text{regular}) = (26.4\%)(40\%) + (73.6\%)(20\%) = 25.28\%$
$P(\text{chocolate}) = 1 - 25.28\% = 74.72\%$

Friday: $P(\text{regular}) = (25.28\%)(40\%) + (74.72\%)(20\%) = 25.056\%$
$P(\text{chocolate}) = 1 - 25.056\% = 74.944\%$

The probability of a student choosing chocolate milk on Friday is 74.944%.

6 Probability Distribution

1. B   2. A   3. D   4. C
5. B   6. B   7. A   8. D
9. C   10. C

11a. geometric distribution   b. uniform distribution
c. hypergeometric distribution   d. binomial distribution

12a. 0.2 ; 0.2 ; 1 ; 0.6
b. $1(0.2) + 2(0.2) + 3(0.2) + 4(0.2) + 5(0.2) = 3$

13a. 20   b. $\dfrac{2}{7}$ c. $\dfrac{5}{7}$ d. 5.26%

14a.

Number of Digits that are 2 or 5	Probability
0	40.96%
1	40.96%
2	15.36%
3	2.56%
4	0.16%

b. $15.36\% + 2.56\% + 0.16\% = 18.08\%$
c. $40.96\% + 40.96\% + 15.36\% = 97.28\%$

15. $_{12}C_5(0.08)^5(0.92)^7 \doteq 0.14\%$
    The probability is 0.14%.

16. $\dfrac{5 \times 13}{52} = 1.25$
    The expected number of cards that are hearts is 1.25.

17. $p = \dfrac{6}{36} = \dfrac{1}{6}$ $\qquad q = 1 - \dfrac{1}{6} = \dfrac{5}{6}$

    Expectation: $\dfrac{\frac{5}{6}}{\frac{1}{6}} = 5$

    The expectation is that you will roll 5 times before rolling doubles.
    So, the expected number of trials needed to get a double is 6.

18a. $p = 25\%$ $\qquad q = 75\%$
    $(0.75)^4(0.25) \doteq 7.91\%$
    The probability is 7.91%.

  b. (All outcomes) – (5 misses)
    $1 - (0.25)^5 \doteq 99.9\%$
    The probability that Matthew hits the target within 5 arrows is 99.9%.

19. $0 \times \dfrac{2}{50} + 1 \times \dfrac{11}{50} + 2 \times \dfrac{23}{50} + 3 \times \dfrac{9}{50} + 4 \times \dfrac{4}{50} + 5 \times \dfrac{1}{50}$
    $= 2.1$
    The expected number of stop signs a student will encounter is 2.1.

20a. $\dfrac{_5C_3 \times _{45}C_3}{_{50}C_6} = \dfrac{141\,900}{15\,890\,700} = 0.89\%$
    The probability is 0.89%.

  b. $\dfrac{_5C_0 \times _{45}C_6}{_{50}C_6} + \dfrac{_5C_1 \times _{45}C_5}{_{50}C_6} + \dfrac{_5C_2 \times _{45}C_4}{_{50}C_6} \doteq 99.08\%$
    The probability is 99.08%.

21a. (All outcomes) – (6 failures)
    $1 - _6C_0(0.9)^0(0.1)^6 = 99.9999\%$
    The probability is 99.9999%.

  b. (All outcomes) – (0 servers online) – (1 server online) – (2 servers online)
    $1 - _6C_0(0.9)^0(0.1)^6 - _6C_1(0.9)^1(0.1)^5 - _6C_2(0.9)^2(0.1)^4 = 99.873\%$
    The probability is 99.873%.

22. Discrete random variables have separated values which are integers. Continuous random variables have an infinite number of possible values over a continuous interval.

23a. All outcomes in a uniform distribution are equally likely. The random variable is a single value for each outcome.

  b. A binomial distribution has independent trials that are either successes or failures. The probability of successes does not change between trials. The random variable is the number of successes in a given number of trials.

  c. A geometric distribution has independent trials that are either successes or failures. The probability of successes does not change between trials. The random variable is the number of unsuccessful outcomes before a success occurs.

  d. A hypergeometric distribution has dependent trials that are either successes or failures. The random variable is the number of successful outcomes in a given number of trials. The individual outcomes cannot be repeated in the trials.

24. A Bernoulli trial has two possible outcomes, success or failure. The probability of the outcome remains the same from trial to trial. The trials are independent.

25. $\$1\,000\,000 \times \dfrac{1}{10^6} - \$2 = -\$1$
    The expected profit for playing the lottery is -$1.

26. $p = \dfrac{6}{36} = \dfrac{1}{6}$ $\qquad q = \dfrac{5}{6}$
    $\left(\dfrac{1}{6}\right) + \left(\dfrac{5}{6}\right)\left(\dfrac{1}{6}\right) + \left(\dfrac{5}{6}\right)^2\left(\dfrac{1}{6}\right) + \left(\dfrac{5}{6}\right)^3\left(\dfrac{1}{6}\right) = \dfrac{671}{1296} \doteq 51.77\%$
    The probability is 51.77%.

27. $0.18522 = _6C_3 p^3 q^3$
    $0.18522 = 20(pq)^3$
    $pq = 0.21$
    $p(1 - p) = 0.21$
    $p - p^2 - 0.21 = 0$
    $p = 0.3$ or $p = 0.7$ (more likely)
    The probability is 0.7.

28. $p = 0.15$ $\qquad q = 1 - 0.15 = 0.85$
    The total probability for n cards is given by:
    $(0.15) + (0.85)(0.15) + (0.85)^2(0.15) + ... + (0.85)^{n-1}(0.15)$
    This is a geometric series, rewrite as:
    $\dfrac{(0.15)(0.85^n - 1)}{0.85 - 1} = 1 - 0.85^n$
    $1 - 0.85^n > 0.5$
    $0.85^n < 0.5$
    $n \log 0.85 < \log 0.5$
    $n < \dfrac{\log 0.5}{\log 0.85}$
    $n > 4.27$
    Joanne should purchase more than 4 cards.

7 Normal Distribution

1. A $\qquad$ 2. D $\qquad$ 3. C $\qquad$ 4. D
5. A $\qquad$ 6. D $\qquad$ 7. B $\qquad$ 8. B
9. A $\qquad$ 10. C

11. $P(6.5 < x < 7.5)$; $P(x < 17.5)$; $P(x > 34.5)$; $P(4.5 < x < 12.5)$

12a. $= P(x < 31.5)$
    $= P\left(z < \dfrac{31.5 - 29}{7}\right)$
    $= P(z < 0.36)$
    $= 0.6406$ or 64.06%

  b. $= P(31.5 < x < 38.5)$
    $= P\left(\dfrac{31.5 - 29}{7} < z < \dfrac{38.5 - 29}{7}\right)$
    $= P(0.36 < z < 1.36)$
    $= 0.9131 - 0.6406$
    $= 0.2725$ or 27.25%

  c. $= P(x > 24.5)$
    $= P\left(z > \dfrac{24.5 - 29}{7}\right)$
    $= P(z > -0.64)$
    $= 1 - P(z < -0.64)$
    $= 1 - 0.2611$
    $= 0.7389$ or 73.89%

13a. $\mu = np = 250(0.35) = 87.5$
    $\sigma = \sqrt{npq} = \sqrt{250(0.35)(0.65)} \doteq 7.54$
    $P(x \geq 70)$
    $= P(x > 70.5)$
    $= P\left(z > \dfrac{70.5 - 87.5}{7.54}\right)$
    $= P(z > -2.25)$
    $= 1 - P(z < -2.25)$
    $= 1 - 0.0122$
    $= 0.9878$ or 98.78%

  b. $P(x = 90)$
    $= P(89.5 < x < 90.5)$
    $= P\left(\dfrac{89.5 - 87.5}{7.54} < z < \dfrac{90.5 - 87.5}{7.54}\right)$
    $= P(0.27 < z < 0.40)$
    $= P(z < 0.40) - P(z < 0.27)$
    $= 0.6554 - 0.6064$
    $= 0.049$ or 4.9%

14a. 12.31 mm is 3 standard deviations less than the mean.
(12.4 − 3(0.03) = 12.31)
99.7% of data values lie within 3 standard deviations.
99.7% ÷ 2 = 49.85%
49.85% of brake pads have a thickness between 12.31 mm and 12.4 mm.

b. 12.46 mm is 2 standard deviations more than the mean.
(12.4 + 2(0.03) = 12.46)
95% of data values lie within 2 standard deviations.
(1 − 95%) ÷ 2 = 2.5%
2.5% of brake pads have a thickness of more than 12.46 mm.

15a. $P(x > 167)$
$= P(z > \frac{167 - 158}{7})$
$= P(z > 1.29)$
$= 1 - P(z < 1.29)$
$= 1 - 0.9015$
$= 0.0985$ or 9.85%
The probability is 9.85%.

b. $P(x < 167)$
$= P(z < \frac{167 - 158}{7})$
$= P(z < 1.29)$
$= 0.9015$
Georgina falls into the 90th percentile.

16. $P(x \geq 6)$
$= P(x > 5.5)$
$= P(z > \frac{5.5 - 7}{2.3})$
$= P(z > -0.65)$
$= 1 - P(z < -0.65)$
$= 1 - 0.2578$
$= 0.7422$
$0.7422 \times 370\ 000 = 274\ 614$
Approximately 274 614 households have at least 6 electronic devices.

17. $n = 450 \quad p = 0.12 \quad q = 0.88$
$\mu = np = 450(0.12) = 54$
$\sigma = \sqrt{npq} = \sqrt{(450)(0.12)(0.88)} \doteq 6.89$
$np = 450(0.12) = 54 > 5$
$nq = 450(0.88) = 396 > 5$
$P(x \leq 65)$
$= P(x < 65.5)$
$= P(z < \frac{65.5 - 54}{6.89})$
$= P(z < 1.67)$
$= 0.9525$
The probability is 95.25%.

18a. This is a sample.
$\bar{x} = 25 \quad s \doteq 3.59$
$P(x > 26)$
$= P(z > \frac{26 - 25}{3.59})$
$= P(z > 0.28)$
$= 1 - P(z < 0.28)$
$= 1 - 0.6103$
$= 0.3897$
The probability is 38.97%.

b. $P(23 < x < 28)$
$= P(\frac{23 - 25}{3.59} < z < \frac{28 - 25}{3.59})$
$= P(-0.56 < z < 0.84)$
$= P(z < 0.84) - P(z < -0.56)$
$= 0.7995 - 0.2877$
$= 0.5118$
The probability is 51.18%.

c. $P(x > 20.5)$
$= P(z > \frac{20.5 - 25}{3.59})$
$= P(z > -1.25)$
$= 1 - P(z < -1.25)$
$= 1 - 0.1056$
$= 0.8944$
$0.8944 \times 10 = 8.944$
He should expect about 9 worms to be longer than 20.5 mm.

19. $z_{\frac{x}{2}} = 1.96$
$n = (\frac{2(1.96)(10)}{6})^2$
$\doteq 43$
A sample of about 43 muffins is needed.

20. In a continuous distribution, probability is measured over a range of values. Within that range there can be an infinite number of values. So, any single particular value has a probability of zero.

21. A bimodal distribution has two modes, so its curve reaches a local maximum value at two separate points. Generally, a bimodal distribution occurs when the results of two processes are mixed together and each set of results displays a normal distribution. (Suggested answer)
Example: There are two peaks on the number of customers of a restaurant: during lunch and dinner.

22. When $np < 5$ or $nq < 5$, the distribution is left-skewed or right-skewed and cannot be modelled by a normal distribution.

23. Continuity correction is used when discrete values are treated as continuous values in order to apply a normal model.

24. Comparing their percentiles:
$z_A = \frac{80 - 75}{3} \doteq 1.67 \qquad z_B = \frac{80 - 75}{9} \doteq 0.56$
Percentile: 95th   Percentile: 71st
According to a normal distribution, the student who is in the 95th percentile is better than the one who is in the 71st percentile. Therefore, the student who is in the class with a standard deviation of 3 can be considered better than the other.

25. $0.75 = P(x < 4.1)$ $0.95 = P(x < 5.2)$
$0.68 = \frac{4.1 - \mu}{\sigma}$ $1.65 = \frac{5.2 - \mu}{\sigma}$
$0.68\sigma = 4.1 - \mu$ ① $1.65\sigma = 5.2 - \mu$ ②
$0.97\sigma = 1.1$ ② − ①
$\sigma \doteq 1.13$
$\mu \doteq 3.33$
$P(2.5 < x < 3.5)$
$= P(\frac{2.5 - 3.33}{1.13} < z < \frac{3.5 - 3.33}{1.13})$
$= P(-0.73 < z < 0.15)$
$= P(z < 0.15) - P(z < -0.73)$
$= 0.5596 - 0.2327$
$= 0.3269$
The probability is 32.69%.

26. This is a normal approximation of a binomial distribution.
$0.68 = P(x < 9)$ $0.36 = P(x < 7)$
$0.68 = P(x < 8.5)$ $0.36 = P(x < 6.5)$
$0.47 = \frac{8.5 - \mu}{\sigma}$ $-0.36 = \frac{6.5 - \mu}{\sigma}$
$0.47\sigma = 8.5 - \mu$ ① $-0.36\sigma = 6.5 - \mu$ ②
$0.83\sigma = 2$ ① − ②
$\sigma \doteq 2.41$
$\mu \doteq 7.37$
$\mu = np = 7.37 \qquad \sigma = \sqrt{npq} = 2.41$
$2.41 = \sqrt{(7.37)q}$
$q \doteq 0.788$
$p = 1 - 0.788 = 0.212$
$n = 7.37 \div 0.212 \doteq 34.76$
There are about 35 passengers on the bus.

27. In a normal distribution, 95% of values fall within $\mu \pm 2\sigma$.
$\mu + 2\sigma = 53$ $P(50 < x < 52.5)$
$\mu - 2\sigma = 45$ $= P(\frac{50 - 49}{2} < z < \frac{52.5 - 49}{2})$
$4\sigma = 8$ $= P(0.5 < z < 1.75)$
$\sigma = 2$ $= P(z < 1.75) - P(z < 0.5)$
$\mu = 49$ $= 0.9599 - 0.6915$
     $= 0.2684$
The probability is 26.84%.

ANSWERS

Cumulative Test

1. C   2. A   3. A   4. D
5. C   6. B   7. D   8. D
9. A   10. C   11. B   12. D
13. C   14. D   15. C   16. D
17a. 11.1   b. 12   18a. -0.85
   c. 12   d. 2.41   b. $y = -1.19x + 106.1$
   e. 9.5   f. 13   c.
   g.

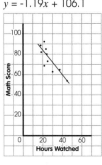

h.

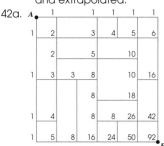

19a. 7   b. 36   c. 840   d. 4
   e. 8   f. 10

20.

$t_{a,r}$	Sum of Terms	Difference of Terms	Value
$t_{3,1}$	$t_{2,0} + t_{2,1}$	$t_{4,1} - t_{3,0}$ or $t_{4,2} - t_{3,2}$	3
$t_{5,3}$	$t_{4,2} + t_{4,3}$	$t_{6,3} - t_{5,2}$ or $t_{6,4} - t_{5,4}$	10
$t_{4,1}$	$t_{3,0} + t_{3,1}$	$t_{5,1} - t_{4,0}$ or $t_{5,2} - t_{4,2}$	4
$t_{8,4}$	$t_{7,3} + t_{7,4}$	$t_{9,4} - t_{8,3}$ or $t_{9,5} - t_{8,5}$	70

21. $2187y^7 - \dfrac{5103y^6}{4} + \dfrac{5103y^5}{16} - \dfrac{2835y^4}{64} + \dfrac{945y^3}{256} - \dfrac{189y^2}{1024}$
   $+ \dfrac{21y}{4096} - \dfrac{1}{16\,384}$

22a. 0.6   b. 2:3   c. 3:2
23a. 5.5   b. 0.67   c. 4   d. 2.78
24. 3780 different sets of teachers are possible.
25. It can be chosen in 12 ways.
26. They can line up in 1440 ways.
27. They can be arranged in 4 989 600 ways.
28. 165 triangles can be formed.
29. The probability is $\dfrac{15}{16}$.
30. A pizza can be ordered in 511 ways.
31a.

S
Extra-curricular   Part-time job
17   13   12
    10   8   14
14   12
     Volunteering

   b. 86 students participate in at least one after-school activity.
   c. 14 students do not have after-school activities.
32. The probability is 14.38%.
33. It is more probable to get fewer than 3 guinea pigs with grey fur.
34a. The probability is 88.4%.
   b. Gina should expect to need about 52 strokes.
35a. The probability is 18.53%.   b. The probability is 95.05%.
36a. The z-score is -1.36.   b. The probability is 32.64%.
   c. The probability is 8.69%.

37a. Use a sample. It would be too much work to test 1000 speakers.
   b. Conduct a census. There are only 12 rabbits.
   c. (Suggested answer)
     Conduct a census. Practice tests are only given to a small number of students, so all the students' scores can be collected easily.
38. (Suggested answer)
   - sample bias: the owner can survey only his frequent customers who are likely to be satisfied
   - measurement bias: ask a leading question, such as "Why do you think that my product is the most effective one in the market?"
   - response bias: give an incentive, such as a discount, to those who complete the survey
39. Advantages: - easier to calculate when the number of trials is large
        - easier to evaluate "more than" and "fewer than" probabilities
   Disadvantages: - only an approximation
        - restricted to when $np > 5$ and $nq > 5$
40. (Suggested answer)
   The sales of ice cream and sunglasses are strongly correlated, but one variable does not directly influence the other. It is more likely that they have a common-cause relationship such as temperature.
41. - The correlation coefficient/coefficient of determination should be strong.
   - The regression model should simulate the initial condition.
   - The model makes sense when the data is interpolated and extrapolated.
42a.

A
	1		1		1		1		1	
1	2		3	4	5	6			
	2		5		10				
1	3	3	8		10	16			
			8		18				
1	4		8	8	26	42			
1	5	8	16	24	50	92			B

There are 92 different paths.
   b.

A
	1		1	1	1	1	
1	2	3	4	5	6		
1	1✕	4	8	13	19		
1	2	6	14	14✕	33		
1	3	9	23	37	70	70	70✕
			70	140	210	210	
			70	210	420	630	630 630 630 630
					630	1260	1890 2520 3150
					630	1890	1890✕ 4410 7560 B

There are 7560 different paths.
43. The probability is 56.89%.
44a. The probability is 0.12%.
   b. The probability is 77.38%.
   c. It is more likely to get one of each flavour.
45a. The mean is 100 and the standard deviation is 14.
   b. 66.94% of the population will score between 90 and 120.
   c. It corresponds to the 95th percentile.
   d. Her IQ score is over 133.
46a. The mean is 45 and the standard deviation is 14.58.
   b. The semi-interquartile range is less than 10.75.
   c. The maximum probability is 53.35%.

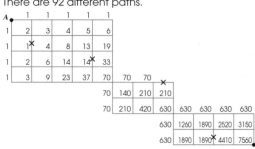

 ISBN: 978-1-77149-223-2